UNION AND CONFIDENCE: the 1860s

UNION AND CONFIDENCE: the 1860s

by HAROLD M. HYMAN

THOMAS Y. CROWELL COMPANY

ESTABLISHED 1834 • NEW YORK

 *Published simultaneously in
Canada by Fitzhenry & Whiteside Limited, Toronto.*

Manufactured in the United States of America

*L. C. Card 75-21840
ISBN 0-690-00987-9
1 2 3 4 5 6 7 8 9 10*

To Ferne
at almost thirty

BY THE AUTHOR:

Era of the Oath: Northern Loyalty Tests During the Civil War and Reconstruction

To Try Men's Souls: Loyalty Tests in American History

Stanton: The Life and Times of Lincoln's Secretary of War (with B. P. Thomas)

Soldiers and Spruce: Origins of the Loyal Legion of Loggers and Lumbermen, the Army's Labor Union of World War I

The Radical Republicans and Reconstruction, 1861–1870 (ed.)

New Frontiers of American Reconstruction (ed.)

Heard 'Round the World: The Impact Abroad of the Civil War and Reconstruction (ed., with Allan Nevins)

A More Perfect Union: The Impact of the Civil War and Reconstruction on the Constitution

Union and Confidence: the 1860s

ACKNOWLEDGMENTS

Every writer accumulates many debts. In order now adequately to record my cumulative indebtedness to colleagues and students for ideas and criticisms, to universities and libraries for essential facilities and environments, to foundations and publishers for support and confidence, I should require a volume larger than this.

Instead I content myself with acknowledging only individuals and institutions who most recently have aided me in special ways. Among them, Dun & Bradstreet's Mr. George Paul recruited me for this writing. Professor Robert Sobel was an especially valuable trailblazer. Professor Glenn Porter very graciously gave me access to his notes on relevant Dun & Bradstreet papers. Mr. Robert Lovett of Harvard's Baker Library guided me through that great collection. Rice University's librarians were extraordinarily effective. The useful wars I fought with Thomas Y. Crowell's editor, Patrick Barrett, and Miss Arlene Reisberg of the copy editing department resolved several tenacious issues of interpretation and style, often, I admit, in their favor. My secretary, Mrs. Sylvia Ross, whose services are another element of the debt I owe to Rice University, patiently worked her way through successive drafts. Research assistants Richard Cole and John Mauer were inventive and energetic.

To all, my thanks.

H.M.H.

FOREWORD

IT IS FITTING THAT *Union and Confidence: the 1860s,* the third volume in a retrospective series commissioned by Dun & Bradstreet Companies, Inc., should appear during our country's celebration of its Bicentennial, for this book scans that darkest decade of our history when dissension and bloody internal conflict threatened the Union's ability to survive to its centennial. Yet these years of despair ended in hope: the reunited states were proud that their governmental institutions had endured the ordeals of civil war, reconstruction, and impeachment of the President, and the rise of industrial technology seemed to promise a future in which increasing material rewards would be shared by all citizens.

To record the achievements of a generation "touched with fire" (as Oliver Wendell Holmes, Jr., characterized it), we selected noted historian Dr. Harold M. Hyman, the William P. Hobby Professor of History at Rice University in Houston, Texas. A former associate of the late Allan Nevins, Dr. Hyman is an acknowledged authority on the Civil War period; seven of his previous books deal with aspects of the War and Reconstruction. Among the honors bestowed on him are the American Historical Association's Albert J. Beveridge Award and the Sidney Hillman Award.

Dr. Hyman was asked to probe the business aspects of the 1860s as well as the political and social history of the era. He has written a work rich in insights into the causes of the Civil War, distinctive, and at times controversial, in its perspective on its subject. His many provocative ideas illumine an age that all too many of us know less well than we think we do.

As we pass the Bicentennial mark, concern is being expressed about the ability of our institutions of government and business to rise to the challenges of the future. But a study of our past is reassuring, for it reveals that each era has had crises that it considered insurmountable and that in times of greatest despair America and its institutions proved equal to almost every challenge.

Harrington Drake

President and
Chief Executive Officer

CONTENTS

INTRODUCTION 1

1. UNCONFIDENT AMERICANS of 1860–61 7

2. THE FAILURE of POLITICS 31

3. SECESSION and WAR: THE SOUTH'S SENSE of TIME and PURPOSE 59

4. MIXED and MULTIFORM POLITICS 77

5. BATTLES and PLEADERS: 1861–62 101

6. FROM JELLYFISH to OCTOPUS: THE LINCOLN HERITAGE 129

7. DEMOCRATIC EXPERIMENT, PRINCIPLE, and MACHINERY 169

8. NO BLUEPRINT for LEVIATHAN 193

9. THE STATES: THE BEGINNINGS of UNUSUAL ENTERPRISES, 1860–70 217

10. 1868—THE CRITICAL YEAR 243

EPILOGUE / CONFIDENT AMERICANS of 1869–70 271

INDEX 291

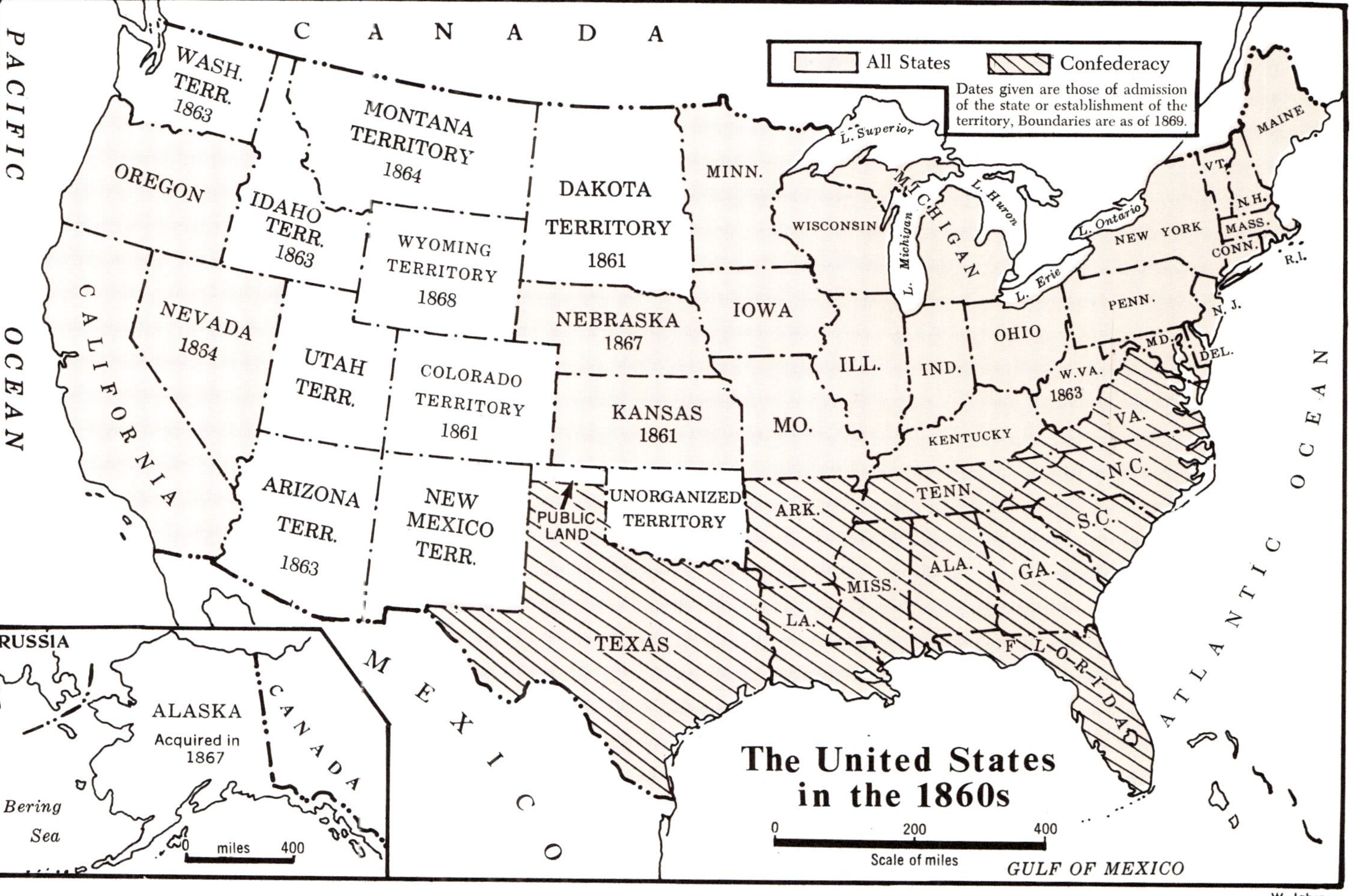
The United States
in the 1860s
All States
Confederacy
Dates given are those of admission of the state or establishment of the territory, Boundaries are as of 1869.
CANADA
PACIFIC OCEAN
ATLANTIC OCEAN
GULF OF MEXICO
MEXICO
WASH. TERR. 1863
MONTANA TERRITORY 1864
DAKOTA TERRITORY 1861
MINN.
OREGON
IDAHO TERR. 1863
WYOMING TERRITORY 1868
WISCONSIN
MICHIGAN
L. Superior
L. Michigan
L. Huron
L. Ontario
L. Erie
NEW YORK
MAINE
VT.
N.H.
MASS.
CONN.
R.I.
N. J.
PENN.
MD.
DEL.
CALIFORNIA
NEVADA 1864
UTAH TERR.
COLORADO TERRITORY 1861
NEBRASKA 1867
IOWA
ILL.
IND.
OHIO
W.VA. 1863
VA.
KANSAS 1861
MO.
KENTUCKY
ARIZONA TERR. 1863
NEW MEXICO TERR.
PUBLIC LAND
UNORGANIZED TERRITORY
ARK.
TENN
N.C.
S.C.
MISS.
ALA.
GA.
LA.
TEXAS
FLORIDA
RUSSIA
Bering Sea
ALASKA
Acquired in 1867
0 miles 400
0 200 400
Scale of miles
W. Jaber

UNION
AND
CONFIDENCE:
the 1860s

INTRODUCTION

The Book's Title: Explanation

In the preceding volume in this series, Professor Robert Sobel aptly titled his first chapter, dealing with the year 1850, "Confident America." He noted in his concluding pages that by 1860 the dominant mood nationwide had become deeply pessimistic. A very great number of Americans were reduced to despair about the prospects of their nation's survival and about their own individual futures.

As an example, in June 1860, Edwin M. Stanton (the successful patent and commercial lawyer, who was to serve in the cabinets of Presidents Buchanan, Lincoln, and Johnson) wrote to his wife from Washington: "Disaster and overthrow impend . . . and no power seems able to avert a danger that can be overcome only by union and confidence."[1]

Confidence in the vigor of the union of states was diminishing so swiftly in 1860 that, paralleling Professor Sobel's chapter title for 1850, I have titled the first chapter of the present volume "Unconfident Americans of 1860–61."

Of course not all Americans were sunk in glum pessimism. As Sobel noted, in 1860 at least one major center of optimism remained. Ironically, it was in the increasingly truculent slaveholding states of the deep South. There, confidence stemmed increasingly from acceptance of the need for disunion—the need for the perpetuation of a legally static class structure based on race, not individual or general freedom. It was a curious, unhealthy, and dangerous imbalance that, in the land of the free, the home of the slave should be the center of bravest estimates.

Yet, ten years later, in the Christmas season of 1869, the decade, that had begun so inauspiciously, closed with the Union and national confidence restored. The enormous centrifugal forces generated during the 1850s had been reversed. Secession had been overwhelmed. The exaggerated constitutional dogma of state sovereignty, which, combined with the commitment to slavery, had underlain the secessions of 1860–61, was buried in history's graveyard. The rock of slavery, that for seeming ages had cleft public opinion and frustrated public policies and private endeavors, was destroyed. Despite the recent history of secession, war, racial revolution, constitutional adjustments, and financial fluctuations, when 1870 began, adequate reasons existed again for confidence in the Union and in progress.

For these reasons, and with apologies to Professor Sobel for the parallelism, I title the Epilogue of this volume "Confident Americans of 1869–70." I hope readers will agree that the progression from the "Unconfident Americans" in the first chapter to the "Confident Americans" of the Epilogue offers insights into both what occurred in this watershed decade and the reasons for these vast changes.

The Book's Theme

In this survey of the epochal decade 1860–70, my essential purpose is to examine the adequacy and appropriateness of certain public and private-sector institutions in relation to the hazards and opportunities of the 1860s. I argue that the Union not only enjoyed but deserved the rebirth of confidence in its durability and utility; and, as confidence returned, both public and private institutions functioned more vigorously and effectively, further strengthening the Union.

The result of the endeavors of this decade was a significant modernization of many aspects of American society. Cyril Black's *Dynamics of Modernization* (New York: Harper & Row, 1966), p. 7, expresses best the sense of modernization: ". . . the process by which historically evolved institutions are adapted to the rapidly changing functions that reflect the unprecedented increase in man's knowledge, permitting control over his environment, that accompanied the scientific revolution." I add to this able definition my belief that a less tangible aspect of the modern way also developed in the Union states from 1860 to 1870. I refer to the renurture of a "can do" spirit that had long been part of American life, but which was so strikingly diminished in the North in 1860–61. This spirit grew stronger as slavery, state sovereignty, and secessionist activism faltered.

The Literature

History has no obligation to be neat. In their search for order, writers tend to divide the past into periods. Almost all accounts break the Civil War and Reconstruction decade into two five-year segments separated by Appomattox. But I argue that the decade does not divide neatly into these phases. Reconstruction began very soon after Fort Sumter's surrender in April 1861, not on the day after Lee's surrender in April 1865.

As I stressed in my earlier books, *The Radical Republicans and Reconstruction* (Indianapolis: Bobbs-Merrill, 1966) and *A More Perfect Union: The Impact of the Civil War and Reconstruction on the Constitution* (New York: Knopf, 1973), I disagree with judgments that secession and civil war and reconstruction were inspired by selfish, economically motivated commercial-industrial interests in the North in order finally to crush and to exploit the South, allegedly already doomed to an inferior, slaveless destiny. I assert that the free states, as a political society, were motivated by complex purposes, including moral concerns as well as material interests. The evidence impresses me that the South was far from the weaker of the two sections in 1861, in terms underscored by recent events in Vietnam.

From my quarter-century of research, thinking, and teaching, I have come to conclusions that gave form to the following pages: Lincoln and his Republican party mates were not "honky" racists who resorted to emancipation during the war, but supported only minimal civil and political rights for Negroes in the Reconstruction, primarily to manipulate blacks. The war and Reconstruction were not vast tragic errors that allowed greedy entrepreneurs to spark what Charles Beard called a "Second American Revolution." A centralized, bureaucratized, urbanized nation was not born by the time Lincoln died or when the Fifteenth Amendment to the Constitution was ratified in 1870, and such a birth did not underly the Republicans' war and Reconstruction purposes.

Recent scholarship has stressed that businessmen were by no means universally pro-war; industrialism may have been retarded rather than advanced during the decade of the '60s. President Johnson's impeachment was not causeless, its mode of conduct was not savage but decent, and it did not injure the Presidency or the society.

Further, it distorts the past to ask of men who lived a century ago to want what we want in the order of our priorities. It is unrealistic to demand of Lincoln's contemporaries that they seek our goals at speeds, and using instruments, whose existence we take for granted, but which, by and large, they could not conceive.

I hope in this volume to account for men's decisions in the 1860s on the bases of *their* information, aspirations, and prejudices, not ours. In no sense do I minimize the primary place the Civil War and its aftermath had for Lincoln's contemporaries. "Here [in America] we read no books," philosopher Ralph Waldo Emerson wrote to Englishman Thomas Carlyle in late 1862. "The war is our sole and doleful instructor."[2] I hope to consider the decade with due attention to the politics and battles of the Civil War and Reconstruction, to national politics, and to the Negro's fate. But, as noted, I intend to place these basic war matters into a broad context of trends involving public and private institutions. I aspire to learn how adequately these public and private institutions, ranging from government bureaus to business corporations to private benevolent and reform associations, coped with that decade's needs. My conviction increases as I study this period that public and private institutional adequacy had a great deal to do with the determination of public policy decisions, many of which still affect us today.

I accept as a constant the clay feet of heroes. But I hope to consider the emancipating hero Lincoln and the impeached President Johnson in light of mid-nineteenth-century realities (including racial attitudes), not ours.

What follows is the story of how disrupted, despairing, free-state America of 1860 raised itself to the confident Union of 1870. As the nation's bicentennial approaches, it is gratifying to note that Lincoln's generation achieved, though at great cost, the rebirth of confidence and Union, which in 1860 Stanton feared was unattainable, and that it has lasted to the present. History will record, I hope, that even Watergate could not destroy what the Civil War and Reconstruction decade restored.

FOOTNOTES

1. June 4, 1860, Brown University Library.

2. *The Correspondence of Emerson and Carlyle,* ed. Joseph Slater (New York: Columbia University Press, 1964), p. 537.

1/UNCONFIDENT AMERICANS of 1860-61

Causes of Former Confidence

By early in the nineteenth century, Americans had become famous—infamous in monarchical and clerical circles—as outrageous democrats, nationalists, and optimists. By all contemporary gauges, white Americans, whether *Mayflower* descendants or recent immigrants, had good reasons for their tenacious optimism and staunch patriotism. Since the Revolution they had enjoyed and come to expect as a matter of right spectacular rises in their conditions of life.

To be sure, irksome setbacks had occurred to the economy, in particular, numerous "boom-and-bust" speculations. Moreover, not only were some Americans enslaved, but full shares in the economy's fruits were denied even to free Negroes, and also to nonhostile Indians and long-resident Latins. Widespread though lesser prejudices similarly affected Catholics and Jews.

Nevertheless, almost all white Americans believed that constant improvement and open opportunity were their manifest destinies. Merely hard-scrabble family origins were no bar to social preferment and political advancement, as, among many others, Abraham Lincoln's career proved. Yet in light of hard data, not sentiment, Americans' ideas about opportunity were reasonable and present rather than sentimental, utopian, and futuristic. And even abroad this was felt to be true: "*Amerika,*" Goethe said, "*du hast es besser.*"

America, and Americans, did have things better. In one of the greatest voluntary mass movements in the world's history, between 1815 and 1860 hundreds of thousands of Europeans came to this "light continent," as popular usage had it, in distinction to the unalluring mysteries of the Dark Continent, Africa. Yet, even when their numbers were added to the astonishing birth rate of earlier residents, there seemed in mid-century no danger that the cities would become overcrowded or that virgin western lands would be filled. Diplomacy, exploration, and war had won a continent so vast as to beggar European-scale vocabularies for a single nation.

Though enormous, the American space was not seen as overwhelming. At least until 1860, city dwellers, frontiersmen, factory workers, trappers, farmers, and urban businessmen assumed that their environments were manipulable and profitable.

In material terms, evidence on hand from commonplace sources in 1860—newspapers, sermons, general-interest periodicals, and businessmen's magazines—makes clear how profitable that manipulation was. Since 1850 the total population had increased more than 35% to almost 32 million people. Enormous applications of free and servile labor, capital, and talent had developed the agriculture, industry, and communications needed to feed, house, and clothe these multitudes. Exports of cotton, foodstuffs, timber, and tobacco had increased greatly. Wheat production soared from 100 million bushels in 1849 to 175 million bushels in 1859. Corn output had more than doubled in twenty years. Total American grain production in 1860 was approximately 25% of the world's output. Beef cattle increased in number from 11 to 17 million head during the 1850–60 decade. Cotton output rose from 1,580,959 bales (of 500 pounds each) in 1839 to 4,309,641 bales in 1859.

Despite the financial uncertainty resulting from the "panic" or depression in 1857, by 1860 unemployment was probably only 6–8%, and per capita real income had been rising since 1840. The outflow of American agricultural and industrial machinery and of finished goods impressed observers at European commercial exhibitions. America was becoming one of the western world's major transatlantic workshops. New staple crops and improved animal breeds expanded demand further here and abroad.

Not surprisingly, real and personal property values soared almost 30% during the 1850–60 decade. From extractive mining to fisheries to finished textiles, industry after industry doubled and tripled output value to a grand total of $2 billion in 1860, and profits rose accordingly. Railroads had already become America's first "big business" and were developing new approaches to capital accumulations, conservation, and use, to management, to labor relationships, and to geographical expansion. Railroad directors and engineers were working to rationalize the industry through voluntary standardization of track gauges, signaling equipment, and safety devices. In the 1850–60 decade, railroad mileage expanded four times. By 1860 route projections for continental lines were no longer visionary but

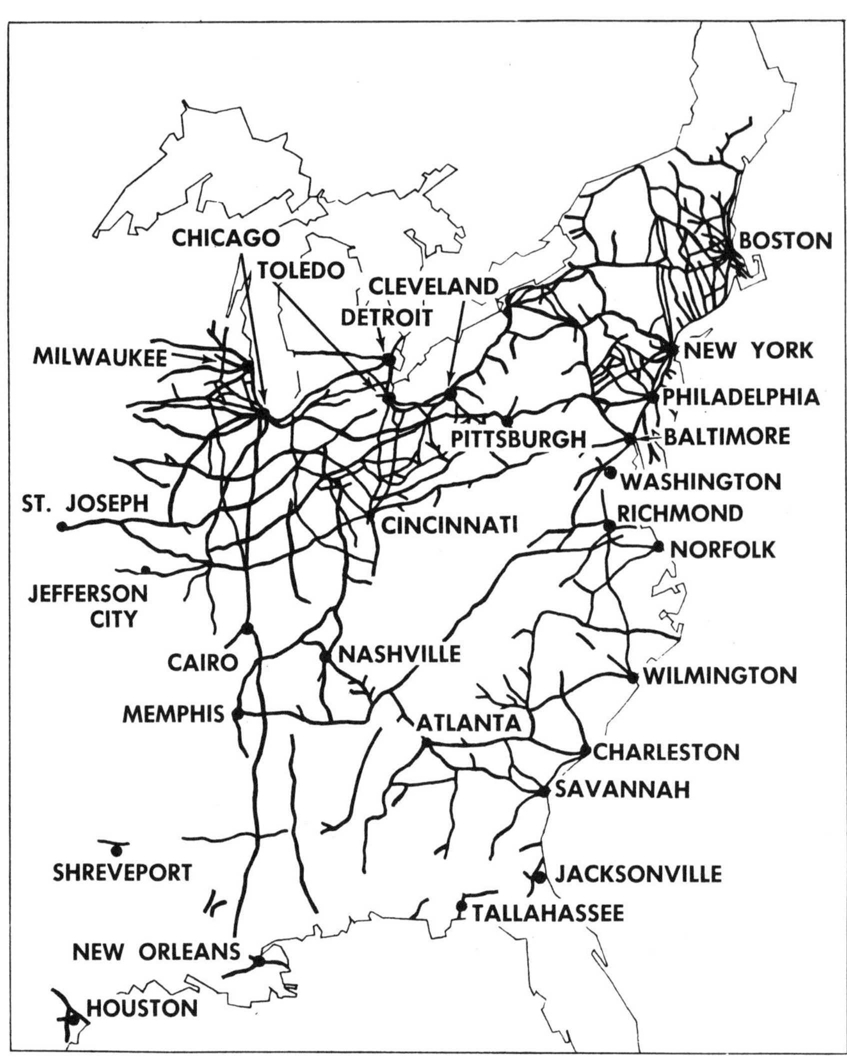

America's railroads in 1860 stretched as far west as Missouri and Iowa. The first transcontinental line was completed in 1869.

practical. The best means for nation and states to encourage rail-line extensions was a leading political issue.

Growth and improved techniques similarly characterized other industries and agriculture and, save in the still small and obscure telegraph business, monopoly conditions did not close off competition. Ordinary capital-light individuals were still able successfully to enter and to compete in agriculture-industry-transportation arenas. Steam engines, which had almost doubled in number since 1850 and had far more than doubled in energy output, were the visible sign of the new America. Inventors abounded, and some of their marvelous devices, like Cyrus McCormick's reaper and harvester and S. F. B. Morse's telegraph, were already profoundly changing the operation of farm and factory.

More complex financial institutions and procedures were needed to accommodate such innovation and expansion, and by 1860 appropriate adaptations were well underway. State-chartered private banks almost tripled in number and in deposits during the 1850–60 decade. Bankers had created a clearing house in New York City, and by 1860 commercial paper movement was much improved, although severe regional inequities remained.

These extraordinary material achievements and institutional rationalizations were the more remarkable (and how Americans remarked on them!) because they appeared to be only a phase in an ascending cycle. Concerning the "condition and progress" of American agriculture, the report on the 1860 decennial census commented:

> It appears from the returns of the last census, that the ratio of increase of the principal agricultural products of the United States has more than kept pace with the increase of population. Indeed, there appears no reason to doubt the continuance of an abundant supply of all the great staple articles, equal to the necessities of any possible increase of population or national contingency for ages to come. It is also gratifying to note the evidences of improvement in some of the most important agri-

> cultural operations, proving that our farmers are fully in sympathy with the progressive spirit of the age, and not behind their fellow-citizens engaged in other industrial occupations. The products of the great west are giving a tone to the markets of Great Britain and the continent. Chicago has become one of the first grain markets in the world, and as the boundless region still further west is being developed, every channel of communication with the Atlantic coast will teem with the products of the soil.
>
> Our reapers and mowers, ploughs, steam engines, and railroad cars have found their way to the Old World, and an American in taking the tour of the continent will, in the great empire of Russia, find himself on board of an American railroad car drawn by an American locomotive on a railroad built by an American engineer. . . . The enterprise of our countrymen, with so wide a scope for its development at home, manifests itself wherever a profitable field opens for its exercise abroad. . . . The increasing annual products of agriculture in our highly-favored country, . . . furnish striking illustrations of the close interpendence and connexion of all branches of the national industry. The dependence of agriculture upon the results of mechanical skill, as well as the astonishing progress of the latter within the last half century, is strongly exemplified in the application of labor-saving appliances, . . . in all the operations of the farm. . . . In nearly every department of rural industry mechanical power has wrought a revolution.[1]

These were sweet words, and Emerson later described to Thomas Carlyle his feeling that the 1860 census was a poem worthy to ". . . inspire a genius like your own. The dismal Malthus, the dismal DeBow, have had their night."[2] Musing on America's bounty after a visit here in the early 1860s, British newsman John Baker Hopkins was moved to comment that "America first appeared [to Englishmen and Europeans] as a dreamland. . . . Are not the realities of the New World more marvellous than the fairy-like fictions of the adventurers?"[3]

The Media

Such happy conditions and auspicious expectations were copiously reported and repeated. General-circulation media included newspapers, literary magazines, book-length travelers' accounts, and religious sermons reprinted as pamphlets. Their messages were disseminated cheaply, swiftly, and reliably via the growing railroad network and even the telegraph. All were frequently graced with news of America's past achievements and favorable prospects. Copyrights were little known or respected then. Almost anything in print was frequently picked up by space-rich, money-short publishers and editors. Postage rates for printed matter were set very low. Alternative distractions were few, and Americans were the world's most literate public. As a result, the printed page had an impact that is difficult to appreciate today.

In addition to general-circulation publications, a substantial number of smaller, specialized, highly influential publications went periodically to bankers, businessmen, farmers, and a growing roster of licensed tradesmen and professionals. The claim was common in these otherwise disparate specialized publications that confidence in continued material advances was justified because desirable modernizations were occurring in the practices of almost all professions and businesses.

Among businessmen, the comfort of more reliable credit reporting was available. The Mercantile Agency, ancestor of Dun and Bradstreet, by the late 1850s had more than two thousand correspondents scattered across the nation, in every state, whose replies to credit inquiries from Agency subscribers required thirty men in the home office to read, copy, and index. Credit reporters in the field usually were lawyers, whose insights into mercantile and industrial conditions and reputations were often very sharp.

The Professional and Business Association Movement

Among the professions, rationalization was manifest in the development of formal associations. By the late 1850s, city- and county-level professional associations were growing in number and influence in several eastern states, especially among businessmen, doctors, lawyers, and educators. Even state-level associations were beginning to be formed from confederations of local organizations; and as the decade ended, tentative regional coalitions were taking shape. The leaders in this movement were entrepreneurs, educators, engineers, physicians, "sanitarians" (public health reformers), and social-science-minded statisticians.

Of course, these diverse associations varied greatly from one another in detail, but they possessed certain common assumptions, purposes, and practices. They tended strongly to create novel links between associated private practitioners and state (including county and city) powers. One of their prime purposes was to improve the quality of government (usually city government, for most business and professional men worked in urban areas). They aimed also to use state powers (many cities and counties were discredited by political corruption) to raise their professions' levels of practice by licensing. A first step in this direction was to raise standards for would-be entrants into the professions. Ordinances and statutes increasing formal-education requirements for practitioners were passed (a trend highly favored by educators' associations), and state licensing procedures in general were increasingly determined by associations' standards. Professionals worked matters out so that they served as the state's examiners for licenses. Urban chambers of commerce, sometimes armed with quasi-government authority, especially in matters of arranging public works contracts, served businessmen in diverse ways.

Higher professional standards sanctioned by state government were directed against the numerous charlatans, confidence tricksters, and malpractitioners who undermined public trust. Professionals were becoming vitally important to the population's interests, health, safety, and progress, and they were very self-conscious about notorious rascals in their ranks.

Civil engineers (although comprising only a minuscule crop of West Pointers and Rensselaer graduates) were reshaping whole landscapes. Their bridges, dams, tunnels, parks, and waterworks were determining the fates of cities, their rail-route decisions were affecting entire regions.

Public health professionals were striving to use state power to check disease, especially cholera and yellow fever epidemics. Social science statisticians, in eastern states especially, were systematically measuring numerous population and economic trends, including insurance and actuarial probabilities, and communities' future needs for jails, asylums, and schools.

A cynical portrait of a lawyer at work.
NEW YORK PUBLIC LIBRARY

In several states, the tax-supported elementary and secondary school systems were the most fully developed in the world, and educators insisted that teachers—keepers simultaneously of knowledge and moral standards—must not be casually licensed. It was argued successfully in locality after locality, and state capital after state capital, that by appropriate regulation worthy doctors would replace "quacks" and honest attorneys would oust "shysters."

It seemed reasonable that such regulations should be devised and administered chiefly by the professionals themselves: after all, only engineers could understand each other, and only lawyers could comprehend "the mysterious science of the law." Each profession argued that its discipline must be outside of ordinary politics with respect to examining and licensing.

Other, less defensible motives spurred association efforts. Elitist, anti-democratic, and bigoted practitioners wished to exclude from entrance "the wrong people," meaning, in 1860, Catholics—especially Irish—Jews, Negroes, and, except in elementary education, women. Paradoxically, elitist association leaders, while asserting that the professions must be independent of politics, established connections with city councilmen, county commissioners, and state lawmakers to create licensing boards staffed with exclusion-minded association members and armed with government authority. But the paradox appeared not to worry even many of those who discerned it.

Associated lawyers, for example, acknowledged that some of their purposes were anti-democratic and elitist. By mid-century, the "right people" were dominating the new bar associations and were influential in sponsoring new law journals and in supplying many of their feature articles and case comments. Law journals aimed at raising standards for all lawyers and judges, even for those in barbaric Ohio or the bookless Arizona Territory (as the western areas appeared to many eastern viewers). Editors culled and pirated case reports from across the nation, stressing those from pace-setting eastern state courts. Innovations in legal education and occupational licensing received special attention. Workmanlike, untheoretical, and "scientific" in tone, the law journals aimed to be ". . . an effective counter-image to the popular stereotype of the [lawyer] as the crafty despoiler of the poor."[4]

Bar association spokesmen hammered the theme of the need for raising the entrance standards for legal education, extending the time spent in studying, and increasing the sophistication of the teaching. Moral standards, too, were to be raised, and lawyers were to exhibit energy and inventiveness in every client's service, and thrift and sobriety in all situations. Poor, worthy recruits into the law, of the Lincoln-Stanton sort, were welcome, if they could make it. But others who did not share in the work-virtue ethic were less desirable, and everyone understood the implication.

Law and the Conditions of Business Freedom

By 1860, American law and lawyers had markedly harmonized the newer production, extractive, communications, and transportation entrepreneurship with state-based federalism and political democracy. In cities, lawyers and leaders of commerce, banking, and industry were benefiting greatly from modernizations of commercial law forms and procedures. Older business arrangements, such as single ownerships and simple partnerships, in which owners were liable to the full extent of their assets for their enterprises' debts, were giving way to corporations. State charters created corporations, which, in law, were artificial persons whose shareholders were liable only to the extent of their investments. Through most of the pre-1860 decades, states created each corporation by means of special legislation. The need for entrepreneurs to win passage of a special incorporation law at a state capital led reformers among businessmen and lawyers to lobby successfully for passage of general incorporation statutes, less cursed by patronage.

In a few leading states, such as New York, by the mid-1850s success had also crowned lawyers' and businessmen's efforts to codify civil and criminal laws. The results were relatively rational categories of statutes, arranged by related subjects, that eased marketplace exchanges. Newer business needs were swiftly and successfully accommodated in contract, equity, and tort laws. With respect to contract, for example, the new steam-powered transport and production technology was easily coped with by extensions of old common-law contract concepts. Persons suffering civil (as distinguished from criminal) wrongs in industrial situations, as in locomotive explosions, found remedies in tort law's swift developments. Equity comforted plaintiffs whose plights fit none of the traditional pleas allowed in courts run by ancient rites.

It was a blessing to American entrepreneurs that the law was property's ally, not foe. The swift growth of American agriculture and business would not have been possible, farmers and merchants understood, if law had blindly and inflexibly protected all property. Society was changing, growing, and interacting swiftly. Sometimes, one property right had to give way to another without violence or commercial disruption.

Earlier, American jurisprudence had accepted common-law notions that virtually isolated property owners from public-interest intrusions and almost immunized private contracts against public-policy challenges. By 1860, property ownership still almost always meant virtually free choice of use; but in special contexts, owners were beginning to be subject to some legal limitations in the interests of society. For example, in the late eighteenth century, Massachusetts had granted perpetual monopoly rights to a private toll bridge company, in order to effect, without tax outlay or assumption of public responsibilities, a connection between Charlestown and Boston. In ensuing decades, growth in Boston's population, commerce, and industry made the old structure obsolete. In defiance of its own commitment to the perpetual monopoly contract, Massachusetts in 1828 chartered a second privately owned profit-seeking bridge company. Protesting litigation begun by the heirs of the first owners went finally to the Supreme Court of the United States. In 1837, in the famous Charles River Bridge case, judgment came down approving as an act of necessary, proper, and creative destruction the diminution of the older company's charter in favor of the subsequent recipient's.

Such commercial law statesmanship became the primary work of the states' highest courts and of the United States Supreme Court. By 1860, business and legal spokesmen were delighted that most important public-policy decisions, such as the rights of the contending Boston bridge companies or of basic patent disputants, were in the hands of judges rather than politicians. But, partially by reason of the jurists' specialization in commercial law questions, in 1860, when the great public-policy question was state secessions, the courts were virtually irrelevant to the situation.

The Government

Government's rights, remedies, and limitations, as distinguished from private rights, in such matters as secession or its frustration had received little attention in the pre-1860 decades. One reason for this inattention was that the swift rise in America's wealth, population, and production involved little government participation. Lawyers, judges, and courts performed in America much of the work that Europeans assigned to large coercive bureaucracies. Americans, it seemed, had achieved government by litigation, had created a non-machine that functioned, had constructed a harmless government.

Indeed, by contemporary standards American government was virtually invisible. Few white Americans were accountable to any government official or agency. Carlyle called our way "anarchy plus a street constable," and only a handful of American cities boasted many even of those functionaries. Immigrants and temporary visitors needed no passports; states handled naturalization proceedings. Persons accustomed to European border delays were incredulous at the unimpeded traffic across state and county lines. Months passed without sight of a national government officer, except postmasters. In the early 1860s, the keen observer Edward Dicey, British journalist and barrister, noted of his first weeks here:

> It seemed hard to realize . . . that I had come into a foreign country. . . . There were neither soldiers nor *gendarmes,* not even a policeman, waiting to receive us on landing. The passports with which I, in common with my fellow passengers, had provided myself, were uncalled for; and we left the ship on our several errands without a question being asked of any one of us. Indeed, up to the hour when I quitted the States, I had never occasion to show my passport, except once, to a banker in the West, to whom it luckily served as a proof of my identity.[5]

The national government's invisibility was a fairly faithful reflection of its relative functionlessness and simple institutional structure. The executive departments were almost unaltered in number and procedures since Washington's administration. Bureaucratic staffs were astonishingly small by European standards and were immersed largely in humdrum, introspective record-keeping assignments. Only the postal service created a national presence in every community, and the postmaster, almost always a local political party leader, was a neighbor, rarely thought of as representing the distant central government. The military establishment was all but out of sight; it functioned only in western Indian-control posts or coastal defense forts or at sea. Diplomacy was an even more exclusive and invisible occupation. Assay, customs, land, and revenue offices did deal with substantial numbers of Americans but almost always in ways that advanced the interests of the persons served rather than those of the government. Federal courts were exotic forums, rarely used.

All in all, the great majority of Americans lived and labored without any intimate or frequent connection with their national government; and even state and local governments were relatively quiescent. This situation, which greatly impressed nineteenth-century visitors (including, in addition to Dicey, Alexis de Tocqueville, Georges Clemenceau, and James Bryce), was the more remarkable because there were so many hundreds, indeed thousands of American governments.

Federalism

The American federal system had started to take form without intention or plan soon after the first English-speaking North American settlements were established. The European habit in the 1700s (and later) was to dismiss federalism as an antique, unworthy curiosity that had fatally undermined the ancient Greek city-states and was ruining contemporary Poland. Federal arrangements were considered suitable only for insignificant, tiny places such as Switzerland or the Low Countries. For Englishmen, the very notion that American provincials could cope even with local problems over such an area, much less with defense or imperial regulations, was ridiculous. Authority-from-the-top-down arrangements were necessary.

It was a historic miscalculation. The North American Britons were by far the most populous, prosperous, literate, expansionist-minded, and politically active of England's numerous overseas colonists. Americans took for granted diverse practices of local autonomy. These practices were nourished by the absence of visible imperial institutions and were fed further by colonists' diverse ethnic origins. By the mid-1770s, colonial practices were incompatible with the mother country's constitutionalism and revenue needs, and vice-versa. Put even to such mild tests as the revenue acts of the 1760s and '70s, Americans proved themselves unwilling to give up any aspect of their federalism. They knew that they governed themselves in a federal structure, without a king or an established church or aristocracy, and they intended to continue the trick.

Americans lived federally. Their decision-making, taxation, and public-administration apparatuses grew from the bottom up; great diversity existed between colonies concerning civil, political, and property rights.

Even the Revolution's pressures for abandoning localism, the better to fend off enemies, failed to diminish Americans' federalistic practices significantly. From 1774, when the Continental Congress assembled, through 1789, when the Constitution was ratified, state-based realities determined and limited the shape of the central administration.

One of these basic realities was that almost all of the public work that was done occurred on local and state (erstwhile colony) levels. In constitutional theory all county and city authority was delegated by the state. As the nineteenth century progressed, cities, counties, and states retained this primacy, save in a few areas of military, postal, and diplomatic responsibilities. By the 1840s political parties had developed—usually two competed in each election area. Generally, party contests were not nationally oriented, but involved intrastate coalitions of local organizations, which met biennially and quadrennially to decide on statewide, congressional, and presidential candidates and platforms.

Jurisprudence had developed in state power doctrine, often called state police power, a constitutional and legal theory that reflected the authority of the states. States—and, by delegation, county and city divisions—were held to be possessed inherently of the duty, right, and power to provide for the health, safety, morals, and welfare of residents.

The law's language concerning state power became impressively plenary and elastic. From reading only legal commentaries, it might seem that state authority was all-encompassing, fully fleshed, and functionally vigorous. One can misconceive that such state apparatuses were armed, like railroad corporations of 1860, with appropriate organizations, budgets, and cadres of expert, trained personnel. But the legal imagery belied reality. The reality is what so impressed Dicey and other visitors: the invisibility of government personnel and institutions.

In most states, counties, and cities, few public responsibilities were in fact admitted before 1860. Taxes supported some road and levee maintenance, boundary surveying, water supply provisions, sketchy law-and-order institutions including asylums, hospitals, and prisons, and spasmodic anti-epidemiological efforts. There were few permanent civil servants, light tax rates, and small bureaucratic apparatuses.

The scant numbers of government bureaus and employees helps to explain why associating lawyers successfully made themselves the staffs of state licensing commissions. There simply was not enough government to do new work. Few persons assumed that the public sector should actually take on new duties.

Users of State Power: Northern Teachers and Truant Officers

Two exceptions existed to this pattern of government invisibility. The first was the public-school systems of certain northeastern and midwestern cities, counties, and states. Public education was hailed generally as the primary source of America's great progress in agriculture, industry, technology, and liberty. Required attendance in secular, English-language schools was

The Country School, 1871, by Winslow Homer. Before 1860, compulsory attendance in public schools was one of the few examples of government intervention in private affairs.

one of the few instances, prior to 1860, in which the law intervened in family or private life. Strong opposition to required public-school attendance grew in centers of minority ethnic and religious populations. Churchmen, becoming adept lobbyists, won approval for parochial schools as legal alternatives to the state's secular institutions. But the public schools remained the primary educational institutions.

The state's coercive arm, which reached out for the illicitly absent public-school child, was personified in the truant officer. Usually he was a county sheriff's subordinate; thus, little or no

THE ST. LOUIS ART MUSEUM

additional bureaucracy was required to enforce the attendance laws. General school administration was in the hands of elected boards, composed usually of nonprofessional citizens, very often unpaid. Professional educators fell directly under these local elected school boards. As a result, the schools abraded community sentiments remarkably little. Rarely did a truant officer put in an appearance, and usually did so only in the interest of transforming immigrant children into good American "reading audiences," to use Lincoln's apt phrase.[6]

In 1860 Americans spent approximately $35 million of public funds on education. Like farmers, lawyers, and merchants, teachers associated professionally, the better to spread literacy and morality. Associated teachers were adept lobbyists at state capitals. Some adventurous educators were testing whether Congress might establish a national university and board of education, like the state boards. But whether in county seats, state capitals, or Washington, teachers aimed to apply government power in the least abrasive way imaginable. In the South, however, the doctrine of state police power was more robustly applied, for purposes opposite to those of associated educators.

Users of State Power: Southern Slaveowners

In slave-owning states, frequent and abrasive government interference with individual rights—even with white men's private rights and actions—was used to protect the slaveowner. The slave, after all, had become the single most profitable property in which an American of 1860 could invest.

In all states, the state defined what forms of property were legitimate. Generally, any property was legal unless otherwise specified in local ordinances—thus liquor was illegitimate in dry

RAN AWAY—On Saturday night, 20th inst., from the subscriber, living near Mount Airy P. O., Carroll county, two Negro men, PERRY and CHARLES. Perry is quite dark, full face; is about 5 feet 8 or 9 inches high; has a scar on one of his hands, and one on his legs, caused by a cut from a scythe; 25 years old. Charles is of a copper color, about 5 feet 9 or 10 inches high; round shouldered, with small whiskers; has one crooked finger that he cannot straighten, and a scar on his right leg, caused by the cut of a scythe; 22 years old. I will give two hundred and fifty dollars each, if taken in the State and returned to me, or secured in some jail so that I can get them again, or a $1,000 for the two, or $500 each, if taken out of the State, and secured in some jail in this State so that I can get them again.

ROBERT DADE.

s23–3f.

A typical broadside notice of runaway slaves.

NEW YORK PUBLIC LIBRARY

counties (no statewide prohibitions of liquor sales existed until Maine went dry in 1864). Local custom, though, sometimes had a force in law equal to ordinances. In slave states, by 1860 it had become all but impossible for any court, any authority, to strip an owner of his complete property rights in his slave. Only if a slave committed a capital offense such as insurrection, murder, arson, or rape involving whites would local or state authority hold the slave personally responsible under law and subject him to prison or execution. To do so in instances of lighter offenses denied the master the fruits of the slave's labor. Plantation punishment or sale to a new, distant owner was generally held to suffice.

By 1860, the protection of masters' rights in slave property had become the primary public-policy purpose of slaveholding states. In an Orwellian manner, the right to own slaves had become more sacred than other civil rights, certainly more sacred than the civil liberties—free speech, petition, and assembly—of those who criticized slavery. Slave runaways, rescues, and uprisings in the 1840s and '50s inspired southern whites to use state police power to fetter freedom, even their own freedom if necessary, to keep slaves docile. In southern states, police powers were applied with unequaled frequency, coerciveness, and intensity.

Rural patrols enforced plantation regulations and public laws against slaves or any Negroes traveling without passports or after curfew hours. In urban centers, the size of any black assembly was strictly limited. Old ordinances and customs that forbade teaching slaves to write or to read (even the Bible) were enforced with vigor. Masters were discouraged from freeing slaves whether in wills or by manumission.

To prevent blacks from acquiring abolitionist texts and ideas, tight constabulary or vigilante controls were maintained on foreign colored sailors who came ashore in southeastern and

Gulf port cities. Police nurtured sophisticated informers' networks of barbers, bartenders, and tavern keepers to keep watch over and inform on itinerant Yankee peddlers and salesmen, who might have abolitionist tracts in their carpetbags. Self-appointed censors cut out antislavery materials from "foreign" letters, newspapers, and pamphlets.

The burdens of these arrangements were borne by existing officials and institutions, especially sheriffs and courts, aided by unofficial coadjutors such as tavern keepers and vigilante patrollers. Defenders of the South's ways referred frequently to the virtues, including budget economies, of as little government as possible; but such assertions ignored the shadow government that slavery inspired and required.

It is difficult to imagine a sharper contrast than that between the methods and purposes of the southern states' protection of slaveowners and the northern states' visible and accountable public-school systems; than between truant officers and slave patrollers; than between the encouragement and the suppression of literacy. Yet both systems fit under the very ample state police-power umbrella.

What Price Union?

The coexistence of free and slave states illustrates one great value of federalism, the tolerance of diversity. In 1860 persons who placed a high value on continued union argued that such diverse state institutions could continue to coexist pacifically. To this argument, the majority of southern whites responded with a flat declaration of lack of faith.

Long before the 1860 election, influential southerners had begun to weigh the value of the Union's diverse federalism. In 1860, as result of the Republican-Lincoln triumph, they decided that the Union was too open-ended, too sensitively democratic, too susceptible to the demands of the wrong people; that, somehow, southern police-power protection for slave property was in jeopardy.

Therefore, in 1860 southerners refused to accept the national majority's election verdict. So doing, they undercut all politics, free state as well as southern. Dixie's stand, as 1860 ended, augured the Balkanization, the Latin Americanization of the un-United States. It was the nightmare of 1787 come true. And because no appeal to government or private institution, to shared history, patriotism, or relationship, appeared able to reverse the South's emphatic negativism, free-state citizens feared for the future of their nation.

This account now turns to the question of how an election came to have this transcendant significance, leading in the South to secessions from the Union and in the North to a collapse of confidence.

FOOTNOTES

1. U.S. Congress, Senate, *Preliminary Report on the Eighth Census.* 1860, 37th Cong., 2nd sess., 1862, pp. 80–82.

2. *The Correspondence of Emerson and Carlyle,* ed. Joseph Slater (New York: Columbia University Press, 1964), p. 542.

3. Hopkins, *The Fall of the Confederacy* (London, 1867), p. 12.

4. M. Bloomfield, "Law vs. Politics: The Self-Image of the American Bar (1830–1860)," *American Journal of Legal History,* XIII (1968), 310.

5. Dicey, *Spectator of America* (reprint ed., New York: Quadrangle Books, 1971), p. 7.

6. Lincoln to Mary Lincoln, March 4, 1860, in *Collected Works, Supplement,* ed. Roy P. Basler (Westport, Conn.: Greenwood, 1974), p. 49.

2 / THE FAILURE of POLITICS

1860–61: The Links of Union Are Broken

IN THE WINTER OF 1860–61, southerners rejected the results of the 1860 presidential, congressional, and northern state elections, not on the basis of fraud but because they did not like the results. Then, as their secessions broke apart the union of states, they perverted some of America's proudest political institutions, including popular elections, constitutional conventions, and constitutional amendments.

The southern defiance of the free-state majorities for Lincoln and the Republicans was deadly for many reasons. Above all, it made likely and imminent ruptures of the only remaining major connectives that, however tenuously, were keeping the American society and economy viable, secure, and growing.

These remaining links were government, politics, and business. Other institutional links between free- and slave-state residents had already sundered on the rocks and shoals of slave-centered issues. Even churches—Baptist, Methodist, Presbyterian—had broken into northern and southern branches (a process that is reversing only in the 1970s). Few professional associations had organized beyond state levels by 1860, but nevertheless, fissures were evident, if less spectacular.

Business Links

Though slave-centered crises and passions were disrupting religious, social, and political ties, until 1860–61 mercantile life had continued with few difficulties. But, that winter, even the most ardent peace-at-any-price businessman worried about the capacity of entrepreneurship to survive if government did not survive. Government, as Americans understood it, could not live unless politics operated in the ordered cadences required by state and federal law. If election politics did not work, if majority verdicts were discarded, federalism and popular government were proved to be as impossible as aristocrats insisted they were. Failed politics logically must lead to the failure of government. Then, the myriads of interconnected relationships that stabilized society must break.

"Been stagnated by the times," the Mercantile Agency, the nation's leading credit rating company, reported in January 1861 of a Charleston, South Carolina, real estate broker. The remark effectively describes secession's effect on commerce.[1]

If marketplace relationships broke, it was feared that all the constraints that kept this mobile, vigorous, often violent society livable would give way. Contract responsibilities, the stability of trusts, conveyances, and estates, the very titles to personal and real property would be weakened if not broken. Criminal law would be undermined. All property, all social stability, all law and order, were defined by the states' presences in the union of states; all were risked by the southerners' stance.

Despair was not an excessive response to the southern position, in light of its destructive implications. The southern decision to reject the 1860 election results more than outweighed impressive material gains of the preceding three-quarters of a century. It nullified the rationalizations under way in the professions, business, and industry. It blocked the progress that was being made toward accommodating the greater demands upon state and federal law for public services.

The Worth of Politics and Government

A century ago (as now), every American lawyer learned early in his training a cliché that, in its many versions, has this sense: "Justice must be visible in order to be acceptable; justice must be accepted if it is visibly to serve."

In Lincoln's America, an equally appropriate popular understanding existed concerning the complex of relationships between politics and government. It may be phrased thus: "Politics must be seen to work, and its results in elections be accepted, else government cannot work."

During Lincoln's fifty-year lifetime as of 1860, politics and the nation had come a long way together. During the age of Jackson, aristocratic property and religious qualifications for voting and officeholding had declined in the states. This increased democratization was vital, given the enlarging population. Despite long-standing fears, the nation's territorial and population explosions and the increase in the number of states had not overtasked the capacity of Americans to govern themselves. Instead, Americans had contrived a succession of workable political inventions that permitted both diversity and stability. These political devices harmonized very well with state-based popular government and with the separation-of-powers and check-and-balance governing arrangements on local, state, and national levels.

These original devices included dual party organizations in each state (until antislavery politics became impermissible in the southern states) ; the parties had developed to the point of being active at all levels of government. Nominating conventions for each party, an American innovation, connected candidates, from obscure sheriff to nation's President, to party, locality, and state. Another innovation, constitutional conventions (legalized revolutions), allowed older states to modernize their governments and laws, and enabled former national territories to transform themselves into states. Through favors, patronage, and individual loyalty, these complex institutions were connected in a personal and flexible manner.

With respect to new states, Americans had worked out yet another creative arrangement. Jefferson's Northwest Ordinance technique, applied to subsequent territorial acquisitions, met successfully the problem that British sophisticates of the 1770s failed really to perceive, much less to solve: the problem of mature "colonies" that refused any longer to be subordinate. The Jeffersonian innovation escalated the nation's territories from mere land and administrative units to incubators of future states: thereby, the territories were introduced early into the larger political establishment. Full equality was accorded new states after population requirements were met and a state constitution properly adopted. The orderly progression of new lands from frontiers to territories to fully equal states encouraged immigration, western migration, property-title stability, and capital investments. By 1860 the United States had become the world's largest duty-free trading area. Goods, people, and livestock traveled freely and inexpensively, if not always comfortably or safely, on the expanding web of roads, canals, coastal maritime routes, and rail lines.

Popular, regular, and universally accepted elections were the basic element in all these remarkable government constructions. To be sure, charges and instances of managed voting were increasingly common by mid-century. County rings and city bosses manipulated men and laws. Disputed local election results were frequent. But rejection on grounds of fraud of an individual election's result never threatened the system.

Faults were realistically perceived, but the contemporary judgment was clear that these election-based governments, better than any abroad, allowed for political diversity and change in a manner that, satisfyingly often, worked to the advantage of all. Elections and the institutions and processes they fed provided opportunities for talent to move upward. Insofar as their results were accepted, however grudgingly, elections were necessary legitimizing and stabilizing occasions in a society that, by any measure, was the most pluralistic, volatile, and complex of its time. Elections provided certainty, continuity, and stability for a people whose very folklore glorified violence, who lacked alternative contraints in the form of national churches or hereditary dynasties, and who good-naturedly ignored the pretensions to natural leadership of lawyers, ministers, or businessmen.

The changes that emerged from the election structure tended strongly toward the political middle. From the lowliest justice of the peace to the United States President, offices could have only one incumbent. In each election district, a party had to attract the votes of at least a bare majority of qualified residents in order to win an office for its candidate. By the 1840s, two major parties were competing for votes in each election district, in part by assembling broad platform appeals that seemed likely to win the largest number of ballots. Residents in an election district who favored policies that a party refused to champion—such as abolitionism, liquor prohibition, or women's rights—usually had unsatisfactory alternatives. They could swallow their resentment and vote a major-party ticket, support a narrow-interest third party which could almost never win elections, or, like Thoreau, drift into anti-institutional individualism.

Elections, parties, and platforms were devices for institutionalizing politically acceptable changes in a huge, diverse, dynamic, and complex society. No one imagined that these devices performed perfectly. Then, as now, every American—bartender, bargee, farm or factory worker, clerk, and businessman—was a constitutional and political expert. Cynicism was the common attitude toward politicos. Exposures of political corruption were frequent; opposition politicians and ubiquitous news reporters saw to the revelations.

But if cynical, Americans were not foolish. Common men understood that orderly political processes based on elections made possible their enjoyment of relative plenty. No politician could ignore the importance of open politics and elections in enabling the nation to adapt to the enormous changes demanded by its hugeness and by the altering and rising aspirations of generations.

Better than many professors and law men then and since, laymen of 1860 sensed the indispensability of the democratized politics of federalism. Everyone knew that election rituals, including parades, barbecues, and rallies, were more than the best free shows in town and that they were not cost-free. Yet it seemed to matter little, in popular estimations, that particular elections and party operations might involve sordid city-hall deals, venal county-courthouse favors, interest-ridden state legislation, or outrageous congressional influence peddling. Such self-serving sins were regarded with shocking smugness, would-be reformers complained.

The venality mattered. But it mattered more that politics-as-it-was-played greased more than individuals' palms. Politics, including elections, lubricated all government and kept the federal system operable, at a time when government's own institutions were minuscule and the popular consensus was that they should stay that way.

Politics and elections provided acceptable policy options and responsible personnel choices on all levels of the federal system. In turn, government-through-politics made decisions (on utility contracts, bank charters, tariff rates, and so on) that in other countries were the responsibility of bureaucratic public agencies from start to finish. Politics were crude, wasteful, and venal, but never irrelevant. Elections were visible signs that government lived.

The Underinstitutionalized Government

Politics' relevance and preeminence stemmed from the fact that at both local and national levels government functions were few in number: budgets were low; permanent staffs were sparse.

Because American government of 1860 was so underinstitutionalized, politics translated directly into government policy. By contemporary standards, there was almost no intervening level of appointive, bureaucratic, impersonal experts. Federal judges were appointed for life, but almost everyone else receiving a salary from tax dollars was subject to the partisan "spoils" system of rotation in public office, the system that so distressed the reformers.

In 1860, none of these relationships between politics, elections, and government was taught in any American college or university (although there were many self-taught experts in the subject). The southern rejection of the 1860 election results inspired Lincoln's contemporaries, for the first time since 1787–89, systematically to study their government. As an example, in 1867 Timothy Farrar, the aged law partner of Daniel Webster, noted how

> the infancy of the nation, the sparseness of the population, the severe pressure of daily toil, the immaturity of our institutions, and the remoteness of neighbors, afforded a favorable opportunity for trying an experiment in the minimum of government by which civil society could, under any circumstances, be maintained.[2]

But even without special tuition, workaday Americans in 1860 adequately understood and were proud of their political and governmental world. Most (white) Americans neither feared their government nor felt fettered by their society's political or bureaucratic institutions, at a time when, elsewhere, ordinary men saw both as overt enemies. This may be why Americans were so anxious to explain to foreigners the nature of their usually happy republic and to learn if others appreciated it. Visiting here for the first time, James Bryce, the British statesman and historian, was asked "by every chance [American] acquaintance," a question he had never heard Englishmen, Frenchmen, or Germans ask foreigners: "What do you think of our institutions?"[3]

After the southern secessions, it seemed very possible that those institutions might no longer function anywhere in the un-United States. The southern defiance undercut all politics, all institutions, all law and order. If politics did not work, if election results were rejected as southerners were doing in 1860, federalism and democracy would be uncontrollable. Nothing could work. Property was a farce—except, perhaps, slave property. Anarchy and socialism, both scare words in 1860, were in the cards.

The Perversion of Federalism and State Police Power

What made the southern rejection of the 1860 election results so destructive was not that the character of the threat was unprecedented. Southerners had been talking about nullifying free-state majorities for decades. In earlier sectional crises, as in 1819—20, 1832—33 (when President Andrew Jackson faced down South Carolina's nullification of a federal statute), 1850, and 1854, southern spokesmen had threatened secession. Men Lincoln's age in 1860 had grown up in a period when southern resentment at election results, and consequent secession threats, had become almost standard fare—as threats.

In the earlier sectional crises, Congress had succeeded in temporarily placating indignant southern spokesmen. Congress accommodated southern threats by means of the miscalled "compromises" ("surrenders" would be a more accurate term) of 1820–54. One way or another, these national accommodations to the South gave specially privileged status to that peculiar form of private property, the slave, not only in the slave states but also in the nation's capital and territories, and, frighteningly, even in the free states.

With respect to the territories—states of the future—the "compromises" diminished sharply the possibility of nonslave states developing there. By the 1820 Missouri Compromise, Maine had been admitted to the Union as a free state, Missouri as a slave state, and slavery was prohibited in the Louisiana Purchase north of the 36° 30′ line. But then, in 1854, by the Kansas-Nebraska Act, the Missouri Compromise was rescinded, and new territories were to decide for themselves whether they would become free or slave states. As a result, "Bleeding Kansas" became an arena of violence between proslavery and abolitionist forces. Finally, in 1857, the U.S. Supreme Court's Dred Scott decision ruled that a slaveowner's rights to slave property extended even into territorial areas where slavery was forbidden by the Missouri Compromise or perhaps even the Northwest Ordinance; it was declared unconstitutional for Congress to limit the privileges of slaveowners; indeed Congress was specifically obliged to protect them.

Thus, it was apparent that in federalism freedom took second place to slave property and servile labor. Federal power could be used only to protect slaveowners, not those enslaved. And in the areas where compromise permitted the existence of slavery, by a kind of Gresham's law, slave labor pushed out free labor, and these territories tended toward becoming slave states.

The Democrats

The Democratic party had been born of Jeffersonian antipathies to excessive central government. States'-rights credos had developed to protect individuals' civil liberties against outrageous infringements. Federalist limitations on speech and dissent, especially the Sedition Act, inspired Jefferson and Madison to appeal to citizens to vote the rascals out in the 1800 national elections. But by 1860 the southern insistence on states' rights had degenerated from a concern for individual liberty and a commitment to political action at the state level, to a single-minded concern for state-defined protection of the property rights of slaveowners, and a deep antipathy to change. Elections and politics represented institutionalized change.

Alternative politics—and thus a viable second party structure—withered in slave states. The southern position of 1860 was far more unified, therefore, than that of any other region. Dissent in southern states had become futile if not dangerous. It was impossible to institutionalize opposition to slave property's

Scenes such as this, depicting the seizure of a runaway slave, were enacted in both slave states and free; fugitive slave laws extended the privileges of slaveowners into the free states.
NEW YORK PUBLIC LIBRARY

advantaged place. Employing this sectional chorus in Democratic party councils, southerners demanded functional immobility on the part of the national government in almost all matters except protection of slave property. On that issue, Democrats demanded national action indeed!

To most free-state residents, the most irritating and visible indications of this imbalance in federalism were the recaptures of runaway slaves. By means of increasingly stringent national recapture laws, which Congress enacted as part of the "compromise" packages, the privileges of slaveowners were extended into free states.

When runaway slaves sought refuge in free states, pursuing federal agents entered private homes and offices, seized persons and papers, and took the slaves back across state lines. Free-state legal procedures, rights to due process, to trials and so on, were ignored. Federal functional vigor in the role of slave catcher at the behest of southern Democrats was ironic indeed, for the southerners had championed states' rights and the inviolability of state law, had opposed almost any function for the national government since Whig and even Federalist times. But free-state property and civil rights were apparently not the kinds of states' rights southerners favored.

By 1860 even the disproportionate successes they had won in the "compromises" failed to satisfy southern Democratic leaders. At the party's national nominating convention, southerners demanded candidates and policies that free-state Democrats, such as Illinois's Stephen Douglas, a front-running presidential aspirant, knew could not carry their own states. Delegates like Douglas were trying to practice politics; the southern delegates were promoting ideology. When Douglas received the nomination, the southerners walked out of the convention.

As result, the Democratic party split three ways. Opposing Douglas, lame-duck President Buchanan backed the southern wing, which, in a splinter session, nominated John Breckinridge. There was also a Constitutional Union group, with John Bell as banner-bearer, which had no policies save "Constitution and Union."

The Republicans

In many northern communities, by 1860, thoughtful, propertied, conservative men, most of whom detested abolitionists and were not Negrophiles, were giving the new Republican organization substantial support. Composed overwhelmingly of good law-and-order citizens, with heavy rural and suburban constituencies, the Republican party also attracted numerous urban merchant and professional supporters. The party's central conviction was that Congress must, and could, create a curtain in the western territories beyond which state-defined slave property must not pass, Dred Scott notwithstanding, when election majorities so demanded.

With respect to economic matters, the Republican basic "can do" constitutionalism was echoed, depending upon the Republican, in demands for the revival in more modern forms of old Federalist and Whig policies regarding a national bank, protective tariffs for American industries, aids to agriculture such as a homestead law and federally assisted agricultural and mechanical colleges, and other internal improvements such as road-building and railroad encouragements. Concerning the overriding runaway slave recapture question, Republicans decried the privileges afforded only to slaveowners, and denied that southern state rights ranked ahead of free state rights. The basic Republican position was that the Constitution, federalism, and politics could balance decently the rights of all states if election verdicts were honored. Incurable optimists, Republicans clung

In this 1860 *Harper's Weekly* cartoon, Columbia admonishes young America: "Well done, Sonny! 'Go it while you're young, for when you're old you can't.' "

NEW YORK PUBLIC LIBRARY

to their faith in the system's workability. By contrast, Democrats repeated negations about the capacity of Congress to put limitations on the expansion of slavery, and abolitionists damned both political houses.

By 1860 the Republican consensus was that the South had few genuine grievances. John Brown was dead; abolitionists were in disarray. Violence against slavery was denounced by leading Republicans. Everything the South had opposed for forty years, including the tariff, homesteads, federal aid to internal improvements, and a more rational national banking system, had been frustrated. Further, the South enjoyed the largest benefits of the "compromises."

Republicans insisted that they were no threat to law and order or to state rights anywhere. The party enjoyed majorities only in the free states. Abraham Lincoln, its presidential candidate from the Illinois semi-frontier, could hope for no votes in the South. Whatever Republicans proposed could be achieved only through ordinary political and legislative processes. Democrats, despite their party's three-way split, retained very strong numerical support in the free as well as slave states. And the 1860 fissures in the party surely would be bridged quickly. The Democrats in Congress, state legislatures, and county and municipal councils would be well able to perform the historical checking function that government-without-politics could not provide.

The 1860 presidential vote totals substantiated the Republicans' assumptions. The Douglas-Breckinridge-Bell Democratic party totals far outweighed Lincoln's, although on the fundamental matter of preserving the Union, Lincoln would not be a minority President. Douglas and Bell also stood four-square on the position that the Union must survive and southerners should show restraint. The Breckinridge votes, concentrated in the slave states, were the only negative electoral judgment on this issue (see table).

Result of the Presidential Election of 1860

States	Electoral Vote				Popular Vote			
	Lincoln	*Bell*	*Douglas*	*Breckinridge*	*Lincoln*	*Bell*	*Douglas*	*Breckinridge*
Maine	8				62,811	2,046	26,693	6,368
New Hampshire	5				37,519	441	25,881	2,112
Massachusetts	13				106,533	22,331	34,372	5,939
Rhode Island	4				12,244		*7,707	
Connecticut	6				43,792	3,291	15,522	14,641
Vermont	5				33,808	1,969	6,849	218
New York	35				362,646		*312,510	
New Jersey	4		3		58,324		*62,801	
Pennsylvania	27				268,030	12,776	16,765	*178,871
Delaware				3	3,815	3,864	1,023	7,337
Maryland				8	2,294	41,760	5,966	42,482
Virginia		15			1,929	74,681	16,290	74,323
North Carolina				10		44,990	2,701	48,539
South Carolina				8		No	popular	vote.†
Georgia				10		42,886	11,590	51,889
Kentucky		12			1,364	66,058	25,651	53,143
Tennessee		12				69,274	11,350	64,709
Ohio	23				231,610	12,194	187,232	11,405
Louisiana				6		20,204	7,625	22,681
Mississippi				7		25,040	3,283	40,797
Indiana	13				139,033	5,306	115,509	12,295
Illinois	11				172,161	4,913	160,215	2,404
Alabama				9		27,875	13,651	48,831
Missouri			9		17,028	58,372	58,801	31,317
Arkansas				4		20,094	5,227	28,732
Michigan	6				88,480	405	65,057	805
Florida				3		5,437	367	8,543
Texas				4		*15.438		47,548
Iowa	4				70,409	1,763	55,111	1,048
Wisconsin	5				86,110	161	65,021	888
California	4				39,173	6,817	38,516	34,334
Minnesota	4				22,069	62	11,920	748
Oregon	3				5,270	183	3,951	5,006
Total	180	39	12	72	1,866,452	590,631	1,375,157	847,953

Lincoln over Douglas	491,295
" " Breckinridge	1,018,499
" " Bell	1,275,821
Other Candidates over Lincoln	947,289

† Electors appointed by state legislature.

* Fusion.

From Edward McPherson, ed. *The Political History of the United States of America during the Great Rebellion, 1860–1865* (New York, 1865; reprint, ed. H. M. Hyman and H. Trefousse [New York: DaCapo, 1972]), p. 1.

Reasonable men saw no reason for southerners to reject 1860's election results. No Republican party policies aimed at abolishing slavery in states where it existed. Patience was in order until the next election allowed another popular verdict. No President since Jackson had enjoyed two White House terms. It seemed unbelievable that the election-rejection gambit would actually be played, instead of merely threatened.

Secessions

The story is familiar—so familiar that its shocking qualities are almost forgotten. News of Lincoln's election immediately triggered radical southern action. South Carolina's legislature unanimously issued a call for a special convention. On December 20, 1860, this convention passed, also unanimously, a resolution severing the state's ties to the nation. The members of the convention justified secession as a right derived from the state-sovereignty thesis given classical expression by Calhoun. They maintained it was a necessary response to the victory at the polls of a party, Congress, and President hostile to slavery.

A Christmas pause followed. Then, beginning January 9, 1861, Mississippi followed South Carolina's example. On January 10, Florida; on January 11, Alabama; on January 19, Georgia; on January 26, Louisiana; and on February 1, Texas. In Congress these states' delegations defended emotionally the necessity and propriety of secession. Then, without impediment, they left the Capitol.

Opponents to secession existed in most southern states. Some were prominent individuals of Sam Houston's stature in Texas. But in every instance antisecessionists failed effectively to organize. No antislavery political parties had existed in any deep southern state for a long time. Other local issues were inade-

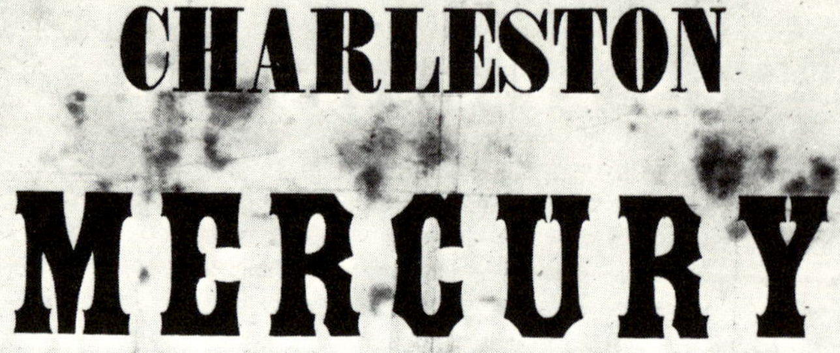

CHARLESTON MERCURY

EXTRA:

Passed unanimously at 1.15 o'clock, P. M. December 20th, 1860.

AN ORDINANCE

To dissolve the Union between the State of South Carolina and other States united with her under the compact entitled "The Constitution of the United States of America."

We, the People of the State of South Carolina, in Convention assembled, do declare and ordain, and it is hereby declared and ordained,

That the Ordinance adopted by us in Convention, on the twenty-third day of May, in the year of our Lord one thousand seven hundred and eighty-eight, whereby the Constitution of the United States of America was ratified, and also, all Acts and parts of Acts of the General Assembly of this State, ratifying amendments of the said Constitution, are hereby repealed; and that the union now subsisting between South Carolina and other States, under the name of "The United States of America," is hereby dissolved.

THE UNION IS DISSOLVED!

A broadside issued by the *Charleston Mercury* announces the secessionist resolution of the South Carolina Convention.

LIBRARY OF CONGRESS

quate to form a base for alternative, antisecession sentiment. The result was that Unionists remained individual opponents to secession, easily isolated and effectively suppressed. Even for brave, patriotic men, it was very difficult to stand against secession in the isolated small rural communities typical of 1860 southern life. To defy neighbors, friends, and families was to incur condemnation as an advocate of race-mixing "black Republicanism." Secessions were horrifyingly smooth procedures.

Only the upper South—North Carolina, Virginia, Tennessee, and Arkansas—hesitated. But even those states issued warnings that they, too, would secede if the national government attempted to reverse secession by coercion.

Secession and Slavery

Economic concerns do not explain the secession imperative. Since 1833, tariff, bank, and internal improvement policies had largely been shaped by southern specifications. Granted, after March 1861 Republicans would have the White House, majorities in Congress, and heavy representation in northern states' legislatures. But, as noted, impressive Democratic phalanxes remained on Capitol Hill, in the Supreme Court, in the federal bureaucracy (such as it was), and in free states' capitals. Blessed with unusual seniority, southern delegates in Congress were expert committee and floor fighters. They would no doubt have been able to take advantage of Republican divisions to prevent a reversal of national economic policies. Without party concert in Congress, no President, however strong, could break out of his very limited functional role—the only kind of role southerners had permitted the federal government. Lincoln was looked on as a weak man.

Southerners' desire to protect slavery was secession's cause. But neither Lincoln nor his party was abolitionist. To be sure, northern states, under local Republican party initiative, had built up procedural impediments against fugitive-slave recaptures. In Wisconsin, for example, state judges opposed recapture agents with state habeas corpus writs. But the runaways were small in numbers; in 1860 perhaps one-fiftieth of 1% of slaves became fugitives, and many were recaptured. Moreover, under conservative pressures that increased after John Brown's violent endeavor (1859), several northern states were preparing to lower impediments against recaptures.

The Republican consensus was that alternatives existed to further extension of slavery into the national territories, and that ordinary politics could develop acceptable options. But slavery extension was not an immediate issue in any territory in 1860, despite the Kansas blood letting. It was a question for the future. The shape of the future was what the territories and secession were all about.

Secession occurred because leading southerners concluded that Republicans, once in power, would become abolitionist. Probably more important, southerners believed that democratic politics would work against them in the long run, no matter how numerically impotent Republicans might be in 1860. The southern form of biracial coexistence would remain possible only if slave states permanently immunized master-slave property relationships from external interference. In 1860 white southerners decided that state secessions and the creation of a new slave-centered federal union (the idea of single-state independence was not seriously entertained) were the only certain way to safeguard the principles of racial superiority and the right to slave property.

In 1860 investments in slave property were the single most profitable employment of capital. And egos as well as profits were involved. Southern whites believed that religion, history, and science proved slavery a benefit to slave as well as to master. Yet every runaway advertised slavery's illogic as well as its inhumanity. No free black ever voluntarily headed southward in order to become a slave; no "fugitive free law" was ever necessary.

Southerners writhed at free-state and European gibes at slave ownership. Emancipations before 1850 in European colonies in Latin America and in independent Latin American republics, especially on Caribbean islands, dramatized slaveowners' encirclement by free labor areas. The emotional defensiveness of southerners may have made national adjustments impossible. They might have created, for example, some form of regional insurance pool for owners of runaways, which could have quietly bypassed the fugitive return problem. But instead, unscientific concepts of racial superiority resulted in hard-line attitudes. Race-ordered moral judgments overshadowed patriotism and respect for common laws and history.

The fear of change through open politics also underlay secession. What the South was defying was history—in particular, the mid-nineteenth-century impetus for reform and modernization. Secession aimed to freeze the future in the image of an idealized past and the slave present. As we shall see, those who attempted to create a "compromise of 1860," to buy off the South with blacks' destinies, were also attempting to freeze the Constitution.

The Secession Winter

Viewed from free-state communities, secession took on nightmarish qualities, but to the deep South, it was a joyous confirmation of southerners' control of their own destiny. On

February 1, 1861, representatives of the seven seceded states assembled at Montgomery, Alabama, as both a "national" constitutional convention and a legislature. By February 8 the convention had produced a provisional Confederate States constitution. Soon after, it named Jefferson Davis president and Alexander Stephens vice-president of the Confederacy.

All this was fully reported in the North. Telegraph and mail communication continued. Also reported were dramatic scenes of Confederate officials lowering the "old" flag wherever it flew —primarily at modest post offices and at revenue, land, navigation, and customs facilities, for, in fact, the national presence was scarcely visible in the South. Many incumbent postmasters, steamboat inspectors, lighthouse keepers, and other minor officials simply transformed themselves into Confederate or state officers with the same duties. There were even fewer military posts, navy yards, and armories. Almost without exception, they surrendered pacifically to the new self-proclaimed sovereignties.

Meanwhile, however nervously, businessmen entered into contracts, delivered cargoes, allowed loans, and pressed lawsuits. Trains and coastal shipping ran on fairly normal schedules. Citizens, who wished to, traveled southward without hindrance to join their seceded states. Those who returned south included United States officials of high rank—a resigned Supreme Court justice (John A. Campbell), senators and representatives, and military and naval officers—and numerous minor functionaries. A great nation was observing its own dismemberment with apparent detachment, while commerce continued almost in a normal manner. In the South and abroad, critics of popular democracy insisted that the grotesque scene proved that craven mercantile ethics dominated the free states, justifying further the slave states' secessions.

No government or political institution seemed to be adequate to the crisis. The President and Congress were lame ducks, involved in discordant recriminations and without positive goals. The Supreme Court was irrelevant and discredited. Still, unhappy patriots looked to the White House for leadership.

President James Buchanan: The Lamest of Lame Ducks

Long before 1860, the Presidency had become the focus of American political life. The Electoral College notwithstanding, the President was the only nationally elected officer. Even United States senators and representatives were states' men. (Only a few became statesmen.) The framers of the 1787 Constitution had tried to create in the office of President an innovation in government: a popularly elected head of state who would be too restricted to be a tyrant yet sufficiently free to govern positively this enormous, ethnically and religiously pluralistic, state-based federal nation. Great Presidents had managed the trick of leadership within the complexities of democratized, state-based party politics. James Buchanan was inadequate.

He knew no ways to focus opposition against secession or to develop alternatives to it. He had been unable to hold together even his own Democratic party in Congress or in the 1860 convention.

If a vigorous policy, capable of eliciting national rather than sectional support, was to issue from anywhere in the 1860–61 winter, it had to be from the White House. Lincoln, the President-elect, had only a sectional mandate, and had to wait in the wings until March 1861 before taking office. Immediate action was up to Buchanan.

But Buchanan was immobilized by his knowledge of the nation's weaknesses and lack of relevant institutions, by his rigid constitutionalism, and by his party's factionalization. Although he stated in his December 1860 State of the Union message that secession was unconstitutional, Buchanan also insisted that no clause of the Constitution permitted the nation to stop a secession by coercing a state. Told of Andrew Jackson's firm stand against South Carolina's nullification attempt twenty-five years earlier, Buchanan alleged that he was ignorant of it because he had been abroad, as United States Minister to Russia. More to Buchanan's credit, he wished not to disturb reconciliation efforts then under way.

A "Compromise" of 1860?

In response to the slave states' extraordinary actions, various groups formed to try to create a compromise formula. What the word meant in 1860–61 was a formula of concessions by which southern whites could be bought off from secession and could be led to obey the nation's Constitution, laws, and customs and to acquiesce in election results.

Special House and Senate committees plus an "old gentleman's convention," chaired by former President John Tyler, groped toward such a formula. Elements in a proposal by Kentucky Senator John Crittenden (since Clay's time border states' men were supposed somehow to be superior exorcists of slave-caused sectional irritants) became common in all deliberations. Crittenden wished to extent to the Pacific the 1820 Missouri Compromise's 36°30′ line, despite the fact that it had been repealed in the 1854 Kansas-Nebraska Act and declared unconstitutional by the Supreme Court in the Dred Scott case. South of the 36°30′ line Congress would be obliged to give positive protection to private property in slaves as long as a region remained a territory. The Kentuckian further asked that the nation guarantee, through an unamendable amendment to the Constitution, never to act against slave property in a state.

In 1860–61 no substantial abolitionist voice enjoyed hearings in any political party. There was no formal or informal provision by which the law of free-labor states could affect slave states. The flow was the other way, by means of the fugitive-slave recapture laws. Crittenden proposed that Congress must perpetually enforce those laws. Similarly, Crittenden's proposals disarmed Congress perpetually of authority to abolish slave property in the District of Columbia.

The Crittenden proposal reversed the free-state majority vote in the 1860 elections. Further, Crittenden's territorial propositions illuminated mercilessly the incapacity of national government institutions to provide local self-determination during the territories' transition into states.

Commenting on these matters, an American expatriate in England, John F. Mercer, noted for foreign readers the immensity of the territories, and stated that a national government "of acknowledged strength, with inherent energy, whose acts could never be questioned," would have no easy task in their governance.

> How then [Mercer continued] can an imbecile government, whose acts are all questioned, and often opposed, dependent on chances or the popularity of its measures for support, hope to control such a wide-spread population? . . . A government that spreads its thin texture over 2,000 miles square, must be united and strong to preserve its own existence.[4]

The Crittenden formulas would have frozen the Constitution and electoral politics into a form agreeable to the regional slave-owning minority. Crittenden's purpose was to remove the central public question of the century from the arena of political democracy. The only similar total prohibition in the Constitution that so intimately affected whole classes of Americans was the First Amendment forbidding creation of an established church. But even this prohibition was amendable. The "compromise" bait, an unamendable constitutional amendment, was aptly called a "Chinese shoe" by the historian Hermann Von Holst.

The depths to which secession sank the constitutional ethics of Americans are measurable by the fact that in the South Crittenden's giveaways were declared to be inadequate. Secession and independence were better guarantees of the perpetualization of slavery than a return to the United States even as altered by such a regressive formula. Even more indicative of the demoralization resulting from secession is the fact that most free-state Democrats came out in favor of the whole Crittenden package.

To their relative credit, Republicans rejected all but one of Crittenden's proposals, holding to a position that was essentially what voters had approved in the 1860 balloting. They agreed only not to interfere with slavery in slave states, maintaining that traditional political processes should determine the destiny of slavery in the territories. Republicans hoped thereby to limit slavery to the states where it existed so that, some distant day, it might die off.

The Abortive Thirteenth Amendment of 1861

Thus, in early 1861, lame-duck Republican congressmen were willing to support an "ordinary" amendment to the Constitution that prohibited perpetually national interference with slave property within states. From President-elect Lincoln down, Republicans saw this amendment, which would become the Thirteenth Amendment when ratified, as an unhappy but bearable price to pay for sectional reconciliation. It reflected what existed. The nation could not prohibit a state-defined form of property within that state. The Supreme Court had even said that the nation could not exclude such property from its territories. A Thirteenth Amendment, limiting forever the nation's capacity to do what it could not at present do anyway, did less violence to free-state sentiments than the attack on all stabilizing institutions that secession represented.

The Thirteenth Amendment proposal passed the Congress and went out to the states for ratification. With the onset of the Civil War, it died. Four years later, a new Thirteenth Amendment was ratified. It abolished slavery in all states and territories. A measure of the distance American society traveled between the secession winter of 1860–61 and the Appomattox spring of 1865 is the style, content, and purpose of the two Thirteenth Amendment proposals. That it was a long distance indeed is apparent in the anxious mood of James Russell Lowell as he measured New Year prospects for 1861 against the sad facts of 1860:

> Is it the effect of democracy to make all men cowards? An ounce of pluck just now were worth a king's ransom. There is one comfort, though a shabby one, in the feeling that matters will come to such a pass that courage will be forced upon us, and that when there is no hope left we shall learn a little self-confidence from despair. That in such a crisis the fate of the country should be in the hands of a sneak [Buchanan]. If the Republicans stand firm we shall be saved, even at the cost of disunion. If they yield, it is all up with us and with the experiment of democracy.[5]

FOOTNOTES

1. Dun & Bradstreet Papers, So. Carolina, vol. 6, p. 77.
2. Farrar, *Manual of the Constitution of the United States of America* (Boston: Little, Brown, 1867), pp. viii-ix.

3. Bryce, *American Commonwealth,* ed. Louis Hacker (New York: Capricorn, 1959), I, 1-2.

4. Mercer, *An Exposition of the Weakness and Inefficiency of the Government of the United States, by a Late American Statesman* (London, 1863), p. 35.

5. To Charles Nordhoff, December 31, 1860, in *Letters of James Russell Lowell,* ed. Charles Eliot Norton (New York: Harper, 1894), I, 308.

3 / SECESSION and WAR: THE SOUTH'S SENSE of TIME and PURPOSE

Secession and a Lost Cause?

SOCIETIES THAT SUFFER deep frustrations, such as defeats in wars, tend to explain failures by bending history. Thus, France after 1871 and Germany after 1918 created and perpetuated self-serving, self-deluding historical fantasies.

The secessionists of 1861 were masterful weavers of history. Looking backward from defeat in 1865, they embedded their Lost Cause approach to the 1860s deeply into American literature. But analysis of the seceders' sense of time, pace, and purpose makes doubtful the accuracy of much of the footnoted folklore about secession.

In the Lost Cause tradition, secession has been seen largely as the prelude to a war—indeed, to the Civil War—that, allegedly, the Confederacy had to lose because of the free states' unbeatable material advantages; a war that became the cutting edge for Reconstruction's supposed excesses. Since, by this kind of reasoning, it was obvious that secession must lead to this war and to this defeat and consequences of defeat, the decision for secession was hopeless and endearingly noble. It was Jeffersonian America's last, best hope to keep the machine out of Eden, and to insulate the southern region against the shopkeepers' standards that were supposedly eroding the moral fiber of the nonslave states' residents.

Secession on Its Own Terms: The Sense of the Future

Despite these protestations, evidence is impressive that seceders were trying to shape a future as well as recover a past.[1] After all, no one in 1860–61 could know that the Confederate States of America was to surrender unconditionally in 1865. Seceders created it to live, not die.

Looking forward from early 1861, when seceders created the Confederacy, rather than backward from our time, there is impressive evidence that secession was not supposed to lead to any war. The scale, duration, and character of the Civil War simply could not be anticipated.

What seceders did anticipate was northern acquiescence in secession, and opportunity to insulate slave property permanently against the vagaries of popular majorities even in the South. The best insulation, it appeared, was in a new national union of slave-owning states. There would be no interruption from Washington, where efforts toward compromise were under way even while secession proceeded. Surely the free states, so accustomed to deferring to the South, would acquiesce in a final severance of the sections.

The idea that free-state citizens would never fight received dramatic support early in December 1860, when Buchanan told

In this Currier & Ives cartoon, South Carolina secessionist governor Francis Pickens' demand that the federal government surrender its facilities in seceded states meets a typically ineffectual response from Buchanan.
NEW YORK PUBLIC LIBRARY

the nation that state secessions were unconstitutional though, in his partisan opinion, understandable, but also that the nation possessed no constitutional means to stop them.

As winter advanced toward spring, the news spread of the flaccid surrenders of national military posts and other facilities inside the seceded states. Only puny, fitful efforts were made by Buchanan, and then, in March and early April 1861, by Lincoln, to resupply two offshore forts, Pickens and Sumter (of which more later). The Washington government could not even effectively sustain a few score regulars in its own fortifications. Could such a government force seven populous states, spread across a veritable subcontinent, into submission? In 1861, and for a long time after, the idea was incredible.

In this context, the seceders' sense of time and purpose deserves further attention. Time was the secessionists' first ally, whether in the peace they anticipated or in a war they did not really expect. Despite southerners' protestations about Republican aggressiveness against slavery, secession had pulled the Republicans' fangs. Coming into office, the new Republican President and congressional majority would be faced not with the issue of expansionist proslavery pressures against which they had campaigned, but with the fact of seceded states. Republicans had no popular mandate on postelection questions, and no way to get one until late 1862. Southern leaders continued to berate the Republicans as unprincipled aggressors against slavery, thereby justifying secession. But at the same time, these leaders argued that the Republicans, and free-state residents generally, would, most unaggressively, accept secession as an accomplished fact.

In this comfortably self-contradictory analysis, it was assumed Lincoln would continue Buchanan's catatonic policy of acquiescence in secessions and the occupations of national facilities. Free-state merchants would insist on keeping open the channels of trade; the free-state population would accept what its leaders knew no ways to prevent. Foreign governments would recognize the Confederacy's independence.

Secession and a War

But suppose that by some quirk the United States tried to coerce the seceded states back into the old Union? Then free-state political corruption, the alleged domination of politics by merchants and spoilsmen, from which the southerners were determined to escape, would soon collapse the effort in scandals. Moreover, in the North, the platforms of both parties committed the White House-Congress leadership to restraint, at least through 1864. Themselves rigid in their political positions, southerners assumed that free-state politics would be similarly inflexible. Therefore, should Republicans shift goals, popular resistance was probable. Slave-owning border states would drop into the Confederate ranks (a correct prophecy). Overly-democratic free-state political processes and institutions would collapse in antiadministration riots, especially where urban Democratic parties were strong (an incorrect estimate).

If, despite all such calculations, a war came, the prevailing assumption North and South was that it would resemble the only conflict Americans of 1860–61 remembered vividly, the Mexican War. The seceders believed they would win such a war.

Brief, cheap, and glorious for Americans, the Mexican War was fought by familiar nineteenth-century military and naval institutions. And the South's martial superiority (enabled by slavery's freeing whites to practice the arts of war) had been demonstrated in that conflict, or at least so southerners believed. A war with the North would lead to a similarly quick victory; the free states would soon accept permanent Confederate independence.

Time: The Southern Asset

In a war, time would serve the South's fundamental purpose. That purpose, permanent independence, required the South to seek no territorial conquest; and no military occupation of free-state areas would be necessary. Indeed, an ultimate Confederate triumph did not require even a single battlefield victory, although southern analysts hastened to add that of course there would be many.

Seceders understood that war (of the sort anticipated) or no war, they had merely to persist, and the South would win its goal. Blessed with unity on the basic racial issue and, consequently, on almost all related policy questions, the South could endure what it must. Meanwhile, northward, free-state society would break into discordant, selfish factions.

It is understandable why secession spokesmen believed that time was the South's natural ally. Time would bring fatal divisiveness to northern democracy; aid for the South would come from abroad; and the labor of millions of slaves would support the South throughout the crisis. Therefore the secessionists' pace was deliberate and dignified. Their purpose was to create (and win legitimacy for) a new nation, not to fight the old. And as the threat of war receded, the self-evident superiority of slave society would lead to increases in its already vast land areas. There was heady talk of Caribbean and Mexican additions to the Confederacy, of slave-owning border-state secessions from the old Union to the new, and of further expansion south of the old 36°30′ line to the Pacific.

The Confederate Constitution

These assumptions and aspirations were central in the constitutional arrangements the Confederates adopted in February 1861, the month before Lincoln's inauguration. The permanent version was confirmed in 1862. The constitution reflects the conviction of the seceders that they were involved in a pacific process leading toward permanent independence and the perpetual ordering of the races in master-servant relationships.

Scholars have long admired certain portions of the Confederate constitution. A number of the clauses incorporate reforms that are still relevant today. However, the reform elements were designed primarily to insulate slave property from politics, from democracy, and from change; they were connected intimately and deliberately to the protection of the institution of slavery.[2]

The framers of the Confederate constitution were enjoying the rare opportunity to replay history and to shape a future. Therefore, they reworked the 1787 Constitution in two ways. First, they limited the functions of the Confederate national government in a manner to prevent future political excesses that might endanger slave property. These limitations on national government are the clauses that have been praised as reforms deserving emulation. Second, the framers tried to improve the structure of nation-state federal relationships, also to achieve firmer protection of slave property.

Perhaps the Confederacy's leaders erred in spending time, energy, and talent in constitution making. Retrospection suggests that they might have been occupied better in readying for war. But, as noted, they did not anticipate any conflict.

Delegates assembled at Montgomery, Alabama, in February 1861 not to theorize but actually to create a southern version of fundamental law that would reform the 1787 Constitution and, most important, settle certain matters that the 1787 framers had skirted.

The two-score delegates who convened at Montgomery began work on February 4. A provisional constitution was in hand, and President Jefferson Davis and Vice-President Alexander Stephens in office, less than a week later. Work was completed on the permanent constitution on March 11, and it went out to the states for ratification.

During this same period, the last United States forts in the South were being snapped up or, as at Forts Sumter and Pickens, besieged. It was consistent with southern constitutional theory for individual states to claim control of all Federal property within a state's jurisdiction. The delegates preferred, however, for the Confederate national authority to assume such control as soon as possible.

During the same February-March period, compromise peace efforts were floundering along. The Confederacy could have existed without a constitution or with only a provisional constitution. But, unless enshrined in permanent manner, the basic purposes for which southerners risked secession might have faded from view. To southern leaders intent on seceding, a Confederate constitution was a symbol of determination for permanent separation and independence.

Casting themselves as guardians of the 1787 Constitution, the delegates in Montgomery followed almost exactly the form and organization of that constitution drafted in Philadelphia 73 years before. Thanks to the extensive and elaborate defenses of their position developed over several decades of political debate, the delegates knew already what they wished substantively to accomplish.

Their first imperative was to define the degree of autonomy to be accorded the states of the Confederacy. Lincoln's March 1861 inaugural address, which condemned the secession experiment, also reiterated the northern doctrine of derivative powers: The Union preceded the states, therefore, the states derive their existence and powers from the Union and from the 1787 Constitution that established it.

Southern detestation of Lincoln's "derivative powers" notion is apparent in the preamble of the Confederate constitution, which declares that each member state is acting in its sovereign and independent character; that membership in the Confederacy is an exercise of a state's sovereignty, not a limitation on it or a surrender of it; that states delegate powers to the nation rather than derive powers from it.

Confederates at Montgomery let pass three times the opportunity to spell out the precise limits on a sovereign state's right to secede from the Confederacy. This suggests that secession was seen as a one-shot weapon. It was a necessity in a Union where free states threatened slavery; it was an irrelevance in a Confederacy where slavery was the norm. Solutions for states' grievances in the Confederacy were to be accomplished by constitutional conventions to be called by the Confederate Congress on demand of any three states.

Slavery, a basic state right by southern lights, received special protection. The Confederate Congress could not deny or impair state-defined property rights in slaves, and, state sovereignty notwithstanding, neither could states. Congress must protect slaveowners' rights in Confederate territories and while in transit across or sojourn in any Confederate state. To be sure, the need to establish diplomatic relations with Europe inspired a prohibition against the importation of slaves from outside the Confederacy except from the United States, and the Confederate Congress was charged with punishing violators of the international slave-trade prohibition. But the Confederate constitution neither concealed nor stressed the goal of perpetuating slavery. It was unnecessary to spell out what everyone knew. Sometimes, however, the desire to do so proved uncontrollable.

On his way home from Montgomery, Confederate Vice-President Stephens offered this frank statement of what he believed had been accomplished:

> The new [Confederate] Constitution has put at rest forever all the agitating questions relating to our peculiar institutions—African slavery as it exists among us—the proper status of the negro in our form of civilization. This was the immediate cause of the late rupture and present revolution. . . . Our new Government is founded . . upon the great truth that the negro is not equal to the white man. That slavery—subordination to the superior race, is his natural and normal condition. . . . It is upon this [assumption that] . . . our actual fabric is firmly planted. . . . The progress of disintegration in the old Union may be expected

> to go on with almost absolute certainty. We are now the nucleus of a growing power, which . . . will become the controlling power on this continent.[3]

Such frankness about the Confederacy's notions of race superiority verged on foolhardiness. There was world opinion to consider as well as domestic. But, proud of administrative innovations, the South's leaders laid bare the primary motivation behind their efforts—the permanent stabilization within a new federal union of white domination in race relationships.

The Confederacy's Constitution, National Functions, and Democracy

The most celebrated "reforms" in the Confederate constitution limited in various ways the functions of national government. With respect to the executive, the President and Vice-President were to have single, nonrenewable six-year terms. The President was given unconditional power to discharge higher appointive officers, although he had to report his reasons subsequently to the Confederate Senate. He could drop minor officials only for reasons of substandard performance or incapacity.

These clauses, designed to diminish the spoils-patronage nourishment of political parties, pointed toward the civil service reforms of the future. The seceders determined to cut connections between party politics and government; to stop the flow of power, funds, and influence to political institutions; and to prevent the accumulation of authority in national government officers. Here lies the basis for claims that the Confederacy's constitution was an instrument of reform.

No "general welfare" clause crept into the Confederate constitution; since 1789 Federalists, Whigs, and Republicans had abused it, southerners insisted. There was to be no Interior Department, and the central government was limited in the internal improvements it could undertake; it had authority only in such obvious areas as maintaining offshore navigation aids, improving harbors, and keeping rivers usable for commerce. But a state, or states, could take over from the central authority even these limited functions. Expenditures for improvements (whether undertaken by nation or state) were to be recouped out of duties on the commerce facilitated by the improvement, with surpluses going to the Confederate treasury.

The postal system was to be self-supporting. Congress was forbidden to tax except for the specific purposes authorized in the constitution's statutes and forbidden to aid any industry by means of an import duty or other encouragement. No extra compensations beyond statutory or contract specifications might go to any officer, employee, or contractor of the national government.

The Confederate President was to have control of the national budget, for southern statesmen believed that the excesses of the U.S. Congress had shown this was necessary. Except to pay its own expenses and claims proved against the government, Congress generally could appropriate money only upon the President's request made as result of estimates prepared by the heads of the executive departments, and agreed to by a two-thirds vote of the legislators. The President was to have an item veto in appropriations legislation. Such laws had to deal with only one subject—the subject to be expressed in the title of the law—and no appropriations were to be permitted except for specified amounts and purposes. If Congress initiated a money appropriation bill without request from the President, it would have to muster an extraordinary two-thirds vote in both houses to pass.

Congressmen were forbidden to hold other national offices

during their legislative tenures. Heads of executive departments had seats in the Congress with privilege to discuss matters affecting their responsibilities.

As for the judiciary, the United States federal court model was imitated, with a significant exception. In the final (1862) draft of the Confederate constitution, jurisdiction was denied to the national courts in cases where the litigants were from different states. This was a severe restriction that southern merchants and staple farmers placed on themselves. It meant that processes of private debt repayments, for example, were returned to the conditions of the 1780s, under the Articles of Confederation. But creditors accepted the retrogression, for it seemed further to magnify the states and to constrain the Confederate nation.

To be sure, some of the reform clauses of the Confederate constitution deserve commendation as improvements in government administration. But, allowing full marks for these advances, it remains hazardous to separate the slave-perpetualization purposes of the Confederacy's creators from the reforms they incorporated into their constitution. The nature of the hazards is evident in a recent judgment by Professor David Herbert Donald:

> The Confederate government, provisional and permanent, was nonpartisan. The question how long it could have continued so is an interesting speculation; but the only presidential election in Confederate history showed all the electoral votes . . . cast for Davis and Stephens. There had been no party nominations in this election.[4]

Professor Donald is correct that in the Confederacy old-line dual political parties no longer existed. But is this to be accounted a reform? Granting defects, the political-party system had institutionalized opportunities to advance diverse views and candidates, and openly to argue policies. By 1860 in the South, options involving slavery were no longer open. The Confederacy's constitution tried to keep them closed by choking off the sources of preferment and funds that in the free states supported political parties. But this purging of politics was to cost the Confederacy very dearly indeed.[5]

Not at first. In February and March 1861, the view from Montgomery was benign. Without interference from Washington, the deep South's states had seceded, formed the Confederacy, and snapped up almost all of the nation's properties in the seceded states. Then, concerning Fort Sumter, President Davis, unfettered by party considerations, chose a road that, four years later, would bring the Confederacy to Appomattox.

Forts Pickens and Sumter: Peace or War?

When in early March 1861, Lincoln took the burdens of the Presidency from Buchanan's inept hands, the new President stated in his inaugural address that, like Buchanan, he considered secession to be impermissible. Lincoln argued that it was also unnecessary. The Republicans were no threat to slavery where it existed, although the party remained dedicated to containing it in the ways approved by the November 1860 majorities. With respect to the numerous national properties already appropriated by Confederates, Lincoln intended no attempts to repossess them. But he would abandon no others.

His reference was to the last two major unappropriated United States properties in the seceded states, the offshore Forts Pickens, near Pensacola, Florida, and Sumter, an island inside the harbor of Charleston, South Carolina. By March, Pickens and Sumter were the only points remaining where United States and Confederate officers could confront one another directly.

From Virginia through Arkansas, the unseceded border states served as a buffer.

Fort Pickens was obscure, way off on the Gulf Coast. Confederate cannon (commandeered along with the mainland navy yard) could not reach the island. Therefore, United States storeships were able to revictual the Pickens garrison. In January 1861, raw Florida militiamen tried to take the fort, but the effort failed, happily without bloodshed.

Florida officials, especially just-seceded former United States Senator S. R. Mallory, fashioned an on-spot "truce" with United States Army and Navy officers from Pickens and the resupply vessels. By its terms, Confederates would allow what they could not prevent, the continuing resupply of the Pickens garrison, and would attempt no further assaults, if federal officers promised not to add to the number of garrison troops.

Pickens was of little strategic or symbolic value. Nevertheless, along with Sumter, its presence under the old flag increasingly irritated ardent secessionists. Confederate President Davis shared the rising impatience. Addressing the Confederate military commander at Pensacola, Davis noted in early April that it would be preferable if the Confederacy could manage to have the United States initiate overt action at Pickens, but that he would assume a truculent attitude in Florida and in South Carolina in order to oust "foreign" garrisons.

The shaky Pickens truce held during the first two weeks of April, primarily because Confederates were not quite ready to push matters in Florida. But in South Carolina, the Confederates were more eager to take action.

Charleston, Calhoun's home and the base of the hottest secessionist firebrands, possessed symbolic if not strategic values that Pensacola lacked. Commandeered shore-based Confederate cannon easily reached Sumter and commanded the channels that supply ships would have to travel. A siege would inevitably lead

The interior of Fort Sumter not long after its bombardment.
LIBRARY OF CONGRESS

to the garrison's bloodless surrender, and a siege was initiated in January.

Lincoln, in his first days as President, had announced publicly that an unarmed supply ship was on its way to Sumter. But, in the face of the Confederate cannon, it could not reach the fort. Then, on April 10, Davis decided not to wait until Sumter's troops were starved out. Instead he determined first to force the Sumter garrison off Confederate soil, then to turn to

Fort Pickens. Two days later Confederate batteries opened fire on Sumter. Its garrison surrendered the next day.

Lincoln, urged by Republican party leaders, had also decided to push matters, but with respect to Pickens not Sumter, and with far greater restraint. He had a Democratic party to contend with also, after all. Very soon after the Confederates began bombarding Sumter, sea-borne reinforcements for the Pickens garrison reached the Florida fort. The fragile Pickens truce had ended with the news of the Sumter attack.

Note that Lincoln ordered no gunfire at either fort. Davis did at Sumter and was prepared to do so at Pickens. War began at Sumter because the United States was weaker there.

Davis initiated the bombardment because he shared the white South's commitment to the Confederacy and its arrogant attitudes toward the North. He aimed to dramatize Washington's appalling weakness for the benefit of the unseceded slave states and potential allies abroad, especially Great Britain and France, and he succeeded. With Confederate soil cleansed of the last United States presence (well, almost the last—Pickens proved to be too tough to assault) the secession movement was now mature. It had forced the Washington government to surrender Sumter, and it had produced a provisional, functioning Confederate national government and constitution.

Twenty years later, Ulysses Grant remembered vividly how the secessions and Sumter appeared to prove the Confederates' contentions ". . . that we had not a nation; that it was a mere confederation of States tied together by a rope of sand, that would give way upon the slightest friction."[6] At Sumter, in mid-April 1861, Confederates applied what in their view was slight friction, confident that, come peace or war, they could not lose.

FOOTNOTES

1. See John Hope Franklin, *The Militant South* (Boston: Beacon, 1956); Emory Thomas, *The Confederacy as a Revolutionary Experience* (Englewood Cliffs, N.J.: Spectrum, 1971); Frank E. Vandiver, *Their Tattered Flags: The Epic of the Confederacy* (New York: Harper & Row, 1970); and Paul Gaston, *The New South Creed: A Study in Southern Mythmaking* (New York: Knopf, 1970).

2. See especially W. R. Leslie, "The Confederate Constitution," *Michigan Quarterly Review*, II (1963), 153–65, which corrects W. M. Robinson, "A New Deal in Constitutions," *Journal of Southern History,* IV (Nov. 1938), 449–61, and Charles R. Lee, Jr., *The Confederate Constitution* (Chapel Hill: University of North Carolina Press, 1963).

3. From Edward McPherson in *Political History of the United States during the Great Rebellion, 1860–1865* (New York, 1865; reprint, ed. H. M. Hyman and H. Trefousse [New York: DaCapo, 1972]), pp. 103–4.

4. In James G. Randall and David Herbert Donald, *The Civil War and Reconstruction* (2nd ed., Boston: Heath, 1961), p. 245.

5. See E. L. McKitrick, "Party Politics and the Union and Confederate War Efforts," in *The American Party Systems,* ed. W. N. Chambers and W. D. Burnham (New York: Oxford, 1967), pp. 117–51.

6. In J. T. Headley, *The Life of Ulysses S. Grant* (New York, 1868), p. 540.

4 / MIXED and MULTIFORM POLITICS

The Emergence of Lincoln

NEITHER FRANKLIN ROOSEVELT during the Depression nor John Kennedy, burdened with the Bay of Pigs, began a new administration with worse prospects than those Lincoln faced in mid-April 1861. Professor Carl Degler has recently remarked that at the time of the Confederate attack on Sumter, the United States government was no more organized than a jellyfish.

Humiliated by secession and shocked by the attack on Sumter and its surrender, free-state citizens reacted initially to the news from Charleston with anger but without much hope. They had few reasons to expect useful action from their national officials. Despairing patriots feared that catatonic quiet would continue along the Potomac. Then, what was left of the old Union would disintegrate, as secessionists anticipated.

Even many free-state residents who had voted for Lincoln and the Republicans worried that they knew relatively little about him or his party. Lincoln's strength and ways were rooted in the small farm and commerce-centered towns of the Midwestern flatlands. "A Lawyer, a Good man, & to be relied on," one commercial-credit rater had described him in mid-1855. "Good for his Contracts and work," stated another credit assessor early in 1856.[1] But were these marketplace qualities, however commendable, anywhere near what the present emergency demanded? Many persons judged not.

Secessionists knew the purposes for which they were striving, and, in mid-April 1861, with good reason, believed that they were all but achieved. Free states' men had not yet formulated even the goal of national survival.

Predictions spread through the free and slave states that Lincoln would be the last President. By 1864 there would be no reason to hold elections for his successor (in 1861 the idea of a second term for Lincoln was incredible). Instead, the Balkanization of the un-United States begun by the South would continue in New England, the Great Lakes area, and the far West.

Then, quiet ended. Within hours after Sumter's surrender, Lincoln acted to restore initiative to, and respect for, the national government. His decision to act, and to act swiftly, was to be his first claim on his countrymen's gratitude.

Resorting to a statute dating from George Washington's administration, he called into national service 75,000 state militiamen, for 90 days. They were to suppress insurrections in South Carolina and elsewhere. Most free-state communities were energized by this unexpected and welcome forthrightness from the White House. They sped hurriedly mustered militiamen toward imperiled cities and to obviously strategic railroad termini, bridges, and road junctions.

The sparseness of American national institutions is revealed by the fact that after six months of crisis including state secessions the regular military establishment should have been all but irrelevant to this initial gathering of force. Instead, state militias, which ranged in quality from a very few expensively clad, mounted, and armed crack units, to the rawest, posturing weekend warriors, for a brief moment bore the weight of the nation's survival.

Lincoln's call for troops excited the free states. But it also immensely strengthened the Confederacy. In quick reaction, the heretofore unseceded slave states, from Virginia through Arkansas, joined the Confederate union. The four-month-old buffer zone that had separated the USA from the CSA vanished overnight. Now direct confrontation was possible anywhere along the Potomac-Ohio-Mississippi River "borderland" and on to the trans-Mississippi West. Scratch pro-Union forces filtered into Washington, Wheeling, Cincinnati, Cairo, St. Louis, and hundreds of more obscure communities.

Washington, as the nation's capital and residence of foreign diplomats, was symbolically too important to become another Sumter. But it could have, easily. Just across the Potomac, Confederate military camps and artillery positions sprang into existence. Concern for the city's security became the highest priority among Union policy makers (the shorthand word "Union" achieved instant popularity in 1861). One aspect of this urgent, ongoing concern was military in a traditional sense. Another aspect, equally urgent and inescapably linked to the military, was novel and endlessly complex. It involved what today is called internal security.

Disloyalty as Actuality

Controversy has existed since 1945 about the need for internal security arrangements, as well as about their procedures and

Marcus Stevens & Co.
ROOMS.
FURNITURE WARE HOUSE.
J.S.JENNESS
LAMPS.
TEAS
FAMILY GROCERIES
H.R.ANDR
RAIL-ROAD
GENERAL STAGE OFFICE

Michigan's First Regiment musters in Detroit's Campus Martius. Lincoln nationalized 75,000 state militiamen after the fall of Fort Sumter.
BURTON HISTORICAL COLLECTION, DETROIT PUBLIC LIBRARY

social costs. Experts abound on security questions and techniques, and many of the experts are dedicated critics. Watchdog libertarian organizations and alert jurisprudents have developed a rich precedential line on security questions, easily traced in any university or law library.

In April 1861, there was no history of controversy and there were no precedents. Free-state white men had known no governmental restraints on their civil liberties since the time of the Sedition Act. Courts had no tradition of civil-liberty defense cases.

Nothing stood in the way of demagogues and vigilantes who wished to exploit what had now become a civil war (but not yet *the* Civil War) in order to pay off personal scores or to choke off dissent. In many places, such exploitations occurred. But in the unseceded states dissent had long been institutionalized through two-party politics. Opposition Democrats, smarting from their public identification with secession and disloyalty, were alert for every Republican mistake and excess. Newsmen were unmuzzled. No mere assertion, from the White House or anywhere else, that national security was threatened by disloyalty could have sustained puffed estimations of the menace.

Lincoln's contemporaries were never divided over the actuality of serious disloyalty. But divisions did occur, frequently along party lines, in reaction to what Lincoln and, later, Congress *did* about disloyalty.

The Lincoln administration's desperate improvisations of 1861, designed to lessen threats to Washington posed by rebel soldiers and disloyal northerners, became a pattern followed throughout the war. As time passed, internal security procedures were refined. Their enforcement continued to depend on uniformed personnel, for civilian police, national and local, were hopelessly inadequate to the task. Abroad, and in the Confederate States, internal security agencies and policies undercut political democracy by equating dissent with disloyalty. In the Union states, Lincoln's security agents, watched over with increasing care from the White House and Capitol Hill, learned to concentrate on actual subversives instead of on open political opponents. The result was that northern internal security expedients did not threaten politics. Instead, political discourse rose from the moribund secession depths. Party spokesmen had to attend to new concerns over civil liberties and the permissible limits of dissent, and the anti-disloyalty efforts ultimately were brought before the voters for decision. A nation that was able to accommodate these tender concerns, by means of open politics, in the midst of a rending civil war, began again to deserve—and receive—the confidence of its citizens.

Baltimore and the Merryman "Case"

Federalized militiamen rushing to Washington in April 1861 had to change trains at Baltimore in slave-owning Maryland. They literally had to fight their way across the city. Pro-secessionist mobs, with the connivance of some state legislators, the mayor, and the police chief, obstructed their progress. Sabotage occurred on the essential rail and telegraph links connecting Washington, through Baltimore, to the rest of the country. There was a real possibility that Maryland and Delaware might secede, physically isolating the capital. Analogous problems festered in many other places.

State and municipal laws against arson, assault, and even murder were going unenforced; no federal criminal law existed relevant to the Baltimore situation or its analogues; no federal civilian police force was on hand. Prosecutions of even the most dangerous disloyalists could proceed only at a leisurely pace.

Moreover, trials for treason had been discredited as ineffective since Jefferson's time, and would only be mockeries where sheriffs, marshals, jurors, and even judges were linked to the offenders. Therefore Lincoln turned to the army. He took a chance that the amateur Union soldiers were "thinking bayonets," in his phrase—trustworthy citizen-soldiers, not tools for despotism. He proclaimed the habeas corpus writ privilege suspended in threatening areas, including Baltimore, and authorized soldiers to arrest actively disloyal civilians.

Much has been written about this and other similar executive orders that were buttressed subsequently with congressional authority. United States Chief Justice Roger B. Taney of Dred Scott fame, in a special circuit court session in Baltimore six weeks after Sumter fell, excoriated Lincoln for the arrests. Taney insisted that only Congress could suspend the privilege of the writ of habeas corpus (a responsibility Congress chose never to exercise), and he required military officers, despite their commander-in-chief's contrary orders, to free John Merryman, an arrested civilian (and by implication all arrested civilians), from his army jail.

Merryman, a prominent Maryland secessionist, had recruited and drilled a troop of men for the Confederate Army. Arrested and imprisoned by United States soldiers, he enjoyed access to eminent counsel and a hearing in a high national civil court, despite Lincoln's suspension of the habeas corpus writ privilege in Maryland. Merryman's case involved issues of constitutional law and history that were far less neat than the Chief Justice claimed. Congress' alleged monopoly over habeas corpus suspensions was an open question then, and it remains open more than a century later.

Lincoln refused to order the army to produce Merryman before Taney's bench. (He did release the miscreant some weeks later, without judicial intercession, after the clear and present

4 / MIXED AND MULTIFORM POLITICS

Chief Justice Roger B. Taney.
NEW YORK PUBLIC LIBRARY

danger of secession in Maryland had passed.) The President avoided a direct President-versus-judge, sword-versus-law encounter of the sort Taney desired. Instead, Lincoln chose to report subsequently on the internal security arrests to Congress, and the lawmakers in effect sustained the President. Lincoln's policies were never condemned by the Congress, repudiated by the Supreme Court (though Taney tried secretly to arrange occasions), or rejected by the voters. The habeas corpus suspensions never closed civil courts or oppressed opposition politicos; newsmen remained ubiquitous and, with astonishingly few exceptions, newspapers were uncensored.

The Politics of Democracy

Ironically, the immediate beneficiaries of the habeas corpus suspension and the arrests were the Democratic politicians of the free states and border slave states. Exploiting this novel issue handed to them by the Republican administration, Democrats demanded an end to both the war and the anti-disloyalty efforts. They cast themselves as defenders of northern states' rights and of white men's civil liberties. The Democrats' new antisecurity posture fit well with the party's traditional opposition to extending the role of national government (ignoring its continuing insistence on vigorous federal activism concerning the return of fugitive slaves). Many northern Democrats, wavering about party loyalty, now felt confirmed in their commitment. The party continued to recruit support among a broad cross-section of the population; and prominent adherents included banker August Belmont, publisher-entrepreneur S. L. M. Barlow, and the West Point graduate and civil engineer George B. McClellan, who was to become commander of the Army of the Potomac and 1864 presidential candidate.

Republicans had to reckon carefully with this suddenly invigorated, newly respectable Democratic organization. And this need served to check excesses in security matters.

It was never easy for Lincoln and his party mates to defend their security operations. The security arrests were overt not covert. They made dramatic, unsuppressed, unmanipulated news. The reasons justifying the arrests, the searches of persons and property, and the travel limitations in unsafe areas, were less dramatic and more complex.

The best defense was the public's general awareness that these policies, however abrasive, were necessary and better than alternatives such as mass executions, star chambers, or concentration camps. The security apparatus was never turned against political foes. Most arrests were for very brief periods and almost always ended with a requirement that the detained person swear to be loyal and keep the peace. Many arrested persons were able, even from military cells, to retain private counsel and to exert political influence. Released individuals suffered no further penalties in terms of business or employment difficulties and the like.

Rather than concealing it, Lincoln leaked news of the security expedients in the hope that persons contemplating disloyal actions would be warned away. As example, in mid-1861, an influential Marylander had his house searched for arms by Union soldiers. He protested to state lawmakers and to Maryland's Democratic congressmen. They attested to his loyalty. Coming from neighbors in the small-town goldfish bowls in which most Americans lived then, such attestations deserved respect. Lincoln came to the heart of these matters in a reply to the congressmen which friendly newsmen printed:

> Yours of to-day, . . . had been received and referred to General [Winfield] Scott, as I knew nothing whatever of the particular case. May I

beg you to consider the difficulties of my position and solicit your kind assistance in it? Our security in the seizing of arms for our destruction will amount to nothing at all, if we are never to make mistakes in searching a place where there are none. I shall continue to do the very best I can to discriminate between *true* and *false* men. In the meantime let me, once more, beg your assistance in allaying irritations which are unavoidable.

Yours, very truly,

A. Lincoln[2]

Saboteurs, spies, and guerrillas apprehended in areas of actual military operations were coped with under the 57th Article of War, part of the statutory authority provided by Congress. Their punishments were not part of Lincoln's security measures. But the public often confused the two, and Democrats encouraged the confusions.

This account is not intended to glorify internal security proceedings. Instead it is to suggest that in the absence of enough government, of adequate alternatives, the Lincoln Republicans worked out a politically tolerable course between either despotism or local vigilante viciousness and Buchanan-like torpidity. There was no political glory in the security arrests. But neither was there shame.

There was comfort. For, along with the evidence of renewed national vigor offered by the armed forces, the anti-disloyalty improvisations were first proofs that the American constitutional and institutional structure was still adequate and sound. Perhaps, as once-despairing patriots noted on news of Lincoln's forceful thrusts, secessionists were wrong that federalism, open democracy, and national survival were incompatible.

Wartime Elections and Politics

In the nineteenth-century world (as now), even nations in which elections were substantively important suspended them during crises. Armies and elections were considered historically to be incapable of coexistence. Beginning in 1861, there were occasional suggestions that perhaps delays, or even suspensions, of elections were necessary. But American constitutionalism was firm. Elections were calendared. The southern rejection of national election results had wounded democracy.

To the astonishment of fascinated foreign commentators, even in the chaotic 1861 spring and summer, local off-year elections proceeded in Union states as though no war were on. Democrats ran full slates, protesting against continuation of the war and the manner of its conduct, especially the security procedures. Then, in 1862, local, state, and congressional contests were held. And, most impressive of all, in 1864 the Presidency came up for grabs.

As always, states and localities set the residence, property, or other qualifications for voting even in the national races. Military interferences with election arrangements occurred only near critical combat areas. The most partisan Democrats failed to sustain allegations of extraordinary election mismanagement.

Many free states devised ways for their soldier-citizens to vote by absentee ballots or when on leave—another American first in history. By and large, Democrats opposed votes for soldiers. In every election, no matter how trivial, antiwar Democrats insisted that the war would lead to military tyranny and race mixing. In short, the wartime Democrats remained tied to a static past and appealed to fears more than hopes. Their party's sole aim was peace, even at the price of permanent disunion and instability.

Republican policies remained relatively elastic and dynamic. Reunion was their justification for struggle and their unaltering war aim. But it was not exclusive. Lincoln and many of his close party coadjutors were educable, "can do" constitutionalists. Change did not oppress them. They were dedicated to accepting the verdicts of elections, to open, two-party politics, to state-based federalism, and to competitive capitalism.

Men of many complementary goals, noble and sordid, found reason to participate in the revived politics of democracy and of federalism, to win what they wanted and to frustrate what they opposed. As always, both parties attracted broad cross-sections of American society. But the Democrats' general antiwar stance appealed primarily to persons who were opposed to changes. The majority of the new business, professional, and political reform association members saw the Republican party as their natural home. Teachers, physicians, farmers, and bankers involved themselves as never before in local and state politics. In addition to patriotic purposes, they wished to gain greater control of state power to further their special-interest goals. Patriotic ministers linked women's church auxiliaries to local Republican organizations and thence to Union soldiers. War work for the nation's survival became associated with local political activism.

Several states reformed penal, educational, and suffrage laws. The rights of persons accused of crimes were increasingly protected. Property rights of women and minors were extended. Electoral districting was adjusted to achieve some degree of greater equity. Efforts proceeded, against great opposition, to end slavery in the District of Columbia, Maryland, and Delaware, and to bring West Virginia into the Union as a free state. Soon after Sumter, the status of the relatively small number of free-state Negroes began to be improved by revisions of municipal, county, and state laws and states' constitutions. In short, reformers, working primarily through the Republican party, began a kind of wartime Reconstruction in some northern states. Democrats stubbornly resisted most of these changes.

In Washington, the patronage business never slackened, but, through party control became manageable. The first waves of avaricious, get-rich-quick vendors of shoddy goods for the army gave way to more responsible suppliers, chosen by regularized bidding and actuarial procedures. Protection-hungry industrialists sought tariffs. Harassed bankers wished to improve the chaotic money market. Working men employed by the federal government were asking for an eight-hour day. Physicians, disgusted by the quality of the Army's medical careerists, brought into the War Department the Sanitary Commission, a semiprivate and largely self-sustaining volunteer operation. Ministers, outraged by vice in military camps, which some local authorities failed or refused to quell, pressured Congress successfully to recognize the Christian Commission, which, in addition to its moral and religious efforts, served as a sort of USO.

On every level of the federal system, party organizations welcomed a wide range of citizens, from altruistic reformers to ambitious businessmen. The striking rise in political activism that began in the war's first months reflected a strengthening of state-based federalism. Through the efforts of individuals and organizations, the interactions between town and county, county and state, state and nation, and nation and the people were elaborated and enhanced. Nevertheless, the resources and influence of the Republican party continued to derive more from local action than central control, despite Democrats' complaints to the contrary. And the Union Army, the most literate army in history, participated in this new political awareness and activity through connections with community-based groups and, often, by voting in local and national elections.

No one planned this complex process. But, to their credit, Lincoln and most Republican leaders quickly discerned its potential for the creation of an army strong enough to crush the rebellion without threatening its own society. Democrats, on the other hand, derided the possibility of a "harmless army" and this question, like the issues of internal security and the ethics and wisdom of the war itself, became part of the two-party dialogue.

The two parties shifted membership. By 1862, Democrats in several states who favored the reunification of the Union by means of continuing the war as long as necessary, and who despaired of moving their party's uneducable leadership toward their views, had joined in a Union party coalition with Republicans. This development heartened Republicans. It appeared to promise that their party, which in 1860 had attracted thin totals of votes in the border states and almost none farther to the south, might create permanent Republican-Union coalition organizations in every state, *if* the war ended successfully.

Open politics was Lincoln's natural arena. Incorruptible, scandal never touched him. He functioned marvelously well in the frequently polluted political pool, mixing with congressmen, courting governors, appeasing county and city party makeweights, pressuring contractors, reining in upstart generals, and leaking hot news to favored newsmen. He had already developed "fixer" techniques to a fine art in Illinois. One of his favorite journalists, Whitelaw Reid, recalled of Lincoln:

> He had small regard for many of the refinements of the modern Civil Service reformer. He knew how to use the Post Offices to secure delegates, and he was ready enough to point out to his Congressman how a judicious use of other patronage would promote the good cause at the next Convention. When he came to great place he still used patronage without hesitation,—to advance high public interests, to gain support for the Union cause, to quiet discontent, to promote recruiting. Honesty he insisted on, but beyond that his official standard was not always the highest, and his judgment of individual character not always safe. Thus, in the haste, he appointed many incompetent officers in the army and elsewhere, and often tolerated inefficiency after others had discovered it.[3]

Among those attracted by the Republican party and/or Lincoln's government were young telegrapher Andrew Carnegie, engineer-entrepreneur Herman Haupt, railroad director Thomas A. Scott, urban reformer George T. Strong, poet Walt Whitman, and the Democrats McClellan and Stanton. Abolitionists, who had long cursed both political parties and all government institutions, now were willing to associate themselves with the Republicans.

The many talented, purposeful individuals who were drawn to support the party or serve in the government had a common purpose, national reunion under the Constitution. But otherwise their interests and aspirations were diverse. The future, or rather many possible futures, seemed to lie with the Republican party. But meanwhile everything depended on the Union Army.

Ralph Waldo Emerson instructed Englishman Thomas Carlyle on these matters when he noted that, as between the two parties, "it is certain that the American nationality lies in the Republican party (mixed and multiform though that party be)."[4]

If Emerson was correct—and he was a shrewd, insightful observer—where, in the Confederacy, which had deliberately eradicated party institutions, was there a basis for "nationality"?

Politics: The Confederacy's Advantages and Hazards

It is easy to contrast North and South with respect to manpower, manufacturing resources, and railroad mileage, among other obvious physical characteristics. These comparisons, reduced to a table, depict the Confederacy as laboring under shocking disadvantages (but Vietnam and similar conflicts suggest that such disadvantages do not predetermine a war's outcome):

Union	*Confederacy*
23 states	11 states (13 if Kentucky and Missouri shadow governments are included)
20,700,000 population	9,105,000 population (including 3,654,000 Negroes, primarily slaves)
110,000 industrial institutions, employing 1,300,000 workers	18,000 industrial institutions, employing 110,000 workers
21,973 miles of railroads	9,283 miles of railroads

It is more difficult to compare and to estimate the effects of differences in government institutions. Measurements are lacking or are too imprecise to describe exactly the elasticity and vigor of the Union's and Confederacy's national governments and of their relationships to their states.

On paper, the two national governments were much alike. Both were central authorities in state-based federal systems, with written constitutions. They were both economic capitalisms. In 1861 even slavery existed as an exceptional condition northward, in Maryland, Delaware, and the District of Columbia.

As noted earlier, the Confederate constitution differed in several ways from the 1787 Constitution. On the surface, these modifications appeared as desirable and substantial reforms. They were supposed to limit patronage and log-rolling party machinations, and to prevent the accumulation of excessive power in the CSA national government.

But in many specific provisions and in the fundamental structure of governments, the documents were virtual twins. Tripartite government, separation of powers, and check-and-balance arrangements were used in both constitutions. (The CSA Supreme Court never came into existence though provided for.) Parliamentary procedures familiar along the Potomac served in Dixie. Cabinet arrangements also were similar, although in fact, there was a greater turnover in the Confederate cabinet than in Lincoln's. There were, though, essential differences between the two governments.

In the North, two-party politics developed by mid-1861 into what Eric McKitrick described as "... the chief agency for mobilizing and sustaining energy in American government." David Potter has suggested "... the possibility that the Confederacy may have suffered real and direct damage from the fact that its political organization lacked a two-party system."[5]

The Confederate constitution did closely parallel the 1787 constitution, and perhaps even technically improved it. But no constitution can create viable, dynamic political institutions; and perhaps no constitution can live without them. The Confederacy, by closing off options on basic issues such as slavery, deadened political life, and made it incapable of sensitivity to the needs of individuals, localities, and states.

Confederates lacked the inspirations that alternative politics involves, as well as the annoyances. Thus, the touted reforms of the Confederate constitution remained mere administrative flourishes, without capacity to invigorate the rebel war effort.

Consider in this respect the balanced-budget requirement. Even the Confederate post office was to pay its way. Obviously this was designed to prevent development of northern-style spoils chieftains who subsisted traditionally on postal surpluses. But this "reform" resulted in curtailment of postal service even to Confederate military posts, while in the North, postal service provided an essential link between home communities and institutions—including political parties—and the literate, voting soldiery. To strengthen that link, Congress and President approved the creation by the Union Army of the world's first military mail detachments.

Bluecoats were never out of politics; graybacks had none in which to participate, even though local, state, and congressional elections continued to take place in the Confederacy. Although as time passed, what historian Richard Beringer called recently "the unconscious spirit of party" manifested itself sporadically in the Confederate Congress—to the distress of some original secessionist zealots—primary matters such as slavery, or reunion without slavery, were effectively excluded from the political arena.

Moreover, without the mediation of political parties, relations between national and local officials became strained. The private political alternatives that Lincoln enjoyed when dealing with Republican and Union party governors and senators, the patronage pressures, the subtle tradings, and the backstage maneuverings were not available to Jefferson Davis.

The South's internal unity steadily declined from the high-water level of 1861. Confederate officials were unrestrained by a dynamic central authority like that, directed by Lincoln, which gained control over internal security procedures and personnel. Therefore, in the Confederate states, dealing with disloyalty remained a local rather than a national problem. Penalties for opposition to conscription were frequently more savage than was true northward, and were always less predictable or rational. Local vigilantes retained the rough ways of the prewar slave patrollers. Fewer political constraints operated in Dixie because political democracy was feebler there.

Southern States' Rights and Police Powers

War functions occupied the southern states, but the states lacked the infrastructure of local, private, and semiprivate associations, tied to local parties, that in the Union was involved in war work. Southern state legislatures voted additional appointive powers for governors and created special councils and commissions to advise the executive on military matters. Legislatures met more frequently and for longer sessions than in prewar times, thus increasing the opportunities for conflict with the Confederate central government.

Confederate states took on the tasks of Indian control and the administration of revenue, collection, the mails, and navigation, which, before secession, the United States government had performed. In some instances states retained these duties in whole or in part after the Confederate nation came into being. The central government called into service the states' militias, and conscripted individuals; state governors and legislators created home guards that sheltered citizens from national military service.

Secession and war caused financial dislocations with which states tried to deal by means of debt moratoria, contract-stay laws, and suspensions of specie payments. State legislatures tried to ameliorate the cotton glut by penalizing overproduction and to stimulate the production of articles in short supply by means of subsidies to manufacturers and importers and the establishment of market monopolies for salt, shoes, textiles, and bread. State penitentiaries were set to producing turpentine, shoes, castor oil, iron, baking soda, and medicine. Louisiana established stores where its depreciating currency was legal tender for scarce items.

To cope with rising costs, the Confederate states passed price control, anti-usury, and anti-monopoly statutes directed against profiteers, but with little effect. These extra responsibilities became heavy burdens. Believing the war would be short, legislators resorted to loans and currency manipulations rather than taxes (Florida retained its 1860 tax rate throughout the war) in order to finance these economic controls. State indebtedness notes circulated in increasing numbers, varieties, and valuations, inviting counterfeiting and inflation. Every Confederate reverse depreciated these issues.

Staffed with intelligent, energetic, opportunistic men, the Confederate state governments surged ahead of the national government, a pattern sharply different from the Union experience. In the absence of a two-party forum, able, ambitious southerners often had no structured political means of advancing themselves and their causes. Only personal attacks on Confederate officials were relevant. Very often, these attacks were made under the banner of states' rights.

As an example, opponents to Confederate conscription and taxation policies took refuge in state courts, behind state-centered constitutional doctrines, and some states' jurists plagued the national government far more than Taney bothered Lincoln. Famous conflicts erupted between the Confederate government at Richmond and North Carolina Chief Justice Pearson. The Confederate War Department, in early 1864, had to decide what to do about a ruling by Pearson against a conscription act that had been authorized by the Confederate Congress. The question came up of what to do if Pearson discharged conscripted individuals from Confederate military jurisdiction. "I will not hesitate a moment to arrest him [Pearson]," said Secretary of War James Seddon. "That is a point to which it is coming," agreed his assistant, former United States Supreme Court Justice John A. Campbell.[6]

Pearson was eventually overruled by other judges, but in the meantime Seddon did not, after all, attempt direct coercion against him. Instead, Seddon could only write helplessly to North Carolina Governor Vance:

> The want of a Supreme Court in the Confederate States leaves them [officers of the central government] unprotected against the . . . actions

> of State Judges by the regular and accustomed course of review by an appellate tribunal. And when the action of the State Judges involves the assumption of powers not conceded to belong to them, . . . this Department cannot discover any course more suitable for making its objections known than to communicate to the Executive of the State those objections in the form of a respectful remonstrance.[7]

Throughout the war, successive Confederate secretaries of war, attorneys general, other cabinet officers, and some congressmen appealed for the Confederate government to create the Supreme Court specified in the constitution. But states'-rights champions delayed the necessary congressional action, and the life of the Confederacy ebbed away while the debate continued.

The Confederacy did not, however, die because of the lack of a Supreme Court. Union military power of a magnitude unimaginable in 1861, sustained by free-state political processes that seceders had seen as a source of weakness not strength, brought Dixie to Appomattox. Northward, where party politics avoided or bridged federalism's worst fault lines, individuals became tied more closely than ever before to their communities, states, and nation, to their Union and Constitution. In the Confederacy, commitment to states' rights and the elimination of the two-party system inspired by the fixation on preserving slavery, impeded the development of unifying political involvements. The causes of secession prevented the more effective conduct of war, as it had frustrated the preservation of peace.

Yet, in the spring and summer of 1861, the Confederacy's self-imposed burdens were less apparent than its advantages. And the advantages became visible as the first Union forces penetrated the South. Bluecoats encountered hard-core problems involving the future of slaves, military administration of local government, and definition of the war's purposes, that Confederates never needed to face. The Civil War and Reconstruction were taking form.

FOOTNOTES

1. Dun & Bradstreet Papers, Illinois, v. 198, p. 176.

2. *National Intelligencer,* August 7, 1861, reprinted in Lincoln, *Collected Works, Supplement,* ed. Roy P. Basler (Westport, Conn.: Greenwood, 1974), p. 86.

3. Quoted in *Living Age* (March 4, 1911), 574, from Reid, *Abraham Lincoln* (London, 1911).

4. *The Correspondence of Emerson and Carlyle,* ed. Joseph Slater (New York: Columbia University Press, 1964), pp. 541–42.

5. McKitrick, "Party Politics," 120; Potter, "Jefferson Davis and the Political Factors in Confederate Defeat," in *Why the North Won the Civil War,* ed. David Donald (Baton Rouge: Louisiana State University Press, 1960), p. 113.

6. *Inside the Confederate Government: The Diary of Robert Garlick Kean,* ed. Edward Younger (New York: Oxford University Press, 1957), pp. 137–38.

7. Seddon to Vance, May 23, 1863, Confederate Secretary of War, Letters Sent, IX, 81, Record Group 109, National Archives.

5 / BATTLES and PLEADERS: 1861-62

War Causes, Aims, and Results

ALTERNATIVE POLITICS could not become an advantage to the Union unless Union soldiers, by military success, made policy alternatives meaningful. Frustrations and reverses could evoke defeatism and dissension. If the electorate turned to the antiwar Democrats, then the Confederacy would win independence, even if it won no battles.

In 1861 the idea of dynamic war was virtually a monopoly of abolitionists. But they hoped, foolishly it seemed, to win over to their view the overwhelmingly unsympathetic or apathetic majority of free and border-state citizens.

The Civil War was, in fact, to become the longest and costliest war, in terms of lives and money, fought anywhere in the world from 1815 to 1914, except for China's Taiping Rebellion. It involved substantial portions of the population, immediately affected the survival of the nation, and for generations in the future affected political realities and the relationships of races.

Of course, this was not foreseen. During the 1861 spring, amassing armies drilled and maneuvered for the anticipated grand clash and final resolution. Confederates remained optimistic. They were sure that their culture produced better warriors, zealous in allegiance to their new nation and in defense of old race relationships. They were unified on fundamentals, undistracted by alternative politics, and masters of millions of slaves. Nature, it appeared, also favored the Confederates, at least in the critical Richmond-Washington heartland.

The East: 1861

Bounded on the east by Atlantic and Chesapeake waters, and on the west by Appalachian highlands, the hundred-mile-wide corridor between Richmond and Washington was beautifully arranged for defense of the Confederacy. No military theoretician could have asked for better defensive geography, topography, and logistics.

Beginning with the Potomac, a dozen great rivers and their innumerable tributaries ran eastward from the Appalachians to salt water. Each was a natural line of defense that could cause attackers great hazard and suffering. The small number of north-south bridges, ferries, fords, rail lines, and roads, crossing the rivers, streams, creeks, and runs, were easily destroyed or blocked. Frontal invaders would have to cut through heavily ravined second-growth forests, cross gullied watercourses, and traverse labyrinthine cultivated fields. They would encounter dust, mud, and rain in summer, ice, sleet, and snow in winter.

In such terrain, a raw recruit was an effective defensive soldier. Military technology made him a formidable one, even in 1861. His gun, although muzzle-loaded, was rifled rather than smooth-bore, relatively accurate, and quick fire. Some breech-loaders were available. Conical bullets had replaced solid shot. Field artillery was a marvel of mobility and close-range deadliness. The result was far greater firepower than had been available in the Mexican War.

Sophisticated entrenchments quickly became a specialty of both armies, but Confederates, aided by slaves, excelled in the technique. In attacks soldiers had to leave cover and face concentrated fire. Little wonder that officers searched for flanking opportunities.

Westward, beyond the Appalachian's first range, the Shenandoah River cut a broad north-south avenue. But this fertile valley was at first far more useful to the Confederates. It angled sharply southwest. Each mile of southward march would draw Union soldiers away from Richmond, the only target in that rural region. There were very few exits from the southern valley, and a few small garrisons could guard them all.

Thus only the coastal plain route led clearly to Richmond. But in this valley, south of the Potomac, numerous exits permitted Confederates easily to flank Union forces. The residents were overwhelmingly pro-Confederate, and Union soldiers would be plagued by guerrillas, spies, saboteurs, and supply scarcities. By contrast, Confederate tacticians saw the valley as a royal road. Friendly residents would provide supplies, information, and labor. The valley angled northeast with numerous exits approaching Washington and the capitals and commercial-industrial-communications urban centers of five politically potent states. All demanded defense, and Washington's security was essential. Therefore many large Union garrisons were needed at these exits, and they were rarely enough.

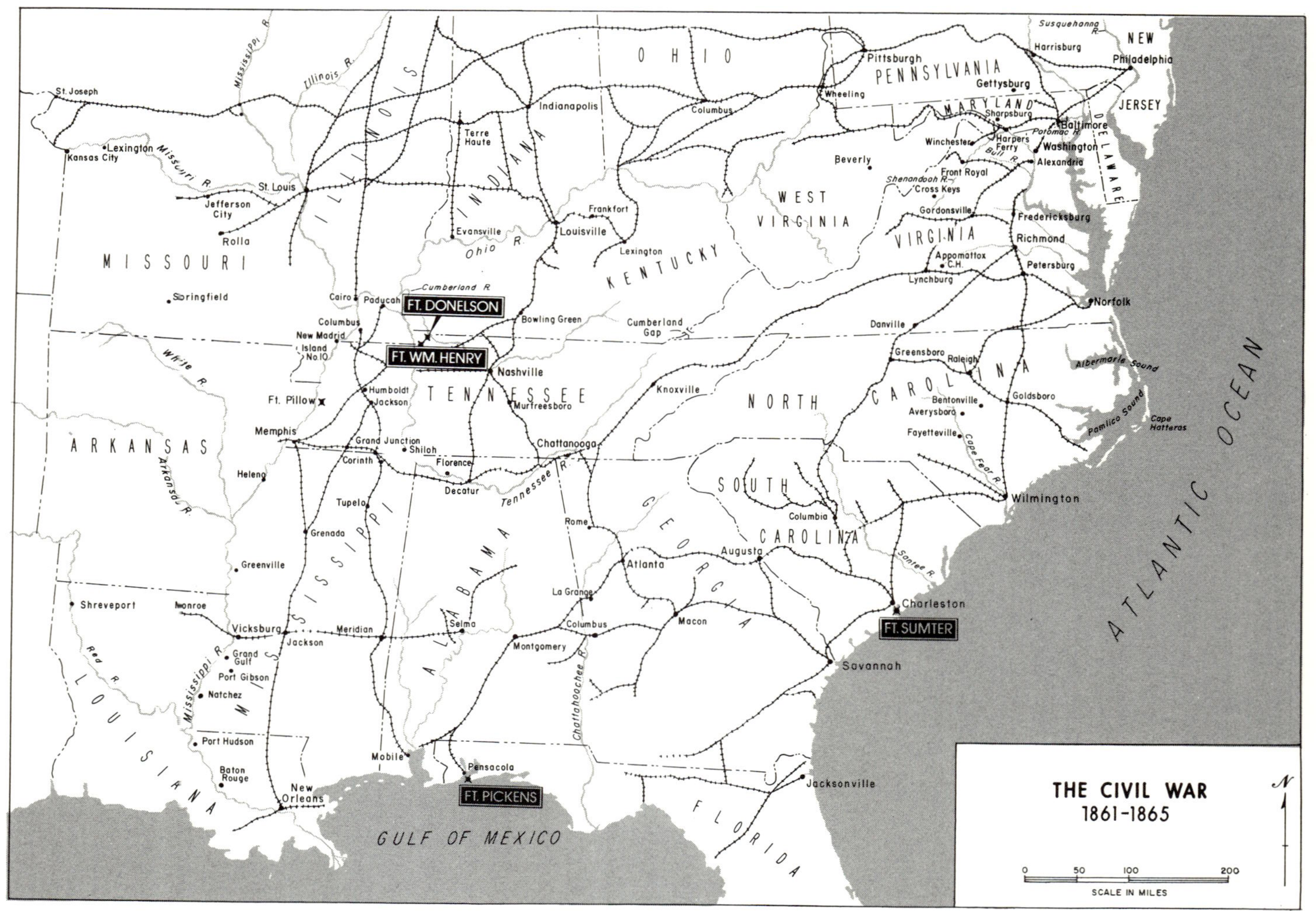
THE CIVIL WAR
1861-1865
SCALE IN MILES
0
50
100
200
N
ATLANTIC OCEAN
GULF OF MEXICO
FT. DONELSON
FT. WM. HENRY
FT. SUMTER
FT. PICKENS
MISSOURI
ILLINOIS
INDIANA
OHIO
PENNSYLVANIA
NEW JERSEY
DELAWARE
MARYLAND
WEST VIRGINIA
VIRGINIA
KENTUCKY
TENNESSEE
NORTH CAROLINA
SOUTH CAROLINA
GEORGIA
ALABAMA
MISSISSIPPI
ARKANSAS
LOUISIANA
FLORIDA
St. Joseph
Kansas City
Lexington
Missouri R.
Mississippi R.
Illinois R.
St. Louis
Jefferson City
Rolla
Springfield
Terre Haute
Indianapolis
Evansville
Ohio R.
Louisville
Frankfort
Lexington
Columbus
Wheeling
Pittsburgh
Harrisburg
Susquehanna R.
Philadelphia
Gettysburg
Sharpsburg
Baltimore
Potomac R.
Washington
Alexandria
Harpers Ferry
Bull R.
Winchester
Front Royal
Shenandoah R.
Cross Keys
Beverly
Gordonsville
Fredericksburg
Richmond
Petersburg
Appomattox C.H.
Lynchburg
Norfolk
Danville
Greensboro
Raleigh
Albermarle Sound
Pamlico Sound
Cape Hatteras
Goldsboro
Bentonville
Averysboro
Fayetteville
Cape Fear R.
Wilmington
Columbia
Santee R.
Charleston
Savannah
Augusta
Atlanta
Macon
Columbus
La Grange
Rome
Chattahoochee R.
Montgomery
Selma
Jacksonville
Pensacola
Mobile
Cairo
Paducah
Cumberland R.
Columbus
New Madrid
Island No.10
Ft. Pillow
Bowling Green
Cumberland Gap
Nashville
Murfreesboro
Knoxville
Chattanooga
Tennessee R.
Humboldt
Jackson
Memphis
Grand Junction
Shiloh
Corinth
Florence
Decatur
Helena
Tupelo
Grenada
Greenville
Meridian
Jackson
Vicksburg
Grand Gulf
Port Gibson
Natchez
Port Hudson
Baton Rouge
New Orleans
Shreveport
Monroe
Red R.
White R.
Arkansas R.

By mid-July 1861, the 90 days for which the first mustered militiamen had been called to serve were running out. In command of approximately 30,000 militiamen, lightly leavened with regulars, West Pointer General Irwin McDowell marched southward into Virginia from Washington, accompanied by sightseers, vendors, and excursionists. Facing them were Confederate General Pierre Beauregard's 25,000 equally inexperienced troopers. At a hill stream called Bull Run, where high banks and thick woods cloaked Confederate movements, Beauregard's and McDowell's men met and fought. After four hours of brave, indecisive close-range combat, Confederate reinforcements from the Shenandoah hit the Union flanks. Green troops broke. Retreat became a rout. The Union's primary army straggled back, a mob, into Washington's streets, in full view of foreign diplomats and American congressmen. "I sat up late last night to write you about a victory," Wisconsin Republican Senator Timothy O. Howe reported from Washington on the eve of the battle; "I got up this morning to hear of a most disastrous overwhelming defeat." But, he added, "The Government is firm and resolute."[1]

Well, that it was. Confederate failure to follow up Bull Run by hitting Washington is explained not only by the exhaustion of the victorious rebel troops, but also by their leaders' assumption that the war was won—that, one battle lost, the Union would quit. Instead, casting off pessimism, Lincoln appointed to command the Army of the Potomac another West Pointer, since become a prominent railroad executive, the talented, vigorous, young (35 years old in 1861), ambitious George B. McClellan. Within a few months after the Bull Run debacle, McClellan's formidable administrative reforms and training programs had cleared Washington of drifters and deserters. His superbly disciplined regiments of volunteers and reenlistees numbered more than 100,000 men. It was hoped that this huge

General George B. McClellan (engraving from a painting by Alonzo Chappel).
NEW YORK PUBLIC LIBRARY

corps, to that time the largest body of troops ever gathered in the Western Hemisphere, would end the war in one massive blow.

Winter intervened. Now a one-year war was a common estimate. Training continued along the again-quiet Potomac.

The West: 1861

Unionists enjoyed topographical advantages in the West. The area was dominated by great, largely navigable river systems that flowed south. Once cleared of Confederate fortifications, the Ohio River, combined with the Cumberland and Tennessee River tributaries, joining the Mississippi at Cairo, Illinois, could transport the Union armies. These river systems, plus complementary rail lines, would link the Old Northwest's agricultural and industrial resources to the Gulf of Mexico, and connect the eastern and western war theaters.

Missouri was especially important. Its eastern border was the Mississippi, extending to the north far past central Illinois and to the south past Cairo. And Missouri was the only slave-owning state north of 36°30′. In the spring of 1861, antisecessionist Missourians at St. Louis had linked with scratch Union forces under General John C. Frémont, the Republican party's 1856 presidential candidate, to frustrate immediate attempts to bring Missouri into the Confederacy.

Kentucky was also a crucial state. It connected with Missouri to the west; to the north only the Ohio River separated it from Ohio, Indiana, and Illinois. To the south lay Tennessee and to the east, Virginia. After Sumter, many Kentuckians aspired to neutrality, but the state was too important. In midsummer 1861, Confederates seized Columbus, Kentucky. Union forces

A Union military telegraphic battery wagon. The need for rapid communication in time of war spurred the already thriving telegraph industry. Significantly, the first message sent across the transcontinental line on its completion on October 24, 1861, was a declaration, addressed to Lincoln, of California's loyalty to the Union.

LIBRARY OF CONGRESS

moved into the no-longer-neutral state, and, as in Missouri, prevented immediate secession, although shadow Missouri and Kentucky state governments became represented in the Confederate Congress. Throughout the war, large Union garrisons were needed in both states to prevent secession, to cope with guerrillas, saboteurs, and spies, and to fend off Confederate invaders and raiders.

Once these garrisons were relatively secure, Union decision makers thought seriously of opening the Ohio and Mississippi river systems for troop movements and commerce. By the end of 1861, the Union was preparing to choke off Forts Henry and Donelson, the last major Confederate strong points on the Ohio's Tennessee and Cumberland tributaries. A shallow-draught navy was hurriedly built, purchased, and commandeered for use on the Ohio and upper Mississippi. Made up of ugly but efficient vessels, it came under the command of General Ulysses Grant, a West Pointer who had resigned from the army after the Mexican War to become an unsuccessful petty merchant. Employing this rough naval force, in February 1862, the general forced the surrenders of Henry and Donelson. Grant became a hero.

Union heroes were in short supply. In 1861, the Bull Run reverse, indeterminate skirmishings in Missouri, Kentucky, and western Virginia, and the internal security measures had produced little to sustain the public's (including soldiers') morale.

Maritime: 1861

Except on the rivers, the Union Navy's 1861 performance was another deep disappointment. There had been high hopes that the Union's deep-water fleet would tightly enforce the blockade of southern ports ordered by Lincoln. Few persons understood how forbiddingly difficult blockading was, and is.

Here again, nature greatly favored the Confederates. Deeply indented, the thousands of miles of Atlantic and Gulf coasts are characterized by long sand islands and peninsulas, shifting and silting river and bay channels, uncertain currents, and capricious, often deadly winds. Confederates darkened lighthouses, removed channel buoys, and set underwater traps and mines. Shallow-draft blockade runners proliferated from the Chesapeake to the western Gulf of Mexico. Cuba, Mexico, and the West Indies were vexatiously close. In such conditions, no navy could end large-scale smuggling.

The Union Navy did work hard, and quickly improved its efficiency. But much of its work was offshore, invisible, dull, and cumulative rather than immediate in effect. Its task was to withhold as many supplies as possible from the Confederacy until Union armies could conquer Confederate ports and make the blockade fully effective.

Meanwhile, the navy could not afford to be reckless. In mid-1861, an American warship stopped a British merchantman, the *Trent*, and removed two Confederate diplomats. The American commander was hailed briefly as a hero. But his achievement almost initiated an Anglo-American armed clash, which would have guaranteed Confederate independence. Only highest-level efforts in London and Washington avoided it.

The *Trent* affair suggests the nature of 1861's frustrations. On land as on water, uniformed commanders had to learn that limits existed on what they could do, and these limits were not written in any West Point handbook or international law manual.

Race Relations and Security Policies: 1861

Problems arising from race relations and security needs involved Union officers inescapably in political decisions; and these decisions complicated profoundly the conduct of military operations, and added greatly to the political hazards—and opportunities—of the Lincoln administration.

For example, unforeseen security and race problems vexed both McClellan and Frémont. Though separated by a thousand miles, each reported analogous difficulties with disloyal white civilians, untrustworthy guides, guerrillas, saboteurs, and spies. Both noted that Union camps drew Negroes like magnets. The individual general's perceptions, and political aspirations, however, created sharply differing race and security policies.

McClellan's secret aim was the White House. His already chosen vehicle was the conservative Democratic party. White southerners would be Democrats again, he was sure, once they gave up the Confederate experiment. He wanted their support, too, for his candidacy. Therefore McClellan wanted to prove to southerners that, in war as in peace, Union institutions, including the Army, would not disturb the practice of slavery. In conformity with the 1850 fugitive-slave law, McClellan ordered subordinates to return runaway slaves even to disloyal masters. Some of these slaves had helped Union soldiers at profound risk to themselves.

In patronizing lectures to Lincoln and congressmen, McClellan maintained that a general must obey statutes. But he was trying to hold the war to policies that would shape a peace on the model of 1860; he wished for a reconstruction that would restore the seceded states to the Union, and nothing more.

Frémont, his White House hopes in the past, was increasingly antislavery in conviction, and was facing even more urgent pressures than McClellan. He had far fewer troops, and he encountered more ferocious saboteur, vigilante, and guerrilla action. The Negroes who flocked to his lines were the enemy's basic capital and labor resource. Therefore, to strike at slaveowners who fed and aided saboteurs and guerrillas, if not worse, Frémont ordered the slaves of disloyal owners freed. He envisaged not only the restoration of the seceded states to the Union, but the end of slavery—the institution that had spawned secession and sustained the rebels.

Both generals' policies, and variants in other commands, swiftly generated popular concern. Frémont's liberation order was a bonanza to Democrats. They argued that "black Republicans" like Frémont were ambitious tyrants who would break civilian control of the military, undermine all property rights, and destroy democracy. The Democrats insisted that, despite the war, Union soldiers must not violate slave-return statutes, made for conditions of peace. McClellan, by contrast, was to the Democrats an ideal general (and in 1864 they would make him their presidential candidate).

Republicans were in a quandary. Their law-and-order, state-centered, Whiggish origins made them suspicious of executive initiatives, resentful of interference with any property, and wary of policy-making generals. Then, reports from soldiers began to influence uncertain Republicans in favor of Frémont's policies. A mass of testimony swiftly accumulated to the effect that the only friends Union troopers had in Confederate areas were black. No Negro guides ever led bluecoats into ambushes. In a hostile land, only blacks offered reliable information and food, or, if masters and overseers were near, at least welcoming smiles.

The public began to become aware of the horrid risks Negroes ran by coming to Union camps and aiding Union soldiers. By slave-state laws and customs, runaways, especially those involved in "conspiracies" against masters, were liable to ferocious corporal punishment, even death. Returning men and women who incurred such risks to disloyal owners, who would impose punishment, was repugnant.

In 1861, very few bluecoats were antislavery; fewer were Negrophiles. Abuse and exploitation of Negroes were common in Union camps. But, aware of these hazards, ever-increasing numbers of Negroes preferred them to slavery. Unprecedented in history, a slave population sought refuge in the ranks of an invading army. Recalling the swelling waves of black refugees, John Eaton, who became responsible for their welfare in the Union's western command, stated:

> Their comings were like the arrival of cities. . . . There was no Moses to lead or plan in their exodus. The decision of their instinct or unlettered reason brought them to us. They felt that their interests were identical with the objects of our armies. This identity of interest, slowly but surely, came to be perceived by our officers and soldiers, and by the loyal public.[2]

McClellan never understood the basic issues. The question was not whether northern whites loved southern blacks, but whether the nation would survive, and ultimately, if it did survive, what social and political changes would result from the war. So long as Union soldiers remained in Dixie, and Negroes preferred any risk to continuing as slaves, blacks and northern soldiers would interact, and some policy was needed to govern this interaction. Would the policy be made by generals or their nominal civilian overlords?

Lincoln and congressional Republicans indicated that they, the civilians, intended to decide policy. The war was educating educable men very swiftly. Lincoln believed that only generals who won campaigns, not merely battles, had a right to stipulate to their civilian government major policy configurations. Thus far, no Union general qualified. And at this time, Lincoln was not prepared to support Frémont. He revoked the general's emancipation order. A decision for or against abolition was the President's, not a general's. Lincoln knew that he must never outdistance northern whites' opinions about race relationships, and like many of his free-state countrymen, he was very uncertain about what should follow emancipation if it occurred. Colonization of freemen abroad? Creation of all-Negro states? Or biracial coexistence in the present slave states on terms other than master-slave?

Congress also had constitutional responsibility to oversee the military. Its duties included confirmation of commissions, budgets, and Articles of War statutes. At the end of 1861, Congress created an investigative committee to watch over the ever larger army and navy. This was the Joint Standing Committee on the Conduct of the War, dominated by moderate Republicans and "War" Democrats. A joint committee for substantive rather than ceremonial purposes was an innovation. Using subpoenas to enforce their demands for information, committeemen grilled high-ranking officers, sometimes very roughly, about civil-military matters.

Although it is often said that Lincoln was at odds with the committee, he worked closely with it, but backstage. He provided members with War Department information when generals would not. When the committee chastised generals, Lincoln did not have to do so himself, and thus conflicts between the executive and military were lessened.

At first Lincoln and the committeemen treated McClellan gently. He was a very effective organizer, popular among soldiers and home constituents, defended by Democrats, and impressive in his martial promises. But Lincoln's decision against Frémont was not a commitment to McClellan's conservative, fixed race views.

McClellan might eventually have had his way on policy matters if he had defeated rebel forces. But the mere maneuvering of Union armies, however well done, did not prove that the best means to peace was to leave slavery untouched.

The East: 1862

Aware of the Confederacy's innate time advantage, Lincoln and his new (appointed February 1862), energetic, efficient War Secretary, Edwin M. Stanton, pressured McClellan to attack directly and to crush the Confederate Army. The rebellion could continue only if the rebel armies endured as fighting forces. The general insisted on an elaborate amphibious expedition to the James River Peninsula, near Richmond, in order to flank the formidable Confederate forces on the coastal plain. Lincoln detached one division from McClellan's army, to insure Washington's security.

Then a basic threat to McClellan's enormous expedition, and the entire Union blockade, suddenly appeared. The CSA's warship *Virginia* had been built on the raised hulk of the *Merrimack,* a vessel scuttled when secessionists overran the Norfolk navy yard. It was crudely iron-plated, armed with numerous, unmatched, immovable cannon, and fitted with unreliable engines and a defective steering gear; it leaked badly even on calm water, lacked adequate ventilation and sanitary facilities, and had almost no cruising range. Yet, with all its comic limitations, the *Virginia* was one of the world's two most powerful warships. On March 8, 1862, it smashed the Union blockade line with arrogant ease.

The world's other most powerful fighting ship appeared on the scene the next day, after being towed from New York City to Chesapeake Bay. Although it appeared equally comic, the armored *Monitor* was a novel, sophisticated design. Among other improvements, it boasted a revolving turret containing only two cannon on its low-lying hull.

For an entire day these ungainly ironclads blasted at each

The sailors of the *Monitor* pose before the ship's revolving turret.
LIBRARY OF CONGRESS

other. Crews on the beautiful wooden-hulled sailing vessels of the Union fleet, and the Confederate cannoneers ashore, were all but irrelevant spectators. Then the wounded *Virginia* withdrew up the James, never again to threaten the blockade. McClellan's peninsular expedition proceeded; its first goal was to take Yorktown.

But the pace was too slow. Confederate General Joseph E. Johnston rushed graybacks from the Potomac area to Richmond's defense, daringly ordering Stonewall Jackson's command to overrun Union garrisons in the upper Shenandoah Valley. The raiders' purpose was to frighten the Washington leaders into weakening McClellan's forces. Instead, Lincoln sent almost the last trained reserves of bluecoats to join McClellan.

McClellan's cautious siege of Yorktown lost the Union its initiative. By early June, Robert E. Lee, the new Confederate commander, had pushed McClellan back to his base at the tip of the James Peninsula, where naval cannon kept the rebels at respectful distances. The Peninsular Campaign was a failure.

Lincoln then hoped that General John Pope, in charge of the Union Army of the Potomac, could drive directly overland to Richmond while the Confederates were divided. McClellan was ordered to return his regiments by ship to Alexandria in northern Virginia to join Pope. At the end of July, Pope, advancing southward, was outflanked by Jackson's Shenandoah troopers at Manassas, again near Bull Run's green banks. And McClellan's

Part of the Federal force of about 40,000 troops in a vast encampment near Cumberland, Virginia, in May 1862 during the Peninsular Campaign.
LIBRARY OF CONGRESS

Alexander Gardner photographed Lincoln and McClellan on the battlefield at Antietam.

NEW YORK PUBLIC LIBRARY

tens of thousands of veterans, hearing the sound of battle, sat immobile by his orders. Pope's men suffered a grievous defeat. McClellan could have saved the day.

Yet Lincoln had again to turn to McClellan. After the second Bull Run reverse, the Union's premier unit, the Army of the Potomac, was demoralized. There was information that Lee was planning to attack Washington. In early August, Lincoln, against vigorous Republican opposition, reappointed McClellan to top field command. The general proceeded again to build an effective army out of a disorganized uniformed mob. Early the next month, Lee started the Confederacy's forces in Virginia marching northward.

Lee hoped to hit the Army of the Potomac while it was still in shock from Pope's reverses. Exploiting the upper valley's tactical advantages for the Confederacy, He intended to threaten northern communications and production centers. If he was successful, northern Democrats would gain in the oncoming fall elections.

In mid-September, at Antietam, Maryland, the two great armies collided, and fought ferociously for two days. Then McClellan again temporized too long, despite Lincoln's pleas that he block Lee's passage back to Virginia, and possibly bring matters to final decision by destroying the major Confederate army. Lee withdrew south of the Potomac.

But the 1862 Confederate invasion proved to be decisive in other fundamental ways. It lost the seceders the right to claim that they were not fighting an aggressive war. And Lee's thrust, carried on at the height of the agricultural season, affirmed the accuracy of the abolitionists' claim that the rebellion subsisted on the labor of slaves. Lincoln became an abolitionist. Late in September, he issued the Emancipation Proclamation.

The Emancipation Proclamation and the 1862 Elections

Since Sumter, Republican unity had been threatened by deep factionalism, involving especially the war's purposes. Adverting to the Confederates' inevitable victory if the Republicans broke, Lincoln described his party's factions as horses in tandem harness, pulling a fragile wagon, the Union. The goal of the Union's survival kept the horses pulling together, but sometimes, as in the case of Frémont's Negro policies, at dangerously differing speeds.

The minority "radical" Republicans were trying to gallop toward a restored Union without slavery. They wanted Frémont sustained, McClellan dropped. The majority middle Republicans were willing to canter toward emancipation, if they could be convinced it was the only way to military victory and reunion. Conservative Republicans and War Democrats walked very slowly and were determined to avoid the slavery issue, but could, perhaps, be persuaded otherwise. Behind the wagon, the regular antiwar Democrats were dragging their feet as much as possible. They wished to go nowhere except back to 1860.

McClellan had insisted that slave property remain unaffected by the war. But his advice to this effect to the President and Congress, offered arrogantly, was, in the outcome of events, not reinforced by decisive military successes. The Radical Republicans' abolitionist position required, by definition, total victory to be effective. Added to his own moral predispositions against slavery, and to his party's commitment against its further extension, Lincoln's presidential responsibilities now pushed him into joining the abolitionist Radicals. Again resorting to the elastic war powers of the commander-in-chief, Lincoln proclaimed that slavery would end in still-rebellious states on January 1, 1863.

As a psychological weapon designed to persuade numerous southern whites to trade allegiance for the right to keep slaves, the Proclamation was no thunderbolt. Southerners were either too fearful to come forward or believed that the Confederacy could not lose.

As a revision of Union war aims, the Proclamation was a potent force domestically and abroad. It almost entirely removed from the generals the power to make emancipation decisions, thereby strengthening civilian control over the army. It transformed the Union Army into an army of liberation, the torchbearer of blacks' freedom. Foreign rulers sympathetic to the Confederacy dared not link destinies with a slave-owning society from fear of adverse domestic reaction.

Critics from the right and the left quickly noted that the Proclamation was riddled with difficulties. It freed slaves only when and if Union armies conquered areas still unwon. Would Union soldiers risk death and injury to free Negroes? The Proclamation might not stand up; it might be revoked by Congress (the 1862 elections were very close), by a successor President (Democrats looked to 1864), or by the Supreme Court (Taney was still Chief Justice). The Proclamation left slavery untouched in the unseceded states. Opportunistic southerners could become suddenly loyalist when bluecoats occupied their communities, thus keeping their slaves and leaving pockets of slavery in the wakes of Union victories.

Moderate Republicans, though fearful, accepted the Proclamation. Lincoln's gamble paid off. The coalition of Republicans and War Democrats did not break. The abolitionists' argument, that slavery was the basic issue in secession, had struck home. If the Union armies won this war, the re-United States would already have undergone a fundamental reconstruction.

The Republicans and War Democrats needed desperately to advance together, for Lincoln issued the Proclamation only weeks before the fall elections. The regular Democrats could hardly have asked for deadlier campaign ammunition.

The 1862 Elections

Stressing as always that the war was hopeless for the Union, the Democrats now charged that it was also evil. Union states' rights and white men's civil liberties were threatened by a centralized despotism. Free-state white youths should not die for the sake of the South's blacks. Democratic campaigners vilified Lincoln for calling up 300,000 more men. They claimed Republicans were opening the way for floods of southern blacks to migrate to northern communities. They raised gross race-sex fantasies to distress voters.

The Democrats buttressed their appeal with references to the consumer price increases, and predicated further drastic rises to come. The uncertain job market and housing shortages made it easy to inspire in workers fears of competition from migrant blacks. The Democrats' economic arguments hit hard.

Republicans responded with exhortations to patriotism. They condemned disloyalists, linking them to Democrats. The Republicans denied that freed southern blacks would migrate northward. And they insisted that the best way to end the war quickly was to win it, by crushing the Confederacy's military capacities.

In ten thousand communities, Lincoln's party mates appealed also to special-interest groups. Professional organizations and homefront war-auxiliary religious and welfare organizations learned of the exciting educational, medical, and missionary opportunities that Union armies were creating in occupied Confederate areas. Congress' legislation in aid of bankers, farmers, railroad developers, and other entrepreneurs (see Chapter 7), was emphasized fully to appropriate audiences.

Admitting the sharp rise in consumer prices, Republicans countered by noting with pride that agriculture, commerce, industry, and labor had increased output and income. Wholesale prices had risen in a manner to benefit industrial producers. Gross output per farm worker and the value of agricultural products had risen about 15–20% in the brief period since Sumter. The values of industrial, milling, mining, and transportation plants had risen at a similar rate. Railroad track mileage was growing steadily despite wartime difficulties.

Pride was the Republicans' best argument. They noted that, only one year after the pitiful Sumter spectacle, the nation had reasserted its strength and that Union soldiers, despite battering reverses, had refused to quit. The vision of reunion and the reformation of the nation through emancipation excited millions of Americans.

Considering the Democrats' easier task, their election successes are not surprising. They cut the Republican majority in the House of Representatives from 35 to 18. Democrats took six of the most populous states that had gone Republican in 1860, including Lincoln's Illinois; and they won hundreds of county and city contests.

The conservative stance of the Democratic regulars had paid off. Risen phoenixlike from 1860's disasters, the Democrats proved that the party was not following the Federalists and Whigs to oblivion. In 1864, the Democratic candidates would have a fair shot at the White House and a congressional majority.

Lincoln, to his credit, resisted conservative pressure to revoke the Emancipation Proclamation in order to still northerners' race fears. Instead, soon after the election results were in, he discharged McClellan. Then, on January 1, 1863, he added to the Proclamation a provision that Negroes henceforth would be recruited into the Union Army.

Here was revolution. Large numbers of Negroes could come only from slave states; relatively few Negroes resided elsewhere. Lincoln's order defied the property and criminal codes of all slave states, for it would arm blacks to kill whites. In April 1861 slavery was beyond the reach of national power. But by the close of 1862 the nation threatened slavery in its heartland.

McClellan's disgruntled supporters whispered that the Army of the Potomac might march on Washington. Nothing so drastic occurred, but for the next two years McClellan did campaign for the Presidency. Democratic party spokesmen exploited racial fears that emancipation fed. They were encouraged by the ill fortunes of McClellan's immediate successors in charge of the Army of the Potomac. In 1862 and early 1863, after suffering bloody reverses at Fredericksburg, Virginia, that army was back where it had started almost two years earlier.

General Benjamin F. Butler, Union commander at New Orleans. Photo by Mathew Brady.
LIBRARY OF CONGRESS

In the west, however, the Union was gaining ground. While McClellan's amphibious Peninsular Campaign stalled, another seaborne Union expedition had bulled its way past the Confederate defenses on the Gulf and Mississippi River and, in April, occupied the South's largest city, New Orleans. Now the Union officers faced new problems: military occupation and urban government.

The Union commander at New Orleans, Benjamin Butler, gained a tenacious reputation as a brute because, to prevent riot, he ordered that white women who insulted, spat on, and otherwise demeaned bluecoats be classed publicly as prostitutes. On another occasion, Butler had a foolish youth, who had cut down a Union flag, shot. That was the extent of his extraordinary law-and-order expedients.

Butler was also alleged to be a corrupt administrator, but without proofs. In order to safeguard his soldiers' health, he initiated enormous improvements in the quality of public services—especially police, public health, and school matters—in New Orleans, which had long been the worst of any American city's, and in the Louisiana hinterland under Union control. Approved by Butler, these improvements were made possible by the efforts, money, and volunteer workers of numerous private associations, such as the Sanitary and Christian Commissions, that trailed close behind the Union troops. Along with the quality of civil life, political activity revived and improved. Thus, a broad-gauged reconstruction began in Louisiana in 1862 under Union Army auspices.

Far northward, Union commanders continued to try to clear the Mississippi. Heavy April fighting at Corinth, Mississippi, was indecisive. Grant aimed at Vicksburg, Mississippi, and the rail line connecting Chattanooga to Virginia. As 1863 opened, the bluecoats had reached Murfreesboro, Tennessee. No one could say that the western troopers were back where they

In the course of the Civil War well over 100,000 Negroes, most of them from the South, entered the ranks of the Union Army, where they were usually assigned the least desirable jobs.
LIBRARY OF CONGRESS

had been when the war started. It became clear in Washington that high officers in the west were blessed with unremitting vigor, not McClellanite "slows."

Lincoln had estimated correctly, and McClellan incorrectly, on whether Union soldiers would accept blacks as comrades at arms. When Grant heard of the Emancipation Proclamation and the provision for Negro recruitment, he spread the word throughout his command that everyone would obey the civilian dictate and that black soldiers would be welcome. The mood of the army on this issue was reflected in a verse by popular humorist "Private Miles O'Reilly":

> The men who object to Sambo
> Should take his place and fight;
> And it's better to have a naygur's hue
> Than a liver that's wake an' white.
> Though Sambo's black as the ace of spades,
> His finger a thrigger can pull,
> And his eye runs straight on the barrel-sights
> From under his thatch of wool!
> So hear me all, boys, darlings,—
> Don't think I'm tippin' you chaff,—
> The right to be kilt I'll divide wid him,
> And give him the largest half!

Soon more than 100,000 Negroes were recruited, most from the slave states. White self-interest accepted the innovation, if meanly at first, according inferior assignments, pay, and rank to uniformed blacks. Lincoln understood self-interest. Racial equality was a muted element in emancipation and black recruitment. But equality was now closer than any sane man had dreamed in 1860.

FOOTNOTES

1. July 22, 1861, Howe Papers, State Historical Society of Wisconsin.
2. Eaton, *Report of the General Superintendent of Freedmen . . . for 1864* (Memphis, 1865), p. 4.

6 / FROM JELLYFISH to OCTOPUS: THE LINCOLN HERITAGE

BY EARLY 1863, the Union jellyfish of 1860–61 was far less flabby. It was developing appropriate organizational structures and administrative systems for fighting the war, amassing experts as well as military manpower, and evaluating war aims in light of wartime reconstructions. The Union's larger government and modernized organizations exhibited themselves strikingly in 1863.

The East: 1863

In late April, the Army of the Potomac, with more than 130,000 troops, moved south again, now under command of General "Fighting Joe" Hooker. It was stopped by elaborate

Three Confederate prisoners, taken at Gettysburg.
LIBRARY OF CONGRESS

Confederate entrenchments at Chancellorsville, near ill-fated Fredericksburg. Lee, with only half the number of soldiers Hooker deployed, risked sending Jackson's crack units through valley passes to flank the bluecoats. By May 5 the severely mauled Army of the Potomac again sounded retreat.

As after the Union's second Bull Run reverse at Manassas a year earlier, Lee determined to exploit the North's disappointments. He again invaded the Union heartland. Perhaps, Confederate leaders hoped, the Democrats' upsurge in the 1862 balloting, and reaction to McClellan's dismissal and the Negro recruitment policy, had caused enough dissatisfaction to topple the Lincoln government, or at least to trigger revolution in Maryland or Pennsylvania.

Early in June, Lee started up the Confederates' Shenandoah highway. No one, Lee included, knew where he would strike. Pennsylvania legislators abandoned the state capital. Hooker resigned because of policy differences with Lincoln. But Lincoln, cabinet, and Congress displayed no panic or irresolution.

Lincoln appointed General George Meade to replace Hooker. Meade, a Pennsylvanian, might fight well on his own "dung hill," Lincoln said. Exploiting rail facilities whenever possible, Meade interposed the Army of the Potomac between Lee and Washington.

The two vast armies blundered into each other at Gettysburg, Pennsylvania, and fought bloodily for three days. Union troops had the advantage of being the entrenched defenders for a change. The Confederate staffs, unfamiliar with large-scale offensive operations, failed adequately to organize troop movements, signals, and supplies. On July 4, Lee broke off battle; on July 13, he and his surviving regiments escaped into Virginia.

Yet Gettysburg was a great Union victory. Lee was stopped; Union institutions did not collapse. While Gettysburg was being fought, terrible antidraft and anti-Negro riots broke out in

Abolitionists and Negroes were special targets during the draft riots in New York City, July 13-16, 1863. This sketch, from the August 15 *Illustrated*

London News, depicts the mob's destruction of the Colored Orphan Asylum. It was one of about a hundred buildings that were burned.
NEW YORK PUBLIC LIBRARY

major northern cities from New York to Chicago. Municipal and county police were utterly unable to cope with the bestial mobs. Governors pleaded with Lincoln for soldiers, but he refused to detach one regiment from Meade until the battle ended. Then Meade sent small numbers of Gettysburg veterans to those cities. The rioters quickly dispersed. Social dissolution was not yet in the cards for the Union; Lee's strategy, as well as his tactics, had failed. To commemorate the failure and to relieve tension, Lincoln scribbled these "Verses on Lee's Invasion of the North":

> In eighteen sixty three, with pomp,
>   and mighty swell,
> Me and Jeff's Confederacy, went
>   forth to sack Phil-del,
> The Yankees they got arter us, and
>   giv us particular hell,
> And we skedaddled back again,
>   and didn't sack Phil-del.[1]

Lincoln's pleasure was heightened by news from the west that on the same July 4—such happy symbolism!—that Lee began his retreat from Gettysburg, Vicksburg, the last major Confederate city and strong point along the Mississippi's great length, surrendered.

The West: 1863

The Vicksburg triumph required six months of complex amphibious and land operations, involving scores of thousands of men, logistical exploitation of rail and canal lines, and sheer hard fighting by Grant's troopers. Despite unending guerrilla harassment and large-scale Confederate raids, Grant persisted. He captured the country's imagination by his transfer of the

Ulysses S. Grant during the Vicksburg campaign, 1863. Portrait by Mathew Brady.
LIBRARY OF CONGRESS

main Union forces to Vicksburg's softer southern flank, using a river fleet that ran past the city's supposedly impregnable batteries. The transfer made possible the battles near Vicksburg that led to its capitulation.

The Mississippi was secure. The trans-Mississippi west, especially Arkansas and Texas, was cut off from the rest of the Confederacy. Grant now turned eastward.

In early September, Union troops, under General W. S. Rosecrans, ousted Confederates from Chattanooga, Tennessee, where vital rail lines connected to Virginia. Lee, who had been idle since Gettysburg, and President Davis rushed 11,000 crack soldiers by rail to Tennessee. The Confederates' powerful fortifications on Lookout Mountain and Missionary Ridge oversaw Chattanooga and its environs. With winter imminent, the Union soldiers in Chattanooga appeared likely to be starved out, redressing the Vicksburg loss.

East and West Bridged

The prospect at Chattanooga was dismal. To prevent disaster, in mid-October Lincoln placed Grant in command of the western armies. In Washington, Lincoln and Stanton sent out telegraphic orders that assembled rail transportation experts, quartermaster officers, and engineer specialists—the cream of the nation's new managerial and communications elite—in the newly created bureau of the Military Director and Superintendent of Railroads. Plans were swiftly made and approved.

Telegrams flashed out to directors of dozens of private rail lines to give absolute priority to emergency government traffic. Hundreds of locomotives and empty cars of all sorts moved, under synchronized orders, to northern Virginia and other eastern army centers. There, the men, animals, and equipment of two entire army corps, plus supplies for the Chattanooga garrison, were entrained.

Through late October and early November, the laden trains ran westward day and night. At crossings where track gauges changed, the men and supplies were transferred to other lines. Re-entrained, the enormous caravan rolled again toward assembly points near Chattanooga. Heavy guards successfully kept away saboteurs, guerrillas, and Confederate raiders. It was a logistical operation unique in military history.

In the last week of November, the reinforced Union forces in Chattanooga drove the Confederates from their positions on the fortified heights. Now the Confederacy was not only split along its Mississippi spine, a rift was opening from the Mississippi to the Atlantic as well.

The Better-Organized War

Such effective, sinewy action on the part of the North required sophisticated, specialized organization, expert staff work, and efficient manpower and security procedures. None of these existed in 1861. Allan Nevins has aptly described 1863 as the year of "the organized war." This improved organization further increased the public's sense of confidence in the nation's adequacy for peace. The prospects improved of the nation's emerging from the war with states and civilians as free and prosperous as when it began.

Manpower and the Politics of Federalism

Initially, the states wholly dominated the supply of manpower. Lincoln's first calls for states' militiamen, and Congress' subsequent provisions for 500,000 war-service-only volunteers, left control of the muster and the selection of officers largely in state hands. In mid-1862, Congress authorized a militia draft of 300,000 more men, in which the states encouraged volunteering with bounties and other bonuses in order to meet quotas set in Washington. By early 1863 it was apparent that such arrangements were inadequate. In March, Lincoln signed the first "national" conscription law in the country's history.

The 1863 statute created a new Provost Marshal General's Bureau in the War Department, with Assistant PMGs in every congressional district. They registered all fit adult males and selected servicemen by a lottery. But state volunteer quotas still prevailed; national conscription occurred only when a state's quota was not met. The basic quota-setting and exemption work was performed by PMG district boards. Each board, headed by the Assistant PMG (usually a former combat officer), consisted also of prominent local citizens, including a physician.

Local-state political machinery was involved in all PMG operations, including personnel choices and exemption appeals. Thus, the PMG Bureau meshed with familiar, local political procedures and institutions. It was a great improvement over previous arrangements, and a more rational, decent system than any other known at that time.

Other Reins on the Military

The new PMG Bureau also assumed effective charge of all anti-disloyalty operations. Since 1861, internal security had been handled primarily by local military officers, with improvised and inconsistent policies. Now, under the PMG statute of March 3, 1863, and another which Lincoln signed the same day,

Recruiters for Pennsylvania's "Bucktail" Regiment.
SY SEIDMAN

the Habeas Corpus Act, PMGs and other uniformed security officers were required to report all security arrests of civilians to federal district and circuit judges, and to initiate civil-court proceedings against arrested persons within a specified time or to release them. Thus, with Lincoln's full assent, Congress placed a judicial check on executive-military power.

The Habeas Corpus Act allowed the transfer to federal courts of certain state-court litigation in which federal military and civil officers were defendants. Usually these were damage suits, directed against low-level internal security and draft officials. In localities where state judges, jurymen, and attorneys were hostile to the war, such suits had harassed officers and officials, and impeded the war effort. The Habeas Corpus Act was a statesmanlike way to provide better justice and to avoid direct confrontations between nation and state, sword and robe. It did not diminish the primacy of local-state justice, for the circumstances in which it applied were very narrow.

Army–War Department Reforms

Throughout the war, Congress, always with Lincoln's cordial support, was concerned with the oversight of the War Department and the army. To this end, it reactivated some moribund military bureaus and created some new ones, such as the PMGs. These new bureaus are often cited as evidence of the increasing growth and power of centralized government during this period. But this claim should be reexamined in light of these bureaus' impact and duration.

To head one of these reinvigorated bureaus, in early 1862 Lincoln appointed William Whiting, a noted Boston lawyer, to be War Department solicitor. Whiting made this formerly peripheral office an influential element in the winning of civilian control over the military. He and his staff served as counsel for officers accused in damage suits in state courts, and in situations in which the defendants appeared to be accused unjustly, Whiting arranged for transfers to federal courts. In 1863 the War Department published Solicitor Whiting's collected opinions and instructions as a book. It was the first relevant guide army officers had available with respect to the procedures they should follow in many civil-military matters. The book's title was *War Powers Under the Constitution of the United States*; the word "Under" in the title is significant.

Long moribund, the Judge Advocate General Bureau, headed since 1861 by former Cabinet officer Joseph Holt, also helped to standardize and refine military-civil legal relationships. The JAG, a civilian, dealt primarily with appeals from soldiers and civilians accused under military or martial law. By statute, the JAG enjoyed direct access to the President, opening the way for Lincoln's numerous merciful intercessions in cases of harsh sentences. Holt's collected circulars to field commanders, entitled *Digest of Opinions*, was also published in 1863, and, like Whiting's book, it served to regularize the military's legal procedures.

Another similar publication was "General Orders #100" (1863) by special War Department adviser and Columbia College professor Francis Lieber. This manual consisted of Lieber's rules for the government of the field forces that systematically defined the limits of permissible military behavior affecting enemy civilians and their property. It was, by all estimates, the best such document in the world, and the nation's generals followed it.

Congress reconstituted the Inspector General's Office, which systematized the accounts of military and civilian contractors. On its own, the IGO court-martialed offending officers. Through the Attorney General, the IGO initiated civil or criminal suits against fraudulent or delinquent contractors. In outrageous instances, "shoddy" suppliers could even be proceeded against under the Articles of War. IGO inspectors worked closely with the House Committee on Government Contracts and the Joint Committee on the Conduct of the War. By mid-1863, the early carnival of fraud had ended.

The new bureau, established in 1862 by Congress, of the Military Director and Superintendent of Railroads had a small but effective staff of civilian and uniformed rail operations experts. They imported private-sector managerial methods into army mass-transit logistics, as in the spectacular 1863 reinforcement of the Chattanooga garrison. Although Congress and President delegated awesome powers to him, the Military Director operated government railroads only near combat areas and in occupied regions in cases where the southern owners and managers had given up control. The Military Director worked primarily with commercial lines, through use contracts, even in the Chattanooga operation. He encouraged them to integrate schedules, routes, equipment, and accounting as much as possible. The result harmonized well with the goals of prewar rail reformers, who had sought such rationalizations. And profits to contracting railroads were very high.

In these and other ways the military's relationships with civilians and private industry and business were greatly systematized. No longer could a Frémont or a McClellan quote scripture, the Constitution, or international law to support opposite policies. Now the President, War Secretary, and Congress had the resources, experts, institutions, and procedures to control policy decisions by officers and profiteering by civilians. The War Department solicitor's authority to decide whether or not to defend army officers, the IGO's authority to investigate officers' and contractors' accounts, the JAG's access to the President, and the PMG's ability to work out satisfactory draft quotas with most state governors all worked to stabilize constitutional government under conditions of civil war.

In order adequately to coordinate the work of these new units with older bureaus and, above all, to learn the needs and conditions of the field commands, Stanton, with Lincoln's encouragement, held regular policy meetings in his office. The meetings anticipated general staff assemblies, with Grant performing as overall field commander. Stanton invited to these policy sessions relevant department and bureau heads, combat officers on leave or convalescing, important civilian suppliers and inventors, auxiliary-association executives, other cabinet officers, friendly congressmen, and visiting governors or other high state functionaries.

Such meetings were fruitful. The new bureau personnel included extraordinarily talented, energetic, trustworthy men, possessing excellent managerial and bureaucratic skills. Most had been drawn to Washington for duration-only service, often at considerable personal sacrifice.

The New Military Establishment as Bureaucracy

By early 1863, the organization of the War Department and of the army met the standards of a modern bureaucracy as defined by political scientist Richard E. Neustadt: the effective combination of ranking agency officials, important legislators, and leaders of unofficial or quasi-official public-interest private organizations. It also met the standard consisting of men of good training and standing (which political theorist Joseph Schumpeter has applied to the definition of modern bureaucracy).

But, unlike most bureaucracies, the Civil War-Reconstruction military establishment was short-lived. Congress and the President designed it to create and coordinate policy for the duration of the war only. To be sure, the IGO and the solicitor endured in the War Department long after Appomattox. But their influence was limited to the army's tightly circumscribed world.

Reconstruction: Lincoln's December 1863 Plan

On December 8, 1863, again resorting to his war powers, Lincoln offered a general sketch of Reconstruction. He wished to harmonize the discordant policies developed in several army commands.

The Union's armies were now occupying whole states. The Emancipation Proclamation had been in effect for a year. Black soldiers had not indulged in orgies against whites, as predicted. Still, the most conservative Republicans and War Democrats were pressuring Lincoln to revoke the Emancipation Proclamation so that the war, the party's fortunes, and Reconstruction without changes in race laws might advance more swiftly. The 1864 presidential nominations were coming up in six months; the elections in less than a year.

Lincoln's December 1863 Reconstruction proclamation offered amnesties to ordinary rebels, and individual pardons to prominent miscreants who swore to loyalty to the nation in the future. Reflecting Republican state rightism, Lincoln stipulated that existing state boundaries should not change in a reunified nation. When, in each rebel state, 10% of 1860's voters qualified for amnesty or pardon, and met their state's voting rules (meaning white voters only), Lincoln would order the Union Army to aid the newly loyal electorate in reestablishing state government. Each restored state government must repudiate secession. Then Lincoln would recognize the state as legitimate, although he noted that Congress had constitutional control over the admission of delegations.

He asked those seeking amnesty to "recognize and declare" Negroes' "permanent freedom." Beyond this, Lincoln agreed that the states' civil and criminal laws and customs should not be impaired—a fault in his program, according to many attentive contemporaries.

At the same time, the President specified that he was suggesting "a mode," not a blueprint, for Reconstruction: ". . . while the mode presented is the best the Executive can suggest with his present impressions, it must not be understood that no other possible mode would be accepted"[2] Like the Emancipation Proclamation, this Reconstruction policy statement was subject to revision via open politics, legislation, and, perhaps, judicial review.

Republican Politics: 1864

Expectably, Democrats stormed at the President for assuming the responsibility for policy decisions involving national stipulations that states must obey. Serious reservations existed also among Republicans concerning Lincoln's approach. Approving his commitment to emancipation and the restoration of states, Republicans nevertheless worried that the lily-white electorates Lincoln's policy envisaged would be unrepentant. What then would be the fates of southern Unionists and Negroes, who had risked so much for the nation's survival? Radical Republicans tried to block a second-term nomination for Lincoln, but he easily outmaneuvered their chosen champions, Treasury Secretary Salmon Chase and old campaigner Frémont. By June 1864, when the Republican nominating convention met, Lincoln had a clear field and received renomination on the first ballot.

As his vice-presidential candidate, Lincoln wanted, and got, Tennessee's Andrew Johnson. Back in 1861 Johnson was the only senator from a seceded state to opt for the Union, at great personal hazard. Since then Johnson had served Lincoln as Tennessee's military governor. Johnson represented the kind of southern Unionist who invigorated the Union party coalition.

Returning in the wake of victorious Union armies, such southern Unionists might, it was hoped, effectively promote the President's Emancipation and Reconstruction proclamations.

The Republican platform stipulated against any military armistice. It demanded the unconditional surrender of all Confederate forces, the obliteration of rebel governments, the end of slavery, and an abolition amendment to the Constitution. It praised the army's Negro troops. And it promised to preserve the party's economic legislation.

Military: 1864

The harmony at the Republican convention soon soured. Grant, who was appointed general in chief of the armies of the United States in March, had developed a grand scheme by which all Union forces would launch coordinated, octopuslike attacks on remaining Confederate troop concentrations and strategic rail and port centers. The War Department drafted and recruited tens of thousands more whites and blacks, encouraged reenlistments by regiments, accumulated supplies, and, very sternly, prosecuted deserters and inciters of draft resistance.

Elements in Grant's complex strategy failed, however. And Grant himself, in personal charge of what became a costly attrition operation by the Army of the Potomac, seemed unable to get beyond the frighteningly familiar Fredericksburg area. In mid-May, after dreadful bloodletting at Spotsylvania, Grant at last pushed back Lee's army and, by early June, was south of the Chickahominy River at Cold Harbor, where both sides endured terrible casualties.

Grant now moved to Petersburg, a railhead 20 miles south of Richmond. Lee was there before him. Both armies dug in.

General Robert E. Lee.
NATIONAL ARCHIVES

Lincoln and some of his military leaders: left to right, Admirals David D. Porter and David Farragut and Generals William Tecumseh Sherman, George Thomas, Ulysses S. Grant, and Philip Sheridan.
LIBRARY OF CONGRESS

Union troopers extended lines around Petersburg, stretching Confederate defenders ever thinner. But this bloody business seemed to bring the Union no closer to final success.

In the west, too, the sacrifices appeared—at least to home-front strategists—disproportionately heavy in the absence of any clear triumph. Early in May, William T. Sherman set out eastward from Chattanooga with 100,000 splendidly trained and equipped men. After a series of intense fire fights, Confederates gave way grudgingly, until a stand-up confrontation, at Kenesaw Mountain on June 27, opened the way eastward. Then

Sherman headed toward Atlanta. Casualties were heavy; results, seemingly, indecisive.

But, east and west, the Union's commanders were exhausting the Confederacy's manpower resources. With the South unable, out of its race views and constitutional-political rigidities, to risk arming its millions of blacks, the great skirmish-battles that Grant and Sherman were forcing upon Confederate commanders had a grimly logical arithmetic.

The question was, Would the Union's citizens accept the casualty lists? Or was the nation growing too weary to go on much longer, at such a costly pace, toward still uncertain goals?

Gambling again on northern fatigue and impatience, Lee sent cavalry commander Jubal A. Early on a large-scale raid up the Shenandoah. By July 11, Early's men were digging in near Takoma Park and Silver Spring, on the Maryland-District of Columbia line. No panic shook Washington. Hurriedly armed government clerks, convalescent soldiers, and raw recruits manned Union trenches. Visiting them, Lincoln raised himself over a dugout lip. An attentive young Massachusetts captain, Oliver Wendell Holmes, Jr., fearing sniper fire, knocked the President aside, earning Lincoln's thanks.

In response to Early's attack, Grant sent two divisions to Washington. In mid-July these rugged soldiers easily pushed Early back to Virginia. But, determined to end at last the Confederacy's advantage in the Shenandoah, Grant had the valley laid waste.

The Wade-Davis Bill: July 1864

While Early was still buzzing on the capital's Maryland border, Republican congressmen, worried at voter response to the costs of Grant's and Sherman's campaigns (the "butcher bills," as they were being called), and dissatisfied with significant details in Lincoln's Reconstruction plan, offered an alternative. Sponsored by Senator Benjamin Wade of Ohio and Representative Henry W. Davis of Maryland, it passed the Congress on July 2, 1864. Lincoln, to everyone's surprise, pocket vetoed it. His action has been seen as a symptom of a basic Republican schism. It was not.

A product not of a Radical plot but of general Republican concerns, the Wade-Davis bill deserved, and received, serious and extended consideration. Aiming to place Reconstruction on a more stable, legislative, civilian base than Lincoln's proclamation had provided, the bill called for 50% of a rebel state's voters, not 10%, to swear loyalty, thus increasing the probability that returning white Unionists could play significant roles. The bill required the pardoned electorate to call a new state constitutional convention, whose members would have to swear to their past loyalty. Slaveowning was to be a new federal crime. A state's civil and criminal law codes and procedures would have to apply to Negroes equally with whites.

These were decent extensions of Lincoln's December plan, especially with respect to biracial equality before state laws. Why, in an election year, did Lincoln pocket veto, and reopen party wounds?

In a curious explanation of his pocket veto, Lincoln noted that he was by no means fundamentally opposed to the Wade-Davis proposal. Southerners could opt for his way or theirs, he said. He vetoed the bill, he said, because the army had already initiated Reconstruction procedures in conquered Arkansas and Louisiana on the terms of his 1863 plan, and he wished not to disturb them. It appears also that he wished to placate northern conservatives, who were riled at racial aspects of the Wade-Davis Bill. Finally, it seems Lincoln wished not to lock Reconstruction into any legislative mode quite yet.

Wade, Davis, and other disgruntled Republicans excoriated the President, which greatly heartened the Democrats. Far more divided than Republicans, Democrats needed heart.

Democratic Politics: 1864

The Democratic party convened at the end of August, and it was quickly clear that its schisms of 1860, though healing, were still deep.

A far-right, peace-at-any-price faction, led by Ohio's antiwar ex-Congressman C. L. Vallandigham, refused to budge from militant defeatism and frantic racism. At this faction's insistence, the platform declared the war a failure. Although thousands of Negroes were serving the Union as soldiers, these conservative Democrats wanted the platform to demand the revocation of emancipation and new national guarantees for slavery. On these points, the platform was equivocal. On the other hand, it declared forthrightly that the Republicans had destroyed state rights and individual civil liberty. It demanded an immediate armistice.

The Democratic majority selected McClellan as the presidential nominee, with Ohioan George Pendleton as his running mate. McClellan publicly repudiated the war-failure plank insisted on by the Vallandigham men, but had no public quarrel with the other items of the platform.

Sherman's entrance into Atlanta in early September, and the Union's subsequent capture of Mobile, one of the Confederacy's last major ports, buoyed up Republican prospects. But Grant's seemingly indecisive, and definitely costly, encirclement of Petersburg served Democratic campaigners.

Vallandigham and his followers swung into line behind

At Atlanta, neat rows of wheels are all that remain of ordnance trains blown up by retreating Confederate troops as Sherman advanced upon the city. LIBRARY OF CONGRESS

McClellan, despite his disavowal of the peace plank. Similarly, Wade, Davis, Frémont, and all other Republican factioneers stopped sniping at Lincoln and united in his campaign. In short, both the young Republican organization and the venerable Democratic party were elastic and healthy institutions. The war had taught even persons of relatively extreme views to work for what they wanted within party institutions. Widespread reports of the imminent death of one or both political parties were very much exaggerated.

Elections: 1864

Here and abroad since 1861, there had been many premature obsequies for American government and constitutionalism. Foreign commentators were shocked that these maverick Americans kept holding elections. Suppose the Democrats now won the White House and Congress, as many persons, sometimes even Lincoln, believed would occur? Then all the war's sacrifices would be wasted, and emancipation revoked. A military armistice would be arranged, and the Confederacy would regain its strength, especially by linking with the new French puppet regime in Mexico.

Early-election states were watched intently for straw-in-the-wind indications. A drift toward the Democrats in Kentucky's local contests resulted in renewed pressure on Lincoln from nervous party underlings to backtrack on emancipation and to lower draft quotas. He rejected both courses. There were predictions of election-day riots worse than the antidraft riots of 1863, especially if soldiers voted. Again, Lincoln rejected proposals for suspending elections and limiting voting by soldiers.

Instead, War Department orders furloughed whole regiments back to their states in order to let uniformed citizens vote; in other instances, states sent vote takers to army camps to record ballots. It was a stirring spectacle, unique in the nineteenth-century world.

Almost every institution and calling in American society appeared to be caught up in the campaign: churchmen, industrialists, farmers, railroad operators and workmen, disabled veterans, Negroes, women, soldiers (some black), college students, businessmen, southern Union refugees—the list of campaign participants is endless. There were no riots, no meaningful mismanagement or corruption of the electoral process, no military interference. The results were decisive. Voters, including soldiers and their families, replied in the affirmative to the basic question: Should the war continue until the Confederacy and slavery ceased to exist?

Lincoln himself offered the best commentary on the meaning of the 1864 balloting, in his State of the Union annual address to Congress, the next month:

Union soldiers cast ballots in the presidential election of 1864.
NEW YORK PUBLIC LIBRARY

CAP WATTSON
CO L
3rd PENN·ARTY
MESS

> The most reliable indication of public purpose in this country is derived through our popular elections. Judging by the recent canvass and its result, the purpose of the people within the loyal States to maintain the integrity of the Union was never more firm nor more nearly unanimous than now. The extraordinary calmness and good order with which the millions of voters met and mingled at the polls give strong assurance of this. Not only all of those who supported the Union ticket, so called, but a great majority of the opposing party also may be fairly claimed to entertain and to be actuated by the same purpose. It is an unanswerable argument to this effect that no candidate for any office whatever, high or low, has ventured to seek votes on the avowal that he was for giving up the Union. There have been much impugning of motives and much heated controversy as to the proper means and best mode of advancing the Union cause, but on the distinct issue of Union or no Union the politicians have shown their instinctive knowledge that there is no diversity among the people. In affording the people the fair opportunity of showing one to another and to the world this firmness and unanimity of purpose, the election has been of vast value to the national cause.
>
> The national resources . . . are unexhausted, and, as we believe, inexhaustible. The public purpose to reestablish and maintain the national authority is unchanged, and, as we believe, unchangeable.[3]

Lincoln received almost 2¼ million votes; McClellan, slightly more than 1¾ million. Of soldiers voting (their votes were decisive in several key states), 116,000 opted for Lincoln, only 33,748 for McClellan. McClellan won only New Jersey, Kentucky, and Delaware; the electoral count was 212–21.

The clear verdict was comforting, and two-party political institutions had proved themselves to be vigorous. The diverse views of Americans remained fairly evenly balanced. In the East, state after state that went Republican did so by a slim margin. Pacific Coast states, once Democratic strongholds, swung Republican. The Middle West replaced the more industrial, urban East as the Republican heartland.

The election results left the course of Reconstruction open for the future. It would be decided by two-party politics in elections to come, because 1864's elections had taken place, were

Result of the Presidential Election of 1864

States	Electoral Vote: Lincoln	Electoral Vote: McClellan	Popular Vote: Lincoln	Popular Vote: McClellan
Maine	7	....	72,278	47,736
New Hampshire	5	....	36,595	33,034
Massachusetts	12	....	126,742	48,745
Rhode Island	4	....	14,343	8,718
Connecticut	6	....	44,693	42,288
Vermont	5	....	42,422	13,325
New York	33	....	368,726	361,986
New Jersey	....	7	60,723	68,014
Pennsylvania	26	....	296,389	276,308
Delaware	....	3	8,155	8,767
Maryland	7	....	40,153	32,739
Virginia				
North Carolina				
South Carolina				
Georgia		....		
Kentucky	....	11	27,786	64,301
Tennessee				
Ohio	21	....	265,154	205,568
Louisiana				
Mississippi				
Indiana	13	....	150,422	130,233
Illinois	16	....	189,487	158,349
Alabama				
Missouri	11	....	72,991	31,026
Arkansas				
Michigan	8	......	85,352	67,370
Florida				
Texas				
Iowa	8	....	87,331	49,260
Wisconsin	8	....	79,564	63,875
Minnesota	4	....	25,060	17,375
California	5	....	62,134	43,841
Oregon	3	....	9,888	8,457
Kansas	3	....	14,228	3,871
West Virginia	5	....	23,223	10,457
Nevada	2	....	9,826	6,594
Totals	212	21	2,213,665	1,802,237

From Edward McPherson, ed. *Political History of the United States during the Great Rebellion, 1860–1865* (New York, 1865; reprint, ed. H. M. Hyman and H. Trefousse [New York: DaCapo, 1972]), p. 623.

honest, and, unlike 1860's, were accepted. The links between politics and government, seemingly so frail in 1860–61, were again strong. They would serve Lincoln well in his second term, which would last until March 1869.

The Thirteenth Amendment: 1865

The decisiveness of the election enabled Republicans, with Lincoln's warm support, to propose through Congress and send out to the states a new Thirteenth Amendment to the Constitution. Unlike the unworthy amendment proposed in 1861, the Thirteenth Amendment of 1865 eliminated the right of any state to define humans as property. To penalize state violations of this constraint, the amendment authorized the use of federal power as deemed appropriate by Congress.

The amendment passed over contemporary suggestions that there should be compensations for loyal slaveholders, or colonization abroad for freedmen. America, reconstructed by the Thirteenth Amendment, would be a biracial land, with whites and blacks sharing a single nation. The stigma of slavery would be ended nationally.

However, unless Confederate soldiers quit fighting, the proposed new Thirteenth Amendment would have little meaning.

Military: 1864–65

To force the South's final surrender, Sherman marched out of Atlanta and headed toward the Atlantic. Save for home guardsmen and guerrillas, he met little resistance west of the Appalachians. To cut off Confederate resources, he destroyed crops, warehouses, rail lines, and so on, leaving desolation in his wake. After taking Savannah by Christmas 1864, Sherman celebrated the new year by turning north to join with Grant. The last major Confederate ports fell to combined Union land and sea pressures. Yet, in a February 1865 shipboard conference between Lincoln and Confederate Vice-President Alexander Stephens, the rebels refused to consider anything less than Union recognition of their national independence.

Lee, having spent more of his irreplaceable resources of men and supplies in efforts to break out of the Petersburg encirclement, finally began to evacuate the city on April 2. He hoped to join the remnants of Joseph E. Johnston's western troops, now trying to keep out of Sherman's way. The same night, Jefferson Davis and government officers fled Richmond. Confederates' efforts to destroy stores of ammunition, food, and other supplies almost leveled their erstwhile capital. On April 9, trapped, Lee surrendered to Grant unconditionally, in a simple capitulation at Appomattox. The terms of the surrender accorded exactly with the Republican party's platform stipulation against any armistice that recognized Confederate civil government. However, Sherman, accepting Johnston's surrender on April 18, "recognized" local Confederate civil officers. This agreement was properly disavowed by the War Department, and Johnston capitulated unconditionally. On May 10, Davis was captured.

In his second inaugural address, Lincoln had called for charity and magnanimity, but also for the Union to finish its work. On April 11, Lee's surrender was celebrated in Washington by good-humored crowds who urged Lincoln to speak to them (no gates barred public access to the White House grounds then). He told the happy throng that he was considering new Reconstruction policies. Referring to Louisiana, and suggesting that the substance of his proposals should apply in the other Confederate states as well, Lincoln advocated tax-supported elementary education for all children (whether racially segregated or not is

In early April 1865 the fleeing Confederate government set fire to its military stores at Richmond; high winds spread the fire, which devastated the city's business district. Photo by Alexander Gardner.

LIBRARY OF CONGRESS

7110

The capture of Jefferson Davis. Many contemporary accounts of the incident featured sketches similar to this one, from *Harper's Weekly* of May 27, 1865. Actually, Davis wore a complete military uniform and cavalry boots. The canard that he had disguised himself in his wife's clothes grew out of the fact that, when he was taken near Irwinville, Georgia, in the chilly dawn of May 10, his wife threw one of her fringed shawls over his shoulders.

unclear) and the enfranchisement of literate Negroes at least and of all black veterans of the Union's armies. Three days later he was dead.

Lincoln was as educable as ever. He had advanced past the Wade-Davis general concern for equal civil rights for blacks under states' laws. He was now concerned in particular with substantial black voting (political rights) and with black access to state-supported public education—a new frontier indeed. In short, Lincoln had become a very Radical Republican. Which explains why he was murdered by the fanatic John Wilkes Booth and his co-conspirators.

The Enigma of Lincoln and the Preservation of Democracy

A globally significant figure long before his death, Lincoln inspired interest here and abroad. His personal mannerisms frequently misled even men of large achievement who knew him personally. For example, Stanton, on becoming War Secretary, retained for a brief time his earlier misconception of Lincoln as a credulous baboon. McClellan thought Lincoln a clod. Stanton quickly learned better; McClellan, never.

Frederick Douglass, the black political activist, understood that Lincoln, although instinctively antislavery, had become an abolitionist only as result of the war's pressures. Further, Douglass noted, he "was pre-eminently the white man's President." But Lincoln's very intensity about saving the nation for white Americans, combined with his educability and decency, had led Douglass to hope that national policy would continue to promote the rising destinies of black Americans. Measuring the President against other whites, Douglass concluded that "Lincoln was swift, zealous, radical, and determined."[4]

One foreign commentator, formerly a correspondent of the *New York Tribune*, and, in late 1862, a columnist for Vienna's *Die Presse*, was Karl Marx. He saw the Emancipation Proclamation as "the most important document of American history since the founding of the Union." Yet Marx was unable fully to understand Lincoln as man or as American. Admitting, ruefully, that "Lincoln was not born of a people's revolution," Marx realized that "the ordinary play of the electoral system" had carried Lincoln to the American summit. To Marx, Lincoln's fight for Union and Emancipation was the final proof that, "thanks to its [America's] political and social organization, ordinary people of good will can carry out tasks which the Old World would have to have a [military] hero to accomplish!" Lincoln was a different, incurably civilian, individualist hero, Marx continued:

> . . . Lincoln is a figure *sui generis* in the annals of history. No pathos, no idealistic flights of eloquence, no posing, no wrapping himself in the toga of history. He always gives the most significant of his acts the most common-place form. Indecisively, against his will, he reluctantly performs the bravura aria of his role, as though asking pardon for the fact that circumstances are forcing him to "play the hero." The most formidable decrees, which he hurls against the enemy, and which will never lose their historic significance, resemble—as the author intends them to—ordinary summonses sent by one lawyer to another on the opposing side, with the pettifogging juridical character, the tangle of petty stipulations of an *actiones juris*. And this is the character the . . . [Emancipation] proclamation bears. . . .[5]

To Walt Whitman, who had served as a nurse in military hospitals (and had resented the systematic, impersonal techniques of his colleagues in the Sanitary Commission), the Lincoln-Union victory showed that ". . . popular democracy, whatever its faults and dangers, practically justifies itself beyond the proudest claims and wildest hopes of its enthusiasts." Whitman wrote in 1865:

Grand Review of the Union armies in Washington.
LIBRARY OF CONGRESS

> What have we seen here if not, towering above all talk and argument, the . . . last-needed proof of democracy. . . ? That our national democratic experiment, principle, and machinery could triumphantly sustain such a shock, and that the Constitution could weather it, like a ship in a storm, and come out of it as sound and whole as before, is by far the most signal proof yet of the stability of that experiment—Democracy—and of those principles and that Constitution.[6]

Whitman's adoration of Lincoln—"O Captain! My Captain!"—needs no retelling. Lincoln had been captain of what had become, by 1865, a vast, complex military-government-industrial establishment. Yet this accumulated power had accommodated itself to, been accepted by, and not threatened our "democratic experiment, principle, and machinery."

An immediate proof of the argument is in the Union armies' Grand Review, in Washington, soon after Lincoln's murder. Bitter southerners prophesied that the bluecoats would overthrow their civilian overlords, and install "Grant I" as dictator. Instead, the proud regiments, white and black, from east and west, paraded past their new President, Andrew Johnson. His installation occurred without crisis; there was no mass revenge for Lincoln's death. The armies disbanded.

The Vanishing Act

Except for the Freedmen's Bureau, the other new War Department agencies formed during the war disappeared as publicly significant units very soon after Appomattox. Anti-disloyalty operations ended, conscription machinery disappeared, prison camps opened, the Sanitary and Christian Commissions disbanded. Jefferson Davis, almost alone among the high Confederate civilian leadership, remained a captive, and for a relatively brief time. One Confederate military officer, the sadistic Andersonville prison keeper, Henry Wirz, was executed after a military trial.

The vengeful slaughters that traditionally followed European civil wars did not occur here. The regular army, reduced to about 60,000 men, vanished, largely into the Southwest to deal with Indians and to overawe French-backed empire builders in Mexico. Only 15,000 bluecoats (New York City today employs almost 30,000 policemen, and they are overtasked), plus a few hundred uniformed agents of the Freedmen's Bureau, remained to "occupy" the South's hundreds of thousands of square miles. In midsummer 1865, Reconstruction was believed to be all but complete.

This belief was essential to the restored confidence of 1865. How happily different everything was from 1861! The ability of American government and society to create appropriate,

Andersonville Prison, in Georgia, crowded almost 32,000 Union captives into its primitive quarters. The camp's commander was executed for murder. LIBRARY OF CONGRESS

effective public and private institutions, to coordinate them with two-party state-based politics, and to avoid military domination of the government made the confidence deserved.

Lincoln, having encouraged these subtle, complex, sophisticated developments that allowed greater efficiency without centralization, and security without tyranny, had earned the respect and affection that his countrymen began to lavish upon him. He comprehended the need for corporate-style expertise in government. A precursor of the modern administrator, he recruited leaders of the nation's first big business, the railroads, as well as volunteers from many other callings, to see to the country's survival. In harmony with Congress, he saw to it that war agencies harmonized with open politics, state-based federalism, and economic capitalism.

Because these innovations worked, there was confidence in the nation that had created them. Confidence was also encouraged by the monumentally important nonwar legislation and institutions developed by Congress, and by the means used to pay the costs of the war and government. Now this account turns to nonwar economic faces of the decade.

FOOTNOTES

1. Lincoln, *Collected Works, Supplement,* ed. Roy P. Basler (Westport, Conn.: Greenwood, 1974), p. 194.

2. *Messages and Papers of the Presidents,* ed. James D. Richardson (New York, 1897), VI, pp. 213–15, and see pp. 189–92.

3. *Ibid.,* pp. 252–53.

4. Douglass, *Oration at the Unveiling of the Freedman's Monument in Memory of Abraham Lincoln, 1876* (reprint ed., New York: Parkway Press, 1940), pp. 12–13, 20.

5. October 12, 1862, in K. Marx and F. Engels, *The Civil War in the United States* (3d ed, New York: Citadel, 1961), pp. 332–34.

6. *Walt Whitman's Civil War,* ed. Walter Lowenfels (New York: Knopf, 1961), pp. 283–90, *passim.*

7 / DEMOCRATIC EXPERIMENT, PRINCIPLE, and MACHINERY

The Celebration of Appomattox: Northern Confidence

DESPITE DEEP SORROW at Lincoln's murder, the celebration of Appomattox was intense in the victorious states. At last, the cancers of slavery and secession had been excised. Unpopular wartime measures—conscription, internal security procedures, and trade controls—were abandoned. The demobilization of the army was orderly, swift, and safe—a far cry from the panicky, amateurish marshaling of troops in 1861. It appeared that the nation's political, commercial, and professional progress would now resume.

After so many hazards and reverses, the people of the re-United States again controlled all their land and their destinies. It was a grand feeling. Thus, former Missouri Congressman

Charles Drake, addressing Chicago sponsors of a ship canal joining Lake Michigan to the Mississippi River, argued that any time before 1861, southern opposition would have killed such a project. "One of the glorious results of this war . . . is our perpetual freedom from Southern dictation and control," he concluded.[1]

Similar sentiments permeated the very popular restoration-of-the-Union literature that began to appear in print within a few months after Appomattox. One title in this literature, *Across the Continent: A Summer's Journey to the Rocky Mountains, . . . and the Pacific States, with* [*House*] *Speaker* [*Schuyler*] *Colfax*, by Samuel Bowles, editor and publisher of the influential Springfield, Massachusetts, *Republican*, is both typical and singular. The book is typical in its focus on economic opportunity, and singular in the author's manifold connections to important politicians and entrepreneurs, such as his traveling companion, the politically potent, business-oriented House Speaker, Colfax.

Sir S. Morton Peto, Member of Parliament for Bristol, whose book *The Resources and Prospects of America, Ascertained During a Visit to the States in the Autumn of 1865* (London and New York, 1866) was widely read here and abroad, noted Americans' economic stability, diffused prosperity, and great expectations. Nothing was beyond this astonishing people, Peto wrote. They would pay their public and private debts. Agriculture, industry, and commerce had become stronger during the war in terms of value output, sophistication of entrepreneurial forms, managerial quality, and responsibility. Pauperism, so common in European communities, was absent. Peto advised Englishmen and Europeans to smile no longer when Americans described themselves as a "great nation." This prewar boast was now a true description.

Lincoln's assassination was commemorated in a mournful drawing at his entry in the Mercantile Agency's credit ledger for Illinois. The darkly penned note beside the cross proudly records the fact that Lincoln, like many other resident lawyers, had once served the Agency as a credit reporter: "This office has had the honor of having Old Abe as a correspondent." The credit notes themselves, written in an abbreviated style, estimate Lincoln's worth at half-year intervals from the summer of 1856 to that of 1858: "5267 Aug. 6/56 W[orth]. $10m—good. #5282 Jan. 1/57 Wor[th]. 12m$, 4m$ R[eal]. E[state]. See 1/262 July 1/57 Lawyers are ordinarily imp(r)udent but seldom ask for credit. w. abt. 12m$ principally in R.E. Jany 13/58 . . . [apparent erasure] . . . 694. #5282 July 2/58 Worth perhaps 15m$—prompt efficient & skillfull."

BAKER LIBRARY AT HARVARD UNIVERSITY

Champions of invigorated private enterprise enjoyed global visions. Secretary of State Seward, for example, bent his scant staff to building foundations for an American commercial empire overseas. Seward's policies led to the Alaska purchase, the acquisition of coaling rights for American ships at Panama, American participation in an international monetary-stabilization conference, and the sometimes belligerent search for trade privileges for Americans in Japan. Less success attended his efforts to encourage formation of a global telegraph corporation, development of a Panama canal, and creation of a unified world coinage.

Appomattox was a signal for the translation of dreams, including entrepreneurial dreams, into realities. Of course, many dreamers wanted only self-enrichment. But it is difficult, and unhistorical, cynically to dismiss the wider motives that inspired mercantile and industrial spokesmen. They had won the nation's reunification. Now they were anxious for other links to be retied, including political, religious, fraternal, and professional relationships. The fashioning, or refashioning, of national commerce was essential to these goals.

Northern Prosperity

Large-scale businessmen with interests solely in the victorious states and territories were among the most unrestrained and joyous celebrants of Appomattox. A new era had dawned, they asserted. Wartime profits had been very great. The national customs-free marketplace had been preserved. There seemed to be almost daily improvement in American business technology, in rail and telegraph communications, engineering skills, extractive mining and metals production, and managerial expertise. Inventors were flooding the Patent Office with ideas and models. From 1850 to 1860, 19,591 patents had been issued for inventions, 8.4 patents per 10,000 population. But in the 1860s, 71,679 were issued, the majority after Appomattox. Even so, between Sumter and Appomattox, inventors patented 22.1 inventions per 10,000 population, a 163% increase over the preceding decade.

The most ambitious entrepreneurs were continentalists; other men aspired within more modest regional or local contexts. There were, after all, limits on vision, investment capital, bureaucratic and technical expertise, and technological sophistication. But the pluralistic nature of American federalism offered appropriate stages for very diverse enterprises, ranging from a transcontinental railroad, an Atlantic cable, and a Russian-American telegraph link to local improvements such as canals and bridges, interurban transit systems, and public utilities.

Promoters touted new machinery, developed during the war, for mines, factories, and farms. There was a surge of competition for investment capital and talent. Army-trained civil engineers and regimental officers were widely sought as managers in growing businesses and industries. The question of the desirable public-sector involvements, if any, with these numerous private enterprises was becoming a new political issue at all levels of government. It was a time of opportunity that had been nurtured in the war years.

Flatland farmers of the Midwestern states had transformed recent frontiers into incredibly productive corn and pig farms. Expensive new harvesters and reapers worked in the place of men who had gone to war. The prospect of large increases in demand encouraged farmers to buy more land and machines, and output soared. In the 1861–65 years, American farmers had been able not only to meet domestic civilian and military needs, but to export mountains of corn, wheat, wool, and meat to England and Europe.

The Union Stockyards in Chicago, 1866. The town's numerous rail links with the rest of the country made it a center of the cattle and grain industries, both of which prospered during the war.

THE NEW-YORK HISTORICAL SOCIETY

The growing number of railroad trunk lines, such as the Baltimore and Ohio, Erie, New York Central, and Pennsylvania, formed a mesh linking the cities and states of the increasingly urban, industrialized east coast, the Ohio Valley, and the Great Lakes to Chicago and St. Louis. Touching every major community in a dozen states, conveying the products of multitudes of farms, and transporting soldiers and military supplies, the railroads had enormously expanded marketplaces. They also developed the institutional model for government and businesses of the future: specialized employees bureaucratically organized in a graded, rational, elaborate hierarchy of skills and authority managed by a new class of administrators.

Railroad routes and stations held the keys to the destinies of individuals, cities, and whole regions. During the war enormous growth occurred where the trunk lines built spurs, stations, and termini. Pittsburgh, Cincinnati, Columbus, and Indianapolis benefited; unsuccessful contenders for such blessings faded into economic obscurity.

Chicago epitomized the process. In the 1830s it was a dismal hamlet on the lake shore. Then railroads linked the town first to the East, later to the new trans-Mississippi states. By rail and river, commerce flowed to and from the South. The Great Lakes market was vast. Chicago benefited hugely, if unaesthetically, from the war, for meat-packing plants and grain warehouses, supplying the Union Army and foreign buyers, drew workers by the tens of thousands.

As if to compensate for Confederate military, strategic, and tactical advantages in the east, Nature had provided invaluable commercial and industrial assets to northern producers. European crop failures in 1861–62 prompted the governments of Britain and France to buy food products rather than cotton. New Michigan salt mines substituted for traditional southern sources of this essential mineral.

A brand-new petroleum industry had grown swiftly in Pennsylvania and supplied essential lubricants for rail carriages and other machinery. Wool treated with new coal-tar dyes took the place of cotton. Confederate sea raiders drove whalers into safe harbors but kerosene was available to replace whale oil for lighting homes and factories. Kerosene, petroleum's first major mass distillate, smelled. When adulterated with cheaper naphtha by unscrupulous refiners and vendors, it was terribly explosive, as Chicago was to learn. But kerosene was cheap and plentiful, and replaced whale oil very quickly. By the time Grant was preparing his final thrust into Richmond, western Pennsylvania was gushing wealth. "Men are flocking in from all points," a young woman living in the new oil center wrote her brother in college, in March 1865. "Well, Thomas . . . you are about to graduate—where next? Why not come out here? I believe I would if I were you. *Oil, Oil, Oil*, is all you can hear."[2]

Oil was, increasingly, what John D. Rockefeller heard. His wartime oil-refining operations were "very successful," according to 1865 Mercantile Agency credit raters. Rockefeller had ". . . made money very fast the last y[ea]r or two. His esti[mate]d w[orth] upwards of $50 . . . [thousand]."[3] Five months later the same estimator believed that Rockefeller had more than doubled his real worth. And it doubled again by February 1867.

The editor of the popular Appleton's *Annual Cyclopedia* noted in his Preface for the 1864 volume (published in 1869), "The unusual enterprise which has been awakened by successfully refining and converting to various uses the article of Petroleum has caused not less astonishment than the unbounded wealth which it is likely to yield to the country."

During the war, increasingly specialized farms and factories made use of harvesters, sewing machines, and other technological innovations. Production of clothing, grains, meats, shoes, and textiles, among other products, rose rapidly. Innovations in

Miller Farm, an oil pipeline terminal near Titusville, Pennsylvania, as it appeared about 1865. The Civil War gave impetus to the country's newest industry.
MATHER COLLECTION, DRAKE WELL MUSEUM

medical anesthetics developed by War Department-Sanitary Commission pharmaceutical contractors became the commercial bases for the B. F. Bache and E. R. Squibb corporations. Profits from investments in farms or factories ranged from 15% to 30% a year with equivalent dividends from investments. Thanks to the resulting thirst for investment capital, the unsystematic state-chartered private banks made huge profits. National banking legislation improved the organization of banks by mid-1863 (see Chapter 7).

War orders undergirded much of the production increase. An unprecedented input of government money was contrived by a combination of taxes and excises, borrowing, and paper money issues. Floods of private investment capital from domestic and foreign sources became available as the Union approached victory.

In May 1865, Jay Cooke's Philadelphia banking house, which served effectively and profitably as a major marketer of Salmon Chase's Treasury bond issues, was rated "First rate in all respects" by the Mercantile Agency; in December 1866, the same report was issued, with "A1 A1" added. And in March 1868, Cooke's firm was estimated as having $2 million in its own assets, plus depositors' totals, and as "perfectly good in every respect."[4]

The demand for investment capital helped to generate inflationary pressures. Prices rose, the value of repayment dollars declined. Manufacturers who had incurred pre-1861 debts gained one-third in value by repaying them in 1863. By 1863, and thereafter throughout the decade, manufacturers were solidly confident of being able to repay their debts.

To be sure, fiscal casualties of the war existed. Inflation hurt people on low and fixed incomes. In New York, wholesale prices rose dramatically between 1860 and 1865: sugar from 7 to 19 cents a pound; butter from 20 to 55 cents a pound; wheat flour from $4.30 to $10.00 a barrel; cotton from 11 cents to $1.20 a pound; wool from 40 to 95 cents a pound; and domestic whiskey from 26 cents to $2.24 a gallon. Shipping fell prey to daring rebel commerce destroyers, but even this profited some opportunistic men, who switched capital to production or transportation investments. Merchants and manufacturers who were owed money (totaling perhaps $300 million) by southern debtors were out of luck, at least until victory restored debt-collection processes, and even then, it was feared that southern debtors would be judgmentproof as a result of bankruptcy, war damage, or the invocation of statutes of limitations on actions for debt recovery.

Southern Problems

Emancipation destroyed the billions of dollars invested in slaves, with unanticipatable economic effects. Southern land values, tied to the production of staples by servile gang labor, declined precipitously in 1861–65. Alert Egyptian producers of the preeminent former southern export, cotton, had taken over in the English market.

Northern merchants and manufacturers with southern interests tempered their victory jubilation with concerns born of numerous unanswered questions. Would prewar contracts, debts, and insurance liabilities involving southerners still hold? Were unperformed slave-sale contracts, entered into before the Thirteenth Amendment was ratified still enforceable? Did war-time tenders of Confederate money, in payment for private debts, erase those debts? Were prewar insurance contracts voided by the secessions, or were northern insurance companies liable for rebels' life and property losses? What *was* the extent of private and public losses?

In the first months after Appomattox, such questions, and numerous answers, flowed northward from occupation soldiers, newsmen, missionary welfare and relief volunteers, educators, politicians, foreign travelers, and commercial-credit reporting agents. Slaveowners had been hardest hit by the Confederate defeat, it was agreed, sometimes in tones of retributive joy. Many whose capital and assets had been tied up in slaves were now "Out of Business," the credit reporters noted.[5] Yet a surprising number of entrepreneurs had survived, adapting profitably first to the Confederate experience and then to defeat.

Concerning assets other than slaves, it became apparent that, except in localized areas, public and private property had not been decimated. The isolated character of many of the southland's agricultural units had protected a significant portion from battle damage. Bluecoats had behaved with considerable constraint concerning private property. The greatest urban destruction, in Atlanta and Richmond, was probably accidental, or even induced by fleeing Confederates.

Continuity in War and Peace

The fact that Union soldiers had been reconstructing portions of the South since mid-1861 meant that many social, commercial, and legal institutions had already been reestablished. In the wake of Union armies, local, state, and even some federal lower courts had resumed sessions. However infrequent and variant, their judgments in contract, real-property, and inheritance litigation helped substantially to reopen and maintain continuity in commercial relationships.

Of course, near battle areas, or where guerrillas or raiders proliferated, or where Confederate civil judges had fled, martial law had superseded local law temporarily. But martial law is a power, not a code. Prevailing international theory and practice was that, under martial law, the authority of the victorious generals extended over all civil and criminal law. All statutes and other public policies created under the rebel authority were wholly void or erased in such part as the victor ordered. Even ordinary private contracts, entered into during the period of rebel jurisdiction, could be wiped out entirely or partially.

Obviously, prewar northern creditors did not want indebtednesses erased. Creditors and other affected persons were greatly relieved to learn that Union Army triumphs were not preludes to wholesale obliterations of their claims. Instead, bankers, manufacturers, and merchants found that bluecoats were creating or preserving remedies against southern debtors.

What occurred was that Union officers, from generals to lowly provost-court sergeants, resorted to the laws, procedures, and customs of the state and neighborhood they were occupying. Slave laws, the rebel confiscation and draft laws, and the special taxes imposed to sustain the rebellion were voided. But almost all other laws remained in force.

This recourse to existing local arrangements reflected the poverty of West Point's resources. There were no special curricula to train uniformed civil administrators. Generals wanted simply to keep conquered civilians calm and to revive marketplace operations quickly. Sergeants had to cope with the pettiest but most numerous civil disputes and criminal matters. It was easy and obvious to use whatever laws, procedures, remedies, and customs obtained in the occupied neighborhood. The effect was to reinstate the validity of all contracts and responsibilities, except for those relating to slave ownership and rebel support. Later, when United States district and circuit courts opened again in ex-rebel jurisdictions, the federal judges reaffirmed these spontaneous policies.

Alternatives to the use of local and state laws and procedures were never seriously considered by the Congress, the President, federal judges, generals, or provost sergeants. Lincoln's December 1863 Reconstruction proclamation specified their employment. From White House to War Department to Congress down to the lowliest provost judge, lawyers were products of state-centered systems. They conceived of few if any reasons to displace local civil and criminal laws and customs. There *was* no national or "common" law of crime, real or personal property, or contract to substitute for pluralistic state and local codes. Thus, except for slave property, the nation as an economic society suffered less from the war and military occupations than many persons had feared. One of the happy results of this continuity was the relatively smooth resumption during 1861–62, of commercial traffic. Therefore, deservedly, by the time of Appomattox, a substantial measure of marketplace confidence had returned to America.

This continuity in local commercial laws and customs helped greatly to reestablish market confidence. The continuing vitality of decentralized federalism greatly impressed attentive foreign commentators on America such as Walter Bagehot, Georges Clemenceau, Karl Marx, Napoleon III, and Sir Morton Peto. A Member of Parliament, Laurence Oliphant, who visited here in the summer of 1865, on returning to England reported:

> There is no country in the world in which it is so difficult to arrive at authentic information upon any point as in America, or in which all one's preconceived ideas are likely to be more completely at fault. It is impossible to judge of it by any historical parallel, because no historical parallel exists. Every political experience through which it passes is novel and unique; and whereas the political convulsions of Europe are almost monotonous from their uniformity, those of America are quite original, and, I may add, highly sensational.[6]

Oliphant was correct. The American Civil War and Reconstruction experience was unique. It was as unprecedented as the tripartition of the national government, nation-state federalism, and the two-party political structures. After four years of civil war, the restored nation of 1865 was strikingly like that of 1861. The war and Reconstruction had not diminished states in favor of nation, Congress or courts in favor of President, politicians in favor of generals, or capitalism in favor of socialism.

It is understandable that foreigners were puzzled over how the complex, delicate American "democratic experiment" and the "machinery" of government and the constitution, to use Whitman's imagery, should have proved so durable; why it was able to engender confidence and to accommodate both "principle" and political procedures. The following pages will try to lessen persisting confusions on these matters.

The Wartime National Government: President and Cabinet

The return to effectiveness and popular esteem of the Presidency, following its decline under Buchanan, served greatly to restore confidence and a sense of continuity with the administrations of Washington, Adams, Jefferson, and Jackson. To a remarkable extent, this recovery was due to Lincoln's skill as a politician. Served only by two full-time private secretaries, Lincoln parceled out executive authority among the heads of cabinet departments, while seeing to it that ultimately the power to make basic decisions remained where it belonged, with him and with the Congress.

An enormous literature testifies to the delicacy and difficulty of the President's task. As of March 1861, several cabinet officers almost equaled him in party influence. Their departments swelled quickly in numbers of employees, contract patronage, and influence with home-state party organizations and constituents. With a lesser President, these cabinet officers would have carved out independent political baronies, perhaps strong enough to displace the President in 1864 or 1868.

This was attempted. Space does not permit recapitulation here of the famous ambitions and maneuvers of Postmaster General Montgomery Blair, Treasury Secretary Salmon P. Chase, State Secretary William H. Seward, War Secretary Simon Cameron and his successor Edwin M. Stanton, and Navy Secretary Gideon Welles. The question of whether emancipation was desirable or when it should come was one of the fundamental issues in dispute. These men had potent party connections in Congress and their home states. They and their organizations could influence both military and civilian sectors by exploiting connections with newsmen, ministers, professional associations, abolitionists, and businessmen.

By 1865, Stanton's War Department alone employed more than 135,000 civilians. At the Treasury, Chase, a former Ohio governor, original Republican, prominent antislavery lawyer, and contender for the 1860 presidential nomination, controlled the careers of well over 100,000 revenue personnel by 1864. Treasury agents had offices in every congressional district, and they followed close behind Union armies occupying the South. Treasury agents affected everyone who paid taxes, imported goods, and published newspapers, and, like postmasters, they were often influential in local Republican party organizations. Open voting at party nominating conventions and in elections allowed Treasury (and other) federal officials who served as party wheels to see to the ballot performance of subordinates. And, of course, many government employees kicked back portions of their salaries and fees to the party organization.

Yet Lincoln kept Chase adequately in harness for three years. In 1864 he pricked the Chase boomlet for the presidential nomination, and on Taney's death named Chase the Chief Justice of the United States. Blair, a pro-McClellan influence in Lincoln's cabinet, went into the army. Cameron disappeared into Russia as Minister. Simultaneously, the President was able to protect in their cabinet posts the men he trusted most and who served him best, the conservative (with respect to abolition) Welles, the mid-road Seward, and the increasingly abolitionist Stanton. Lincoln managed to control his cabinet without interfering with the essential functions of the various departments, antagonizing excessively cabinet members' congressional or state party phalanxes, or publicly exhibiting too much dirty party linen. By the spring of 1865, as Lincoln's administration —by now truly "his"—began its second term, the President controlled a smoothly running, sensitive, and responsible executive apparatus.

President and Congress: Fruitful Partnership

Lincoln's gradual achievement of mastery over his cabinet enabled him to use his executive war powers (exercised, for example, in the cases of the blockade, internal security measures, and emancipation) when and how he chose. But to flesh out and continue these policies, the cooperation of Congress was necessary.

Lincoln and his cabinet worked effectively with the legislature. Implicitly, as with provision of budgets, or explicitly, as with resolutions or statutes, Congress backed up every one of Lincoln's policies. At the same time, Congress created an array of unprecedently rich legislation for both war and nonwar purposes (see Chapter 8).

Lincoln was no legislative leader; none of the great Civil War statutes is connected with his name. But neither was he a foe of the legislature, nor it of him. Despite considerable opinion to the contrary, Lincoln and the "Union" party majority in the Senate and House engaged in no sustained feuds. To be sure, Congress did poke into every aspect of war administration. That was its right. Democrats sniped and obstructed, as was expected. But Lincoln himself respected Congress' separate-but-equal responsibility to govern.

It was the Union's great fortune that the President and Republican party leaders in both houses of Congress understood so well the need for accord between White House and Capitol Hill, and perceived so clearly that all policy matters were part of the politics of democracy. It was thus they achieved unity on such basic issues as restraint of the military, emancipation of slaves, and the use of Negro troops. In short, acting in essential concert, President and Congress, the civilians, served as commander-in-chief over the military in more than symbolic or rhetorical terms.

The Civil War and Reconstruction Congresses deserve respect. They were blessed with an unusual number of energetic, talented, and perceptive members, especially in Republican ranks. Despite Democratic nay-sayers, these Congresses accelerated internal reforms that greatly improved their effectiveness as a modern legislature, i.e., as a producer of significant legislation and as a public-interest watchdog.

In part this invigoration was a factor of the absence of the seceded southern delegations, which in the 1850s, had deadlocked Congresses. The processes of democracy had appeared to be unworkable; there were disgraceful, violent floor fights. It was feared Congress might become obsolete and, in a crisis such as war, fall prey to a man-on-horseback.

These concerns spurred wartime congressional leaders to look to their institution. The House Speaker and, to a lesser extent, the Senate President became better monitors of legislative traffic. They developed equivalents to the modern party floor leader and whip.

In both houses, committee life experienced a great upsurge. Certain committee chairmanships and memberships became prestigious plums, fought for by ambitious congressmen. Investigations by some committees, such as the Joint Committee on the Conduct of the War, the House Appropriations Committee, and the House Committee on Government Contracts, greatly increased the inflow of information. Committee efforts allowed President and Congress to evaluate the competence of high military officers to regulate their influence in political and civil matters, and to limit the exploitation of the government by contractors.

Congress' constitutional powers to provide revenue, approve officers' commissions, and establish executive departments enjoyed new significance as the war dragged on. If the President felt it necessary to extend his executive powers and leadership, Congress felt it proper, one way or another, to share in and shape his policies, and indeed did so.

Congress and Wartime Reconstruction

With respect to wartime preparations for Reconstruction, the Congress had enacted and Lincoln signed two classes of laws. The first were loyalty-oath statutes (the most rigorous, enacted in July 1862, was known as the "ironclad test oath"); these were designed to exclude voluntary Confederates from federal civil or military employment and from service as judges, attorneys, or jurors in federal courts. In 1864 Congress extended the oath test to its own membership, and, in 1865, the Supreme Court applied it to lawyers practicing before that tribunal. The penalty for false swearing to the prescribed oaths was that for perjury.

The second class of laws Congress passed during the war were confiscation acts. These aimed to punish selected prominent secessionists and rebels through individual prosecutions in the federal courts; their accumulated wealth, including slaves and landed property, would be liable to seizure (but the title to landed property was to be returned to heirs after the deaths of the offenders). Of course, Union victory had to occur before these prosecutions could proceed.

Lincoln's contemporaries favored these laws because they created a Reconstruction without further national interventions. The test-oath and confiscation acts required no new bureaucracies or taxes. The federal courts would handle the perjury indictments for false-oath takers and the confiscation act proceedings, and that would be that. Excluded from federal elective and appointive positions by the oath barriers, and stripped of property by the confiscation laws, leaders of the Lost Cause would fade into obscurity, and southern Unionists would replace them. Thus, it was hoped, two-party politics would revive in the rewon South.

The Federal Courts: Prudent Jurisprudents

It is often claimed that Lincoln and Republican congressional leaders conducted persistent assaults on the federal judiciary, especially the Supreme Court. Not so. Chief Justice Taney's 1861 Merryman decision evoked and deserved Republican criticism; but note that it was not a Supreme Court judgment. Taney did oppose many Republican policies, and was hoping to have the chance to rule on cases involving confiscation, conscription, emancipation, or reconstruction. Nevertheless, Taney and his brethren explicitly sustained Lincoln's blockade order and refused to rule on other war matters. And, in their other capacities as judges in the federal circuit courts, Supreme Court justices sanctioned many other wartime executive expedients and legislative innovations.

Rather than attacking the federal judges, Congress and President substantially increased their number, circuits, jurisdictions, and functions. These changes had been needed long before the Civil War. Population and commercial shifts had made older patterns obsolete. Businessmen involved in interstate (diversity) litigation had found federal justice slow, often distant, expensive, and uncertain. But, as Lincoln noted in his 1861 State of the Union message to Congress, improvement had been blocked by southern leaders.

During the war there was a substantial improvement in the efficiency and usefulness of the federal judiciary. As if to symbolize this progress, in 1863, for the first time in its history, the Supreme Court accepted jurisdiction in a case in which a city—in legal theory a municipal corporation, a creature of its parent state—was defendant. In a landmark decision as contemporaries measured it, *Gelpcke* v. *Dubuque*, the Court overruled Iowa's supreme court, and decided that the city could not by popular vote repudiate bonds, the proceeds of which were to build terminal and warehouse facilities and so attract a rail line. Thus, while war continued, the Supreme Court restrained the fiscal and political irresponsibility of a northern city. Fiscal morality was to be upheld, in the courts at least, war or no war.

Stability during the war, however, would have been won at a high price if the vigor of the nation had been gained by a corresponding weakening of the states. Was the federal government, the object of patriots' hopes, becoming a Leviathan deserving patriots' fears?

FOOTNOTES

1. Drake, *Union and Antislavery Speeches* (Cincinnati, 1865), p. 265.

2. Bessie Murphy to T. M. Murphy, March 11, 1865, Civil War Papers of Thomas P. Murphy, Newberry Library.

3. Dun & Bradstreet Papers, Ohio, vol. 41, p. 228.

4. Dun & Bradstreet Papers, District of Columbia, vol. 3, p. 88.

5. Dun & Bradstreet Papers, any Confederate state volume. Professor Glenn Porter kindly allowed me to see his notes referring to this matter.

6. Oliphant, *On the Present State of Political Parties in America* (London, 1866), pp. 6–7.

8 / NO BLUEPRINT for LEVIATHAN

Dual, Not Dueling, Federalism

THERE IS A TRADITION, inspired originally by antiwar Democrats in the 1860s, that the Civil War greatly centralized American government and society, demeaning the states in favor of the nation. But recent reexaminations of the Civil War and Reconstruction cast considerable doubt on this thesis.

The powers of states did not diminish as the nation's war functions increased; a neat seesaw model does not apply in these matters. States participated as partners with the nation in many war matters, including manpower supply, control of vice and epidemic diseases as these affected soldiers, and control of contagious diseases such as "Texas fever" among cattle destined for army use. There was cooperation also on many nonwar issues including, in some states, policies affecting banking, public-land disposition, and public works.

Prewar precedents existed for effective dual federalism, but nation-state cooperation during the Civil War and Reconstruction was more frequent, effective, and significant than ever before.

To advance informal cooperation, Lincoln encouraged governors' conferences. He used these rare assemblies to sound out opinion, to send up trial balloons on controversial projected policies, and to smooth ruffled tempers. Far commoner and more effective, however, were the traditional nation-state connectives forged within the two-party system.

The Two-Party Politics of Democracy and Federalism

"Old party organizations and associations are strong," marveled crusty "Neptune" Welles in mid-1866.[1] The Democratic party enjoyed a rapid, phoenixlike renascence from the shock of secession: by 1862–64 it again had solid, broad voter appeal. At the same time, the Republican party demonstrated an unanticipated capacity to hold together. For forty years, parties had been casualties of sectional tensions. Men Lincoln's age in 1865 remembered antique Federalists, Whigs, Know-Nothings, and Constitutional Unionists.

Neither major party collapsed during the war, which was an enormous comfort, for instability in party organizations had preceded crisis, secession, and war. Further, Americans understood and were accustomed to winner-take-all politics. Political parties were seen to provide essential connections between localities, states, and nation. The nation's ability to amass a great army and to control its generals was significantly dependent on state and local party organizations, which, in turn, interacted with citizens' volunteer associations.

Volunteer Societies, the States, and the Military

This interaction was fostered by the President and Congress, who accepted or recruited semiofficial volunteers, on local and state levels, to supplement official, sometimes inadequate, bureaus of the War Department. The famous Sanitary Commission came into being in 1861 because civilian medical professionals were disgusted at the ineptness and obsolete techniques of army career physicians. By early 1862, White House and Capitol Hill pressures forced the Army Medical Bureau to accept Sanitary Commission participation in its work and to accept the commission's standards for licensing medical personnel. These standards were those of the most rigorous state licensing minima.

The Christian Commission was concerned primarily with soldiers' morals and managed to effect unprecedented exertions of state police powers for the control of prostitution, pornography, and liquor near military installations. The Christian Commissioners were an inspiration to Anthony Comstock. The pressures the commission generated arose mostly from the efforts of local auxiliaries.

The Freedmen's Bureau

Local auxiliaries were also important in the Freedmen's Bureau, although, administratively, it was a division in the War Department, and the highest personnel and some field supervisors were uniformed army officers. Established by statute in early 1865, for one year, the Freedmen's Bureau illuminates the

By 1867 the Freedmen's Bureau had established schools for Negroes in almost every county in the South. They were attended by both young and old.
LIBRARY OF CONGRESS

inexpensive, uncoercive, voluntaristic approach to public policy that Republicans preferred, even for the vastest enterprises.

By early 1865 it was clear that the millions of freed Negroes would not emigrate. For the first time in the world's history, large numbers of former masters and recent slaves, of different races, would retain residence as neighbors. In formulating the Freedmen's Bureau statute, Congress considered reports from military officers, government commissions, and private educational, medical, missionary, and welfare associations. But, though the bureau had to deal with millions of people, Congress provided it almost no budget.

Recently, this parsimony has been derided as an alleged proof of Republican racist perfidy. But such judgments ignore compelling aspects of Republican thinking that determined the configurations of many war policies. Republicans were incurably state-centered constitutionalists. They stubbornly assumed that the crumpled Confederate states would treat freed black southerners decently, in terms of rough equality in economic and legal (civil) rights and responsibilities. Republicans' Victorian fiscal conservatism made them fretful at every outgoing tax dollar not essential to military operations. The Republicans' (and Democrats') conviction that private-sector operations were preferable to public-sector commitments was a persisting factor in Reconstruction policy evolution.

With respect to the Freedmen's Bureau operations and budget, Congress and President expected, correctly, the bureau to do no violence to state civil or criminal laws. They assumed, incorrectly, that white southerners and southern states would do no violence to blacks freed by national edicts and laws. Further, Lincoln's Republicans depended on local private associations (primarily educational, missionary, and benevolent) chartered in northern states to supply the bulk of the bureau's funds and personnel. It was assumed that volunteer schoolteachers, preachers, and charitable society agents, backed by a handful of soldiers, would within one year transform millions of recent slaves into free citizens, sharing the rights and opportunities accorded all citizens.

Naïve? Yes, retrospectively. But no other emancipating nation before then had ever done anything at all for recent bondsmen. The United States was embarking on an unprecedented social experiment. The assumption prevailed that emancipation would proceed as quickly and smoothly as commerce had resumed. Volunteers, drawn from many parts of the nation, would work with the bureau. The role of the national government would be secondary, brief, and inexpensive. Having no precognition of the violent reaction of southern whites, the creators and supporters of the Freedmen's Bureau expected it to work similarly to and as well as the Sanitary Commission, the railroad Military Director, and other new war agencies. Speaking in support of the Freedmen's Bureau bill, Massachusetts Senator Charles Sumner insisted that, temporarily, the nation must

> . . . supply the adequate machinery, and extend the proper network of assistance. . . . The National Government must interfere . . . precisely as in building the Pacific Railroad. . . . The President [Lincoln] in his Proclamation of Emancipation has used the following language: "I recommend to . . . freedmen . . . that . . . they labor faithfully for reasonable wages." But the President does not undertake to say . . . how the laborer['s civil] . . . rights shall be protected, and how his new-found [economic] liberty shall be made a blessing. . . . Faithful labor and reasonable wages: let these be secured, and everything else will follow. But how shall they be secured? Different subjects, as they become important, are committed to special bureaus. I need only refer to Patents, Agriculture, Public Lands, Pensions, and Indian Affairs—each under the charge of a separate Commissioner. Clearly, the time has come for a Bureau of Freedmen. . . .[2]

National Nonwar Agencies and Policies

Like moraine deposits after a glacier passes, Congress' nonwar creations far outlasted the more spectacular military innovations. Provost marshal operations ended within days, even hours, after Appomattox. The huge civilian bureaucracy of the War Department all but vanished. In the North the only military employees having any impact on civilian affairs were contract-termination specialists and the staff of the new Freedmen's

Bureau. However, several wholly civilian, nonwar bureaus and institutions, created and/or augmented since Sumter, continued in force.

A National Academy of Science now existed. The Steamboat Inspection Service and the Coast and Geodetic Survey, prewar divisions of the Interior Department, were retained and slightly enlarged. The Treasury housed the headquarters of what was popularly miscalled the "national banking system." Indeed, the Treasury Department, far from shrinking after the war, continued to expand. Its personnel had to operate the nation's first income tax (1862), numerous excise and stamp taxes, and import tariffs set in laws of 1861, 1862, and 1863.

In other executive departments, functionaries dealt with the new laws on homesteads (1862) weather reporting (1862), land-grant aids to state-supported colleges (1862), subsidies to transcontinental railroads (1862, 1864), and encouragements to domestic and international telegraph development (1863), among many others. The national government was now more directly involved with agriculture, education, and transportation-communications technology than ever before.

Seemingly, by 1865, a "second American Revolution" had occurred. As interpreted by Democrats of the 1860s (an interpretation repeated by many scholars for almost a century), this revolution favored the federal government over states and individuals, businessmen over farmers and workers, and money over morals.

In preceding pages it has been suggested that even the direct war duties the nation performed brought neither tyranny nor centralization. A proposition that both occurred as a consequence of economic legislation and the creation of related nonmilitary institutions bears a heavy burden of proof. Impressive evidence suggests instead that the new nonwar economic legislation and institutions were not intended to and did not diminish the rights of states or individuals' liberties, including economic liberties.

None of this legislation was revolutionary to congressmen who debated it. Innovations of the kinds that, allegedly, revolutionized American society, had, with few and minor exceptions, been advocated for decades before Sumter.

The North's Empty Purse

To understand how inappropriate it is to argue that a revolution favoring the federal government occurred, consider the starved condition of the United States Treasury, especially from 1861 to 1865 but also throughout the decade. Whatever was done by the federal government in nonwar matters had to involve as little expense as possible, and perhaps even generate some income. In March 1861, Chase, upon opening his portfolio, found the following, according to a memorandum (unpublished, now the property of the Huntington Library) kept by his Assistant Secretary, George Harrington:

> An empty Treasury; a limited public debt; A seriously impaired public credit, . . . ; A prospective war of unknown magnitude in the near future, with a total revenue of about thirty-six millions *per annum.* Ere he left the Department he was called upon to provide for expenditures amounting to sixty millions *per month* [see chart below].

Chase, and William Pitt Fessenden of Maine, the Senate majority leader and the administration's chief fiscal spokesman on Capitol Hill, were confirmed Victorian balanced-budget, hard-money fiscal moralists. Chase insisted on paying all Treasury indebtedness in gold, as had been the practice since 1846, until Congress stopped this antique reflex. His successors as Treasury Secretary to 1869, William Fessenden and Hugh McCulloch, followed Chase's hard-money policies. Moreover, the President, all the cabinet, almost all congressmen (including Radical Republicans), and the great majority of their constituents, were predisposed against the use of government funds to intervene in matters that concerned states and individuals.

Federal Expenditures by Major Function, 1861–65°

(MILLIONS OF CURRENCY DOLLARS PER FISCAL YEAR ENDING JUNE 30)

Fiscal Year	*General Government*[a]	*War and Defense*	*Veterans*[b]	*Interest*[c]	*Miscellaneous*	*Total*
1861	$13.8	$ 32.9	$1.3	$ 3.7	$14.1	$ 65.8
1862	13.9	401.4	1.1	12.2	9.0	437.6
1863	16.3	628.1	1.3	33.6	7.8	687.1
1864	20.4	756.4	4.9	82.4	6.8	870.9
1865	31.9	1,127.9	9.0	126.8	10.9	1,306.5

Miscellaneous Expenditures

Fiscal Year	*Commerce and Transport*[d]	*Postal (net)*	*Indians*	*Health, Education, Welfare*	*Agriculture*	*Foreign Indemnities*	*Other*	*Total*
1861	$2.6	$5.8	$2.9	$0.1	$0.1	$ —	$2.6	$14.1
1862	2.0	3.0	2.3	—	0.1	0.2	1.4	9.0
1863	2.1	0.4	3.1	—	0.1	—	2.1	7.8
1864	2.2	0.4	2.9	—	0.1	—	1.2	6.8
1865	2.7	1.1	5.1	0.3	0.2	—	1.5	10.9

° Administrative overhead has been allocated to function wherever possible.

[a] Includes government overhead not allocated to functions. Congress, courts, Treasury, diplomatic service, etc.

[b] Includes pensions, expenses of soldiers' homes and asylum, bounties paid to servicemen after discharge.

[c] Net of receipts; excludes interest on Pacific Railway bound issues; gold values have been converted into currency equivalent.

[d] Includes interest on Pacific Railroad bonds, river and harbor expenditures.

— Less than $50,000.

From Paul B. Trescott, "Federal Government Receipts and Expenditures, 1861–1875," *Journal of Economic History*, XXV (1966), 206–22.

In relationship to outgo, federal government income 1861–65 from all sources was never enough, as these estimates indicate:

FEDERAL RECEIPTS AND PAYMENTS, CASH FLOW 1861–65

(MILLIONS OF CURRENCY DOLLARS PER FISCAL YEAR ENDING JUNE 30)

	1861	1862	1863	1864	1865
Receipts					
Taxes (net)	$38.3	$ 48.0	$130.7	$293.0	$ 382.0
Land sales (net)	0.8	0.3		0.9	0.5
Total	39.1	48.3	130.7	293.9	382.5
Payments					
Wages and other compensation	27.2	133.4	244.9	313.4	422.2
Purchase of goods or services (net)	30.7	281.2	400.3	463.7	735.2
Interest (net)	3.7	12.2	33.6	82.4	126.9
Transfer payments	2.8	1.8	3.1	8.1	15.7
To state govts. (net)	0.2	5.9	2.6	1.6	1.6
To foreign recipients (net)	0.7	1.1	0.4	1.1	0.4
Total	65.3	435.6	684.9	870.3	1302.0
Surplus (+) or deficit (−)	−26.2	−387.3	−554.2	−576.4	−919.5

Trescott, *loc. cit.*

Congress kept special watch on money matters. A mixture of Burkean conservatism, Millsian liberalism, and proto-social Darwinism dominated the thinking of American leaders on the proper role of government. In such a climate of opinion, creation of a large, permanent, centralized expensive bureaucracy, armed with coercive powers, was hardly in the cards.

Federal Subsidies and Fiscal Interventions

In spite of congressional watchfulness, the shortage of public funds was distressing enough to justify resort to novel, distasteful, politically dangerous, but unavoidable revenue measures, including income and excise taxes and import duties. The new tariffs subsidized favored industrial producers, especially metals, leather, and textiles manufacturers, among many others, who lobbied effectively in favor of tariff rises. But the protection was also seen as essential to the Union's cause; at that time, selfish and patriotic purposes marched along together.

Internal taxes were the important revenue producers. By 1865, there were new taxes on incomes, sales, occupational licenses, and manufactures. Individuals felt the bite of the first income tax in the nation's history. Incomes over $600 a year were taxed at 5%; over $5,000, at 10%. With Congress' authority, Chase, who abhorred paper money, resorted to borrowing. Over $2 billion of Treasury bonds were issued (a monumental sum for the time) through favored banks such as Jay Cooke's in Philadelphia, which took very high commissions.

The pessimism resulting from Union battlefield frustrations in 1861–62, prompted individuals to squirrel away as much hard money, especially gold, as they could lay their hands on. Serious runs on deposits in private, state-chartered banks forced many to suspend payments or to close. There was no deposit insurance or central-bank controls on commercial paper flow. Bank closings and suspensions of payments seriously undercut investors' confidence, industries' stability, and, therefore, government operations.

The "National" Banks: 1863

In view of the gap between federal government receipts and expenditures, the gold flight, and inflation, reluctant Republicans at the Treasury and in Congress admitted the need for greater government involvement in the money market. In 1863,

Congress created so-called national banks. Actually, these were private banks which, chartered by Congress as members of an association, served the Treasury (very profitably for the banks) in several ways.

In order to obtain a congressional charter, the member bank had to agree to sell Treasury bonds and to turn over to the Treasury a portion of its gold assets in exchange for other Treasury indebtedness. In fixed ratios, member banks could issue "national bank notes," which circulated as money. The Treasury also printed $450 million of its own "greenbacks," which lacked specie backing altogether—a grating recourse indeed. Legal-tender laws stipulated that paper money, which swiftly dropped in value in the inflationary marketplace, must be accepted at face value for debts; such laws irked even ardent patriots. And Congress taxed the commercial paper issues of state-chartered private banks, in order to force unsound local institutions out of business.

Thus, the war forced the government into greater interaction with the economy than at any time since 1792. But this development did not lead to a centralized bank in the European nineteenth-century mode or forecast the 1913 Federal Reserve system.

States continued to charter private banks. And before and after Appomattox, states' men in Congress saw to it that the "national" bank system remained private, if less anarchical than in prewar years.

But one monetary innovation was to have considerable social and political impact. Americans were becoming aware of the potential uses and abuses of greenbacks. Farmers, perennially in debt for new machinery and land, and many businessmen-borrowers came to like "cheap" paper money. By 1865, greenbacks were beginning to concern local, state, and national political parties; and politicians and constituents were edging toward awareness of the complexities of fiat money. A new thirty years' money-morality political crusade was in the making. By the 1890s it would take on the flavor of an epic.

Federal Aids to Agriculture, Education, Industry, and Transportation

It seemed natural to Lincoln's contemporaries that both self-interest and patriotism should inspire persons of diverse views to try through politics to influence fiscal policies. Similarly, it was expected that individuals and groups should seek, through politics, legislation favorable to their special interests.

During the war years, farmers, industrialists, and transportation entrepreneurs, among other influential segments of the loyal population, lobbied with great success in Congress and in state capitals for aids, subsidies, and other encouragements. None of the aids involved large Treasury outlays, the creation of bureaucracies and federal watchdog agencies or offices, or the application of coercive powers. Instead, as Professor Willard Hurst has perceived so brilliantly, Lincoln's Republicans aimed to release entrepreneurial energy and talent, not constrain it; to encourage, not to supervise; to expand marketplaces, not to increase government functions.

For example, encouraging homestead settlement of untilled national lands rated a high priority for Lincoln's contemporaries and reflected the admiration for bucolic virtues that Jefferson had expressed so well. Republicans perceived the national territories as an area of opportunity for free (white) labor, and as a barrier against the further spread of slavery; this view had generated futile prewar proposals for encouraging homesteading. In an 1862 statute, Republicans redeemed their party's 1860 platform plank favoring homesteading. The statute allowed inexpensive (not free) land grants to settlers and improvers of public land. The homestead law, which became effective January 1, 1863 (the same day as the Emancipation Proclamation), was a fitting complement to the basic democratization that abolition sparked. The Republicans were already committed by statute to the concept that freed slaves would take over confiscated rebel lands and thereby attain economic and social equality through their own efforts. The homestead laws arose from the same attitude. The role of government was to prove the encouragement that would make self-improvement possible.

This approach to public land use, and to the government's role, was evident also in the 1866 Mineral Land Act (and, in the next decade, in the 1873 Timber Culture, the 1877 Desert Land, and the 1878 Timber and Stone acts). Congress assigned almost no watchdog, supervisory, coercive role to government officers. Existing agencies performed essentially bookkeeping roles. Government opened doors and then largely bowed out.

Farmers, a voting force in every state, did win the establishment of a new cabinet post for agriculture. But the new department did little more than collect statistics and distribute seeds to congressmen's constituents. Half a dozen clerks handled its business. Primarily, the Agriculture Department performed its modest tasks through private, state-based organizations of farmers. It had no coercive powers.

Since Jefferson, some Americans had dreamed of national aid to higher education. In 1861, associated teachers, especially in eastern states, and politically activist farmers, especially in the Midwest, lobbied for this purpose within the Republican party. With Lincoln's warm support, their congressmen pushed through the Morrill Land Grant College Act in 1862. (Buchanan had vetoed essentially the same act in 1857.) It offered each state 30,000 acres of federal land per congressman from that state. In return, the state was to establish and maintain a college of agricultural and mechanical arts for its "industrial classes," in the phrase of the Illinois pioneer of the idea, Jonathan Baldwin Turner. "Industrial classes" included those involved in both agricultural *and* mechanical work.

Relatively well supplied with private colleges, New England and other Atlantic coast states declined to participate. Later, Harvard's president tried to discourage the development of such tax-aided competitors as Cornell University. But from New York westward, states took advantage of this pioneering statute. America's unique, locally tax-supported, low or free tuition state universities were in the making.

Neither homesteads nor state-college aid resulted in expanded federal or state bureaucracies. There was only nominal supervision concerning compliance with the provisions of the statutes. The nation quite freely gave away part of its seemingly limitless resource, unimproved land, in order to advance the broadest social purposes.

However, when associated teachers, appetites whetted by the state-college law, lobbied for creation of a tax-supported national university and a new cabinet portfolio in education, Congress was unresponsive. Some federal tax money went to a deaf-mute school, to establish and support Howard University, and to finance Freedmen's Bureau elementary schools. But these projects involved special, limited purposes and low budgets. Otherwise, education was up to individuals and states.

Beginning in 1860, with the threat first of war and then conscription, immigration declined sharply. But despite the pressing need for farm and factory workers and for soldiers, Congress did not create a special agency to deal with the problem. Instead, Congress reacted with adjustments in naturalization proceedings and encouragements for private employers, such as railroad builders, to import foreign labor. For example, in 1861 Congress lowered federal naturalization standards for aliens who entered the armed services. In 1864, in response to a report by Lincoln on labor shortages, Congress enacted a contract labor law, by terms of which large-scale employers could recruit groups from abroad; the employers were supposed to pledge wages, and sometimes transportation costs, in advance. Again, though, Congress provided for little if any supervision of these programs; it was primarily concerned to open ways for solutions to occur via free, individual action.

The immigration laws and the Union's increasing martial success and stability gradually helped to revive immigration even while the shooting lasted. But it did not exceed the 1860 level until after the war ended.

National government aid and service to merchants and manufacturers were very substantial, and profound in their effect. For example, average tariff rates increased more than 45% over prewar levels. But, as with all the other Civil War and Reconstruction encouragements to agriculture and industry, this led to little enlargement of government bureaucracies and little coercion. Instead, the government performed largely with on-hand executive and/or judicial staff and traditional techniques. Congress tended to slough off the extra work onto other shoulders, and, unless scandals inspired Congress to investigate performance, the precise quality of compliance to statutes was rarely known to legislators. For example, under the Morrill Land Grant College Law, state agencies were made responsible for attesting that the use of the donated national land was in compliance with the statute. With respect to direct aids to industry and transportation, private-sector institutions, such as railroad corporations, were required, nominally at least, to meet certain minimal requirements before receiving benefits. But the nation shied off from developing either a national university system or a government-owned rail or telegraph organization.

The national government's unobtrusive, uncoercive posture concerning railroads, as later generations judged it, becomes comprehensible when considered in the context of the '60s. Consider military mass-transit needs. When the war came, railroad corporations, not government, possessed staffs of experts, a specialized bureaucratic apparatus, and the capacity to manage and transport masses of people and goods. Railroads aided the government—with loans of experts, techniques, and services—not vice versa.

Rail directors had wanted for a long time to extend lines across the continent. The South's secession and the wartime consciousness of the need for links across the nation allowed plans for these continental lines to proceed. In Europe an effort of equivalent scope would have been a national enterprise. Not here.

The Pacific Railroad Act (1862) committed private companies to the development of the Omaha-San Francisco route. Congress chartered two corporations to do the work. One was to head inland from the West Coast, the other to advance west to meet it. Both companies had to build over unsettled land that could not immediately generate revenue.

Earlier, several states had helped private, state-chartered, intrastate lines finance construction, with money grants, bond guarantees, and other aids. Congress' subsidies, as with the Morrill Law, consisted primarily of land, which the railroads could sell: 6,400 acres (doubled in 1864) for each mile of track laid. Secondarily, there were money loans graduated to topographic conditions: from $16,000 per flatland mile to $48,000 per mountain mile. Again, there was to be virtually no national supervisory presence, no bureaucratic coercion.

Only preliminary work was done prior to Appomattox. Then great gangs of army veterans and contract immigrants began to alter the face of the land. Skills developed during the war, in engineering, control of epidemic disease, and mass labor

Locomotives of the Union Pacific (background) and the Central Pacific edge toward each other after the joining of the transcontinental rails at Promontory, Utah, on May 10, 1869. Shortly after photographer A. J.

Russell took this picture, Central president Leland Stanford took a hefty swing at the golden spike—and missed it.
THE OAKLAND MUSEUM

management, allowed swifter tunneling, bridging, and track laying than was conceivable before 1861. The lines joined in 1869; the coasts were linked with very little Treasury expenditure for such a vast enterprise.

Later generations would condemn this flaccid government stance toward the railroads as a deliberate giveaway. But men of the time believed otherwise. At incredibly small public expenditure, they had worked out ways to develop enormous public works. That railroad investors and land speculators reaped great profits from the enterprise was not a matter to regret.

The Telegraph: Too Slippery for Congress

Beginning in 1865, congressmen tried to work out a similar program of national encouragement of the telegraph. As with the railroads, the Civil War accentuated the telegraph's importance to the public. And like rail companies, telegraph companies were state-chartered, private, profit-making entities. In Europe and England, governments controlled both rail and telegraph development by national agencies. Here, congress wished to keep government intervention to a minimum. But politically acceptable means for promoting the development of the telegraph eluded Congress for three decades. Why did Congress experience such difficulties?

Probably the basic reason was that the telegraph differed from the railroads in some significant ways. Telegraph operations required far less capital investment, land, and personnel. A small corps of skilled operators, sending and receiving equipment, and connecting wires were all that was needed. Telegraph signals were not tangible properties of the sort railroads carried. Although rail companies were a much bigger business, telegraph companies developed toward monopoly situations far faster, which generated sporadic political pressures for government intervention.

In 1865–66, Congress required interstate railroads to allow rights of way for telegraph lines, and approved resolutions applauding English and American promoters for their exertions on behalf of the Atlantic cable, and Russian and American entrepreneurs for their efforts to create a telegraph link through Alaska and Siberia. Beyond this, congressmen thrashed in a jungle of conflicting jurisdictions and ambiguities. Did sending telegraph messages qualify as interstate commerce? If not, were such messages private property, under the jurisdiction of states' commercial laws? Did telegraph companies come under states' laws on common carriers? under agency laws? under contract? Telegraphers, for example, frequently distorted contract tenders and acceptances in ways that raised legal problems. State contract laws and customs allowed time intervals before offers and acceptances took effect. Railroads had cut that interval, to be sure, but telegrams erased it almost to zero.

No national law existed in these matters. Abroad, a national statute or a national agency's bureaucratic ruling would have established a uniform policy. Here, Congress created neither a statute nor an agency. Therefore, states remained unconstrained in dealing with telegraph companies. This meant that, as in virtually all public-policy questions, great diversity characterized the American way of dealing with, or of not dealing with, this significant new communications technology.

The American Achievement: 1865–66

In the months after Appomattox, the American industrial, financial, and political phenomenon—general prosperity, economic stability, and preservation of governmental and institutional variety and flexibility—increasingly impressed sensitive observers. For instance, bankers had feared economic collapse, or at least, great monetary fluctuations with the outbreak of peace. And between April 1865 and mid-1866, some unsettlements did occur. They would even have appalled prewar monetary theorists, editorialized a bankers' magazine, the *New York Commercial & Financial Chronicle*. But, the author noted, "the shock was comparatively slight, our financial barque soon righted itself, and is now progressing . . . more hopefully and cheerily than before she was struck by the storm."[3]

Foreign admiration is reflected in a series of rhetorical questions posed by Prince Albert de Broglie, chairman of the 1866 meeting in Paris of the international Antislavery Conference:

> Has American society come out less strong, less vigorous, from that great trial? On the contrary, has she not tempered herself in the struggle? Has not this American union, which everybody thought was to be shattered by emancipation, come out of the crisis with the glory of not having sacrificed one of its liberties, of having carried to the extreme of scrupulosity the love of law, acquiring, in this unexampled trial, a new title to the admiration of the world?[4]

Little accustomed to praise from overseas, Americans reveled in it. Many well-to-do Americans celebrated the first post-Appomattox summer by touring Europe. Returning, one such traveler, William Blodgett, an organizer of the Loyal Publication Society, reported happily that Europeans ". . . cannot understand us, and wonder to see . . . steps taken toward Reconstruction, and stocks advancing daily—and the people [of Europe] . . . notice every detail."[5]

What were the essential details? To find them, one must look at state policies, North and South, from 1865 to 1870, and at certain national attitudes that shaped post-Appomattox Reconstruction.

8 / NO BLUEPRINT FOR LEVIATHAN

FOOTNOTES

1. *Diary of Gideon Welles,* ed. Howard K. Beale (New York: Norton, 1960), II, 542.

2. Sumner, *Complete Works* (Boston, 1900), VIII, 480–81.

3. "Lessons from the Panic," *New York Commercial & Financial Chronicle,* IV (Feb. 2, 1867), 125–26.

4. In Committee of the British & Foreign Anti-Slavery Society, *Special Report of the Anti-Slavery Conference Held in Paris . . . 1867* (London, 1867), p. 40.

5. In W. W. Broom (alias Eboracus), *Great & Grave Questions for American Politicians* (New York, 1865), p. 67.

9 / THE STATES: THE BEGINNINGS of UNUSUAL ENTERPRISES, 1860-70

The Great Transatlantic Workshops

"HAVE THEY TRIED IT [i.e., any reform] in America? How does it work [there]?" asked the editor of England's prestigious law journal, the *Law Magazine and Review*, in 1868. Partially because of the Appomattox vindication of the American Union's political democracy, the editor advised readers that parliamentary debaters on home rule for Ireland, on a degree of federal autonomy for Canada, and on political democratization (1867 Reform Act) for Britain, among other subjects, should resort to American analogues. Englishmen interested in business corporations, penology, public health, or transportation felt impelled to consider how Americans handled such matters.

Before Parliament decided which reform alternatives to adopt, the same law-journal editor advised his readers, it should look to America's states for ". . . models in good working order of all our projected reforms." In his opinion, the American states had become the "great transatlantic workshops" of innovations in public policy and government action.

This perceptive Englishman noted that such innovations issued from localities and states more than from the national government. He reminded his readers that in America the city, town, and county divisions of the states determined the quality of daily life and labor. This localism was exciting, he continued, because it produced diverse responses to problems. The American states were virtually laboratories of policy alternatives:

> The United States are generally the vile corpus out of which by dint of many an experiment, essay, and strange vagary, the good comes by which we tardily profit. The American loves to dabble in those subjects which are somewhat vaguely known as "Social Science," and we believe that in one State or another of the Union, . . . education, criminology, legal reforms, sanitary reforms, and so on [have] been further sifted than [they have] at home.[1]

State Power

In the years following the war, it became clear that traditional state "police" power, as defined by the Constitution and cleansed of the concept of state sovereignty, was adequate to meet all appropriate wants. State power was robust, but could be restrained within sound limits as understood in contemporary economic and political thought, and was comfortingly familiar. States, and, by delegation, county, city, and town divisions, were capable of doing whatever public work was needed to maintain the health, safety, welfare, and morals of its residents.

Before the Civil War, however, there were relatively few applications of state power, despite rhetoric about its plenary character. As noted in Chapter I, there were exceptions to this pattern, notably, the public school systems in some states and slavery protection arrangements in others. Beyond this, providing for asylums, canals, street paving, water supply, and the like, had involved many cities and counties in social experiments, and, during the unstable 1850s, in calamitous fiscal risks. A number of cities had repudiated bonded debts incurred in efforts to attract railroad lines and termini. Although the Supreme Court had barred such repudiations in the wartime case of *Gelpcke* v. *Dubuque* (see p. 191), the disturbing possibility remained that, in granting municipal corporations the right to incur such debt, the states had delegated powers just as excessive, although not as dangerous, as the assertions of sovereignty and secession by the slave states.

The use of state power greatly increased during the Civil War and Reconstruction. Thus in *Appleton's Annual Cyclopedia* for the year 1869 the editor's preface included, for the first time in the book's long and influential career, an appeal for regular reports from public officials:

> State officers, committees of [state] legislative and other public bodies, principals of public institutions, whether benevolent, educational, reformatory, scientific, etc., will confer a favor by sending their printed reports and documents to the Publishers.

But the war and Reconstruction did not greatly alter the fact that compelling, tenacious constraints operated on applications of state power. These constraints severely limited its theoretically plenary power. City ordinances, which were expressions of delegated state powers, were often rendered ineffectual. For example, municipal public health measures born of insights acquired during the war, such as those forbidding dumping of sewerage in a manner that would foul sources of drinking water, were countered by strong emphasis in law that favored unrestrained entrepreneurial growth.

The new, more active roles that states and localities assumed to try to limit or eradicate prominent social sores sometimes obscured the presence of these constraints. Beginning in 1861, the public's demands for essential services rose swiftly. Awareness of social distresses, evils, and ills increased dramatically. It was felt that *some* authority must prevent these ills or punish their antisocial authors.

Confidence in local and state authority grew as the odds favoring the nation's survival improved. The traditional concept that state power could cope with all public needs was extended to new problems as they arose. And the inventiveness displayed during the war by local and state organizations and by public, private, and mixed institutions in the accommodation of wants and the frustration of evils greatly encouraged public-spirited persons to continue to seek similar solutions by the use of state police powers.

As noted, states could delegate powers to county and city subdivisions. Therefore, it was reasonable to assume that each level of government could effect whatever inprovements its constituents felt were desirable or necessary. Wagoneers and laborers, as well as jurisprudents, expressed a "can do" confidence. At the end of 1865, the authority of the states was as great as it had been before the war, except for the ban on slavery in the new Thirteenth Amendment, and no one knew that a Fourteenth and Fifteenth Amendment were to come.

However, as was true of Congress, state policy makers remained very reluctant to allow coercive powers to new state or local public agencies and officials. Only very thin budgets were accorded state and local boards, commissions, and other bodies that ran public institutions; most states' tax bases did not rise dramatically. Almost no permanent bureaucracies came into existence. Such institutions were held to be too unaccountable, aristocratic, dangerous, and foreign. Almost always, the courts or other traditional, low-budget sectors of the government bore the weight of enforcing new policies. Individuals, alleging damages due to the operation of a public policy, sued for compensation, injunctions, or other remedies. In this manner, private lawsuits shaped the public sector. In general, enforcement was sketchy.

With very few exceptions, state, city, county, and town officers, including judges, were elected. Inevitably, public-interest issues, and the enforcement of new public-interest laws and ordinances, were bound up in majority politics. Enduring antipathy toward experts and distant bureaucracies, and Victorian reverence for low-tax, balanced-budget government, were expressed on election days.

Therefore, although there was much more work for the increased number of state and local public and quasi-public agencies to do, it remained largely in the hands of amateur, elected volunteers. They staffed the new public-school boards, asylum and prison committees, and fire departments. Remuneration was small, staffs minuscule or nonexistent.

With very rare exceptions, governments worked out ways for private-sector institutions to do public work. For example, states and localities did not create or operate urban trolley lines or statewide trunk railroads, any more than Congress built or operated the transcontinental railroads. Instead, during the '60s, local government franchised private enterprises, usually as corporations, to serve public needs. This avoided substantial investments of public money, resort to higher tax rates, and the need to hire any significant number of new personnel. In short, if in the 1860s states' rights and powers were exercised more frequently, visibly, and extensively, this did not much alter the voluntaristic, low-budget, uncoercive character of government.

States, War Work, and Rising Expectations

During the war, in both the Confederacy and the Union, states engaged in many activities aimed at sustaining soldiers and their families. State bonuses to volunteers and aids to soldiers' dependents supplemented strained private and public local funds and charities. In the North, states, cities, and counties cooperated vigorously in the efforts of the Christian Commission, the Sanitary Commission, and the Freedmen's Bureau. For example, local governments raised money for public health work by sponsoring sanitary fairs, usually in partnership with Protestant churches and neighborhood Republican party officials. These efforts involved, often for the first time, the contributions of experts in a variety of fields. Notably, statisticians were beginning to be valued for their skill in measuring and predicting social trends and needs.

With the end of the war, these experts were diffused nationwide. Recent commanders of regiments, managers of military railroads, military welfare administrators, and the like, expected decent and efficient fire, police, sanitary, and water-supply services in their communities. These higher expectations applied especially in the large cities, to which numerous ambitious men and their families chose to move after Appomattox.

Humanitarianism did not end with reunion and emancipation. War work had illuminated awful conditions, close to home, that had long been invisible to the "best people," and that now cried for improvement. Humanitarian work during the war suggested that ancient scourges—epidemic diseases, alcoholism, vice, venereal diseases—could be checked, if not obliterated, by rigorous applications of government power and scientific techniques. After Appomattox, most Union states and all the ex-rebel states involved themselves in searching internal examinations and "reconstructions," in the form of revisions of state constitutions and state and local laws.

New State Constitutions and Laws

Reforms of states' constitutions and criminal and civil law codes and procedures were enacted during and just after the war in Union states, including new states created during the '60s from recent territories. Analogous reforms occurred in West Virginia, which had spun off as a Union state from its Confederate origins, and, finally, in the ex-Confederate states.

Everywhere, the war accelerated trends that had been underway since Jefferson's and Jackson's times, in particular, diminutions in property and residence requirements for voting. Some states admitted Negroes as voters, and, in rarer instances, women. Electoral districting and property-tax rates were brought into somewhat better correspondence with new population concentrations and real-estate valuations.

On the other hand, several states disfranchised ex-rebels or rebel sympathizers. Loyalty tests became popular, especially in the border states and in West Virginia. Often, loyalty requirements were also added to qualifications for professional licensing.

The supervision of electoral and licensing requirements was handled by relatively small numbers of state and county officials. And the supervision of laws relating to new entrepreneurial forms, such as corporations, required at first almost no additional government personnel at all. This changed somewhat, however, when, as will be seen, states such as Illinois and Louisiana attempted more active roles in the regulation of private businesses.

States, Business Corporations, and the Marketplace

In the 1860s, the large majority of Americans were farmers of one sort or another. But an increasing and influential percentage of the population was involved in nonagricultural work. By 1865, business corporations, which were usually based in urban centers, needed a more clearly defined place in the American system.

The capacity of states to accommodate new business needs, forms, and processes comforted entrepreneurial-minded Americans, from farmers to manufacturers, from merchants to miners. This was a time when little hostility was acknowledged between profit seekers and idealists, when Lincoln, approving the Morrill College Act, described farming as "a field for the profitable and agreeable combination of labor with cultivated thought."

None of the sporadic efforts by states to shape corporation configurations and procedures reflected antibusiness sentiment. Business forms and methods were developing far more swiftly than those of government. Efforts by legislators and judges to soften the craggiest faces of business enterprises reflected concern over the quality and openness of the competitive arena. Fear of negative public reaction should businesses be unaccountable also justified public-sector interventions. But encouragement to entrepreneurship, not constraint, remained by far the major purpose of states and localities.

Until the 1860s, as noted earlier, relatively few private business corporations existed. Before the Civil War, states created corporations by special legislation, ostensibly in order to advance specified public purposes. Often, these corporations undertook expensive engineering projects such as the Warren Bridge, the Hoosac Tunnel, or the Roeblings' Brooklyn Bridge.

Aqueducts, banks, canals, railroads, and streetcar lines were initiated by a state's charter of incorporation, encouraged by state underwriting of a corporation's bonds, and stimulated by direct state investments. (Such investments were specifically forbidden by several states under reformed constitutions of the '60s and '70s.) In general, states restricted their involvement in public works largely to initiating and supporting work by private firms and corporations. Wholly governmental, tax-supported projects were rare indeed.

New state constitutions of the 1860s required general, as opposed to special, incorporation laws. States were adapting their contract, property, and corporation laws to accommodate new managerial and technological styles. At constitutional conventions, champions of the newer general incorporation statutes insisted that they would release the energies of inventive, hard-driving entrepreneurs who, pursuing private goals, would greatly benefit the public. By the mid-60s, state-chartered corporations engaged wholly in private, for-gain business, were common. By the end of the decade, John D. Rockefeller's Standard Oil venture illustrated spectacularly the advantages possessed by a corporation's management, capital, and procedures, within the general corporation laws of a complaisant state.

Farmers, meatpackers, millers, railroad operators, and textile manufacturers, among men of many other callings, were as anxious as Rockefeller to enjoy the benefits of state incorporation, the better to exploit the enormous free marketplace preserved by the Appomattox victory. But men of predatory principles, as well as those of superior goals, associated in corporations. Some entrepreneurs pillaged captive corporations, as in the outrageous despoiling of the Erie Railroad by securities manipulators. Other corporations pillaged customers, as in the Munn Brothers' Chicago grain-warehousing operations. Louisiana state

A sectional view of caissons and mason work on a tower of the Brooklyn Bridge, 1870. The bridge's corporation was formed in 1867; Brooklyn subscribed for $3 million of the stock and New York (they were separate cities

until 1898) for $1.5 million. The bridge, opened in 1883, cost $15.5 million.
MUSEUM OF THE CITY OF NEW YORK

legislators gave favored incorporated meatpackers a monopoly of lucrative butchery. The public ultimately paid the costs. But, save in Illinois and, in a sense, Louisiana, there was little pressure for states to use the same source of authority, the revised constitutions that had spurred corporations' growth, to monitor corporations.

Instead, some states' lawmakers and judges tried to assure more acceptable behavior by increasing entrepreneurs' accountability to investors without diminishing their freedom. For example, several states attempted to outlaw watered stock. Illinois's 1870 constitution forbade railroads from issuing stock except on assets; but assets were undefined. During the '60s, no states created watchdog boards or commissions to systematize the issuance and trading of securities or to enforce standards. Federal bankruptcy law (1867) made many corporations judgmentproof in state courts. In any event, litigation was costly and slow.

Some state legislators and jurists encouraged stockholders' suits, ancestors of today's class actions, against allegedly piratical corporation officers. Would-be reformers of corporate practices rediscovered the *ultra vires* doctrine. A corporation might carry on business only as specified in its charter; all else was "beyond the powers."

But it proved to be impossible to apply this effectively. Some corporations, comprising subsidiary enterprises, as Standard Oil and Western Union did, displayed early holding-company and monopoly characteristics. By the 1860s, prohibitions in states' laws and court decisions against corporations owning stock in other corporations were giving way partially, then totally. At the same time, Massachusetts and New York tried by statute to limit the capitalization of corporations. Migratory corporations evaded such restraints by establishing home offices in friendlier places, such as West Virginia, which in the late '60s charged only $6 for incorporating and a $50 annual tax. Little wonder that businessmen felt unimpeded by state restraints.

Entrepreneurs were also greatly heartened by improvements in the property and contract laws of several states. Some western territories and states adopted the sophisticated New York code of laws. At the same time, new states were adapting their laws to reflect the particular economic needs of their regions, whether mountainous or arid, whether suited for mining, grazing, or timbering. Traditional credit and marketing practices were successfully accommodated to the new West. Laws were changed to allow legitimate homesteading of land, while retaining the capacity to punish intentional claims-jumping. Water rights in semiarid regions assumed new importance in law codes. And labor law (in some areas conditions of slavelike peonage had been inherited from Spanish times) was in the process of improvement during the last half of the '60s.

Public Nuisances

During this decade, however, hostility to certain private enterprises arose in numerous American communities. Factories, mills, mines, and slaughterhouses were springing up in and around cities; and cities were expanding to encircle once-isolated mines and abattoirs. Concern over ecological damage had been expressed earlier only in individualistic protests, which had proved to be wholly ineffective. In the 1860s, such protests continued, but in addition lawsuits based on common-law precedents for seeking redress from public nuisances began to appear in court dockets.

To succeed, suits based on nuisance concepts had to overleap formidable obstacles. A common-law tradition, going back to medieval times, stressed the right of an owner to use property as he saw fit. Further, the Bill of Rights in many instances protected homes, offices, factories, and so on against searches for proof in such cases. Third, proof of damage was often difficult to establish by expert testimony. For example, physicians could offer little evidence that courts would accept about the relationships of individual or group ailments to industrial emissions, no matter how noxious.

During the Civil War, patriotism had begun to affect nuisance-law concepts. It was obviously undesirable, if technically legal, for a textile mill to pour coal tar dyestuffs, which frequently contained arsenic, into water supplies for Union Army training or convalescent camps. Liquor sales near military units were hindered, not always legally, by state and local officers. Similarly, when soldiers' interests were involved in the disposal of human sewage or slaughterhouse offal or mine detritus, critical reaction became respectable. Years earlier, it had become respectable to discuss slavery as an evil, though slaves were legitimate private property under states' laws. Was it not now desirable to reconsider other legal protections of private property that adversely affected the essential quality of life?

In the early 1860s, these concerns expressed themselves primarily through minute improvements and adaptations of existing constitutions and laws, and through individual litigations. No need was seen for new institutions, government functions, or supervisory bureaucracies. But by the last half of the decade, it was becoming clearer, albeit intermittently and imprecisely, that individual litigations were inadequate to cope with the cost to the public at large of irresponsible business practices, such as those of the Illinois Central Railroad or the Munn Brothers' warehousing company. These companies overcharged users, falsified weighing and quality records, and made rational agriculture and commerce very difficult to achieve. The costs in money and health of Louisiana's state-authorized slaughterhouse monopoly distressed not only excluded butchers, but also New Orleans residents newly sophisticated about urban public health.

Concern over abuses of this sort was expressed by the most respectable citizens, whose motives included both idealism and selfishness. The participation of the "best men" in the unsystematic, yet energetic and inventive efforts to achieve a measure of reform was essential to such successes as these efforts enjoyed. By the same token, however, beyond a point this leadership would not let public policy impede private owners. What that point should be, and who should determine it, were prominent political questions in 1865–70.

Interstate Diversity

In response to social evils such as epidemic disease, urban slum housing, prostitution, abuse of animals, and so on, the typical pattern of public response involved resort by concerned persons and associations to traditional political-party apparatuses, and then, if consensus politics worked, local authorities invoked state powers and created an institution or adapted an existing one for the new work. But such adjustments occurred in a federal system in which officials felt no need to harmonize their efforts with those in other states, or to be consistent within a state. Counties, cities, and towns had no reasons (or ways) to coordinate public work with other counties, cities, and towns. In short, within states as well as from one to another, federalism resulted in a great diversity of programs and institutions, aiming, often, at similar purposes.

Many would-be reformers were baffled by this disinclination to synchronize ways and means. But diversity was a factor of federalism's continuing vitality. Interstate diversity, in particular, suited a generation that was seemingly intent on healing many sore spots in American society, yet that valued appropriate limits on government above efficiency in reform.

Intrastate diversity was something else again. Before the 1860s, it was considered normal and acceptable, primarily because few interests were affected by its existence. But as states and local governments began to interact more and more with the public, sharp, sometimes irrational, policy deviations from place to place were seen as less charming. Questions began to arise concerning the desirability of diversity within states in matters of bedrock social significance.

State Power and the (Evil) Cities

In law, cities were municipal corporations, akin to private entrepreneurial corporations. While business corporations became more flexible and free, cities and towns fell under increasing restraints imposed by states and counties.

As with businesses, states' special incorporation laws for cities gave way by the '60s to general incorporation statutes. By and large, these statutes restricted the functions of cities to basic law-and-order policing and the provision of public health minima. Some states (Maryland and Texas) placed city police departments under state authorities. No states gave cities general powers to increase tax bases or to extend their functions or institutions. As cities' populations soared, metropolitan centers fell ever further behind in their capacities to perform public work.

However, the sparse structure of city charters encouraged some urban policy makers to take action in directions not foreseen by the drafters of their charters. Boom-town zealots over-extended urban tax bases and resorted to repudiation of bonded debts. Urban political corruption contributed to the growing cities' incapacity to cope with their problems, ranging from police work to garbage removal.

In the late 1860s, advocates of home rule for the largest cities began to be heard. Other, louder voices stressed the need for states to keep a tight hold on urban governments. This was the message of John Dillon's *Law of Municipal Corporations*, published first in 1866. An Iowa judge, Dillon had observed the transgressions in Dubuque that resulted in the Gelpcke litigation. His book, the first full study of the city in American law and history, was a lawyerlike plea for strict limitation of cities' rights and powers.

Case law, deriving in part from Dillon's views, resulted in courts holding cities more rigidly than business corporations to the *ultra vires* doctrine. Perhaps this judicial position occasionally constrained some cities' bosses. But it also impeded the delivery of necessary public services. As a result, even in the largest cities, public work was either not done or was excessively dependent on political deals.

Nevertheless, the attractions of the great cities was undeniable. Not only immigration from abroad swelled urban populations, there was a heavy drift toward the cities from rural areas in spite of corruption in urban politics that was being revealed in regular exposés of graft and defective public services.

Members of wartime soldiers' aid societies had discovered the health menaces in cities' insanitary markets, vile slum conditions, ineffective disposal of garbage and sewage. By the end of the war, new local associations, ancestors of modern nonprofit corporations, were coming into being. They aimed to correct particular community ills first through political action, then through the creation of private institutions that would perform public service and be armed with public power. Their goals were often not grand but rather local, concrete, and, often, united to a single interest.

State Power and Local Associations

In the spring of 1865 a new, reform-minded Citizens Association formed in New York City. Its membership included a wide range of leaders from the army, Sanitary Commission, Christian Commission, and other auxiliary associations, and businessmen and professionals from a dozen fields, including engineering, publishing, education, medicine, and law.

Wartime Sanitary Commission investigations had revealed shocking practices in New York wholesale markets. Pigs and fowl were boiled alive, for example, to loosen bristles and feathers. The filth and odors were incredible. Diseased beasts and animals injured in the long march to midwestern railheads or on the journey east were usually slaughtered along with healthy stock. Medical men and laymen were outraged; humanitarians were disgusted. All were fearful for the health of their families. New York City women, sickened further at the frequent sight of draymen beating overtasked work animals, and of injured or dying beasts left to fester in the streets, joined in a loose coalition with Citizens Association members, to demand reform.

A returned expatriate, Henry Bergh, who was familiar with England's Royal Society for the Prevention of Cruelty to Animals (chartered 1833, the same year Britain abolished slavery), attempted to create a similar organization here. The Royal Society enjoyed noble patronage and, by an Act of Parliament, had been accorded nationwide authority. Here, the best that could be arranged was an incorporated private association, chartered (1865) by New York State, with authority in New York City only. This Society for the Prevention of Cruelty to

An early horse ambulance of the S.P.C.A.
CULVER PICTURES, INC.

Animals was staffed only by unpaid volunteers; but they did possess deputy-sheriff (county) powers to issue summonses and to arrest offenders in New York City. Thereafter, other communities in New York and in other states created SPCAs, but like the parent, none were budgeted from tax sources and their authority was limited.

A basically similar pattern characterized anti-vice efforts by Anthony Comstock and his followers. Comstock, a Brooklyn YMCA activist, had been an enthusiastic Christian Commission war worker. After Appomattox, he turned his attention and skills to vice in the big city. With support from Protestant and Catholic clergymen, Comstock pressured city councilmen to outlaw prostitutes and liquor. He wanted ordinances against newspaper advertisements for feminine underwear, Sabbath entertainments, and other satanic devices. New York, and other cities and counties, acquiesced to some parts of his extensive program against evil. Comstock's crusade spilled across several states, and as the decade ended, he was preparing to invade Washington, in order to seek postal censorship of sinful matter; in this he eventually succeeded.

A few states, with Maine leading the way, translated anti-vice moralism into state policy. In 1864, Maine created the first statewide "blue laws," most notably the prohibition of liquor sales. Counties in many other states followed suit, but no other entire state attempted to copy Maine's noble experiment. Prohibition in Maine generated no new enforcement bureaucracy. Police officers, primarily county sheriffs, town constables, and the ubiquitous justices of the peace, enforced this statute, as they did most others in the state.

The war had also illuminated grave deficiencies in the quality of engineers, lawyers, pharmacists, physicians, and teachers. By constitutional or statutory changes, made at the request of professional-association leaders, several states created new licensing boards staffed by prominent members of the profession. In effect, the professions made the state's authority their authority; professionals, usually unpaid, became the state licensing bureaucracy. Often the licensing boards worked in close harmony with the new state colleges and universities growing up under the terms of the Morrill Act. But the licensing boards were small in size, and, fundamentally, represented the "regulated" profession more than the public.

New York's Public Health Board

In a very few instances, for highly specialized purposes, states did create tax-supported regulatory commissions with coercive powers, staffed with appointive experts. These deviations from amateur voluntarism brought government to the brink of modern times.

Urban problems and the impact of corporations inspired the innovations. For a brief while in the latter half of the '60s, it appeared that extended use of state power was the right way to cope with increasingly massive cities and business corporations. But the exceptional character of the pioneer state commissions suggests that they were outside the contemporary limits of acceptable public-sector action.

New York's Health Board was one of the first new regulatory bodies. In the autumn of 1865, news filtered in from Europe that a cholera epidemic was likely. Memories of devastation by cholera in 1833 were still frighteningly vivid. But now, physicians in New York's Citizens Association believed that public health techniques developed during the war might work even against cholera. These techniques involved quarantining exposed persons and closing ports. If necessary, destruction of whole corridors of homes and other buildings by controlled fires or explosives and temporary resettlement of displaced persons, in order to create a scorched-earth barrier against the contagion's spread, were envisaged.

These were drastic recourses for propertied men to suggest. Only the scientific, statistical proofs of their importance that physicians provided swung the association to favor such Draconian extensions of state power.

In late 1865, Citizens Association lobbyists headed for New York's City Hall, the state capital, and the White House. At City Hall, Tammany politicos refused to cooperate. At the White House, President Johnson would not provide the requested surplus navy hulks for use as temporary barracks and isolation facilities, or order navy patrols to blockade ports. But at the state's capital, legislators from overrepresented rural districts were willing to let New York City cleanse itself, so long as state tax loads were not increased. They hoped the measures suggested would even prevent the "urban" infection from polluting the countryside.

New York State created a Metropolitan Health Board for New York City. Its medical and administrative staff was salaried, professional, and vigorous. Costs were met by rises in property taxes in New York City's counties. Armed with delegated state powers, staffers could order owners of private property to remove accumulated filth or to destroy unsavable property. Board officers might issue summonses in the case of violations of their orders, or call on city policy or county sheriffs to arrest offenders.

As events worked out, the anticipated cholera epidemic failed to materialize. But the New York City Metropolitan Health Board endured; its powers were little used, but were not repealed.

Many other cities, by exercise of (presumably delegated) state authority, or by direct state action as in New York, created urban boards of health, ostensibly on the New York pattern. Some states established statewide boards. But no other city or state allowed its new health board anything like the coercive authority, staff, or tax budget that the pioneer enjoyed. Almost all became mere statistics-gathering, unobtrusive bureaus.

Illinois's Granger Commission

Before the Civil War, some states, notably Massachusetts, had set up state railroad boards. Under the guidance of such eminent patricians as Charles Francis Adams, the Massachusetts board and its imitators collected, and sometimes published, invaluable data on rail operating costs, rates, and profits. This was as far as men of Adams' mind wished public-sector institutions to go with respect to private entrepreneurship. Marketplace economics, not public policies, must decide rail rates, Adams insisted.

Unscrupulous operators of the eastern Erie Railroad and the Illinois Central, among others, had won enviable profits, in part by corrupting state and local legislators. In the late '60s, in Illinois, exposures of railroad corruption were accentuated by the extortions practiced by private grain warehousemen and elevator operators, such as the Munn Brothers, in the railroad's Chicago terminus. Down-state Illinois farmers, who were uniting in the new (1865) benevolent association commonly known as the Grange, felt victimized by the multiple cost gougings performed by rail, elevator, and warehouse companies. Respectable Chicago businessmen, organized in a city Board of Trade, joined with the politically active Grangers in demanding, and shaping, a new constitution (1869) for the state. The new Illinois constitution required creation of a tax-supported commission, staffed by permanent functionaries, one of whose duties was to set maximum rates that railroads, grain elevators, and bulk farm warehouses might charge. Public scales were to be established. State officials were to check books, prescribe standard accounting systems, and initiate lawsuits to compel obedience.

Louisiana's Slaughterhouse Monopoly

Similarly, in the late '60s in Louisiana, the state legislature took cognizance of New Orleans' difficulties with certain nuisances. In public health matters, the city had backslid dreadfully since the withdrawal in 1865 of Union Army-Sanitary Commission contingents. City growth had continued, however. Slaughterhouses, once suburban, were now within dense population areas. Offal was still cast into the city's major water supply, and butchering odors were obnoxious. By statute, state lawmakers created a monopoly of slaughterhousing in favor of certain named corporations, ostensibly as a public-health measure. Whatever the element of corruption in this statute, it was also a step in the direction of establishing and coordinating, by state law, urban food-supply, pricing, and sanitation policies.

The Southern States' Black Codes

In 1865–66, every ex-Confederate state, obedient to White House dictates, revised its constitution and laws. Many of the revisions brought the governments and laws of these states into closer harmony with those of the Union states and the federal government. At the very least, slavery and secession were renounced.

But in reshaping civil and criminal laws, the lily-white lawmakers sanctioned by President Johnson's Reconstruction proclamations created a new form of citizenship in American law, halfway between slave and free status. This was accomplished via the "black codes," which will be discussed in Chapter 10.

How to Limit State Powers?

In Illinois, Louisiana, and New York, critics of those states' innovative extensions of government authority resorted to the courts. With respect to the New York Health Board, state courts sustained its rulings, and the board carried on its work. The Illinois commissioners and the Louisiana slaughterhouse monopolists defended the laws favoring their interests in state and federal courts. Finally, in the '70s, the United States

Supreme Court, deciding the landmark Slaughterhouse and Granger cases, held that the uses of state power established in these laws did not transgress limitations stated in the Thirteenth and Fourteenth Amendments.

By their very exceptionality, the Health Board, Slaughterhouse, and Granger innovations reaffirmed prevailing imperatives limiting state power. Nevertheless, it is significant that, even in a limited way, state authority had been invoked to cope with novel problems arising from mass urban public-health needs and new technology and business forms. Thus, Americans continued to experiment with diverse institutions and to settle peacefully disputes that arose from such experiments. Moreover, the Union was saved, the nation prosperous, slavery obliterated, and secession reversed.[2] Only the resurgence of institutionalized racial attitudes, in the southern states' black codes, threatened the Appomattox triumph.

FOOTNOTES

1. *Law Magazine and Review* (London) XXV (1868), 51–52, 57–58.

2. H. M. Hyman, *A More Perfect Union: The Impact of the Civil War and Reconstruction on the Constitution* (New York: Knopf, 1973), Chaps. 18–21.

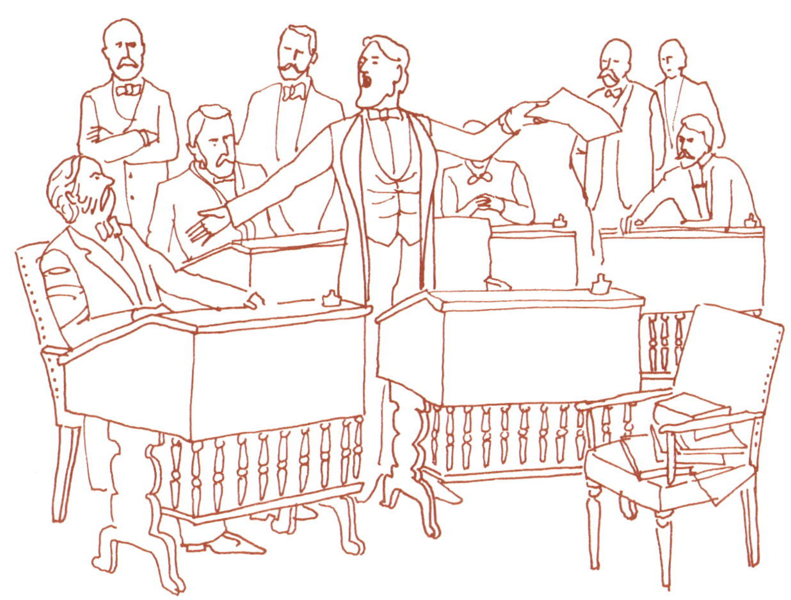

10 / 1868—THE CRITICAL YEAR

Black Codes and the Limits of Presidential Powers

THE SOUTHERN STATES' black codes and President Johnson's intervention in their support spawned the Watergate of 1865–70. Nothing else that decade, save for secession itself, so abused state powers as the black codes. By executive, "war-power" orders, Johnson had, in the May December 1865 months, created the southern state governments that, in turn, produced the black codes. This involved him in fateful misconstructions of nation-state relationships, and in unprecedented extensions of presidential powers. These abuses of state and presidential power fostered deadly combats between President and Congress, and in 1868 resulted in Johnson's impeachment.

At stake was the freedman's fate and the nation's precarious stability. By denying freedmen the same legal rights and responsibilities as free men, the black codes perpetuated race as the determinant of an American's status under the laws and customs of his community and state.

The black codes seriously diminished the Negroes' capacity to compete on equal terms with whites in almost any economic endeavor, and put them at a grave disadvantage in criminal cases and civil litigation. Laws relating to apprenticeship, inheritance, divorce, and vagrancy were written so as to discriminate against Negroes. Long-term contractual commitments, such as real estate mortgages, were virtually denied to freedmen. Blacks were also exploited in lesser contracts, especially management-labor relations, for, in effect, blacks were prevented from testifying against whites in lawsuits. Criminal penalties for Negroes were far heavier than for whites. In short, the state black codes, while acknowledging, if grudgingly, the Thirteenth Amendment's prohibition of slavery, denied the beneficiaries of that amendment anything approaching the equal privileges, immunities, or protections of states' laws.

The regressive black codes repelled northern whites, not because they loved Negroes; that was not the issue. Instead, the central concern in the victorious states was to maintain nation-state stability, and, simultaneously, to continue the progressive commercial and industrial surge that was transforming the continent. Individual initiative and self-help was seen as the key to both stability and progress. Those who were disadvantaged or aggrieved were expected to seek remedies either in the marketplace or the courts. To Lincoln's generation, equality before law —state and local law—was precious because it allowed individuals to compete. Government action was not seen as a proper substitute for lawsuits and economic competition. Unsophisticated men simply assumed equality. Educated persons recalled Cicero's *De Republica* (I, 32, 12): "If the fortunes of all cannot be equal, if the mental capacities of all cannot be the same, at least the rights before the law of all those who are subject to the same state ought to be equal."

If southern blacks could not defend themselves, as whites did, in state courts, a federal presence might be called for endlessly, with consequent tax rises and impediments to commerce and industry. Moreover, southern Negroes had been the most dependable and numerous southern Unionists by far. Patriots and humanitarians could not easily ignore evidence of the inequities they suffered in southern states.

The black codes were the more exacerbating because they were unexpected. Leaders, white and Negro, military and civilian, had assumed that, with slavery abolished, all state residents would automatically possess the same formal rights, remedies, and responsibilities under state civil and criminal laws. West Pointer General A. H. Terry, in charge of United States troops in Virginia in mid-1865, expressed this consensus in the following order. Note the handwritten subscription, by his colleague General O. O. Howard, just named head of the Freedmen's Bureau:*

Headquarters Dept. of Virginia

GENERAL ORDERS
No. 77

RICHMOND, VA., *June* 23, 1865

The Laws of the State of Virginia, and the Ordinances of the different Municipalities within the State, having especial reference to, and made to restrain the personal liberty of free colored persons, were designed for the government of such persons while living amid a population of colored slaves, they were enacted in the interests of slave owners, and were designed for the security of slave property: they were substantially parts of the slave code.

Slavery has been abolished in Virginia, and therefore upon the

*Owned by and used with the permission of Mr. W. E. Layton, Washington, D.C.

principle that where the reason of the law ceases, the law itself ceases, these [slave] Laws and Ordinances have become obsolete. People of color will henceforth enjoy the same personal liberty that other citizens and inhabitants enjoy; they will be subject to the same restraints and to the same punishments, for crime, that are imposed on whites, and to no others.

Vagrancy, however, will not be permited; neither whites nor blacks can be allowed to abandon their proper occupations, to desert their families or roam in idleness about this Department; but neither whites nor blacks will be restrained from seeking employment elsewhere, when they cannot obtain it with just compensation at their homes, nor from traveling from place to place on proper and legitimate business.

Until the Civil Tribunals are re-established, the administration of criminal justice must, of necessity, be by Military Courts; before such Courts, the evidence of colored persons will be received in all cases.

By command of Major General A. H. TERRY:

[Subscribed]

I like the letter and spirit of this Order, and wish it were universal

O. O. Howard, Maj. Gen. &c.

Formal equality in economic relationships was seen as basic to equality. It was all, for example, that Negro leader Frederick Douglass sought for southern Negroes. Northern states had repealed their last black codes during the 1840s and early 1850s. By mid-1865, the citizens of these states, at least, were disinclined to sanction laws that insensitively committed state power to perpetualizing second-class status for millions of Americans to whom the nation was peculiarly indebted.

Probably the majority of nonsouthern whites would have accepted unofficial discrimination against blacks in the ex-rebel states. Only a small minority of whites were concerned about private racist acts, and they had little national influence. But official state discrimination was another matter.

By December 1865, when the Thirteenth Amendment was ratified, and the Thirty-ninth Congress assembled for the first post-Appomattox session, the southern states' black codes posed questions that gave form to the ensuing half-decade. First, should the nation, which so desired stability, accept from recently seceded states such unsettling expressions of state power? Second, must the Congress accept both the President's nonenforcement of lawful national statutes, especially the confiscation and test oath laws, described earlier, and his positive actions, which created a dozen new state governments in the South, by his fiats, thus establishing a White House monopoly in shaping Reconstruction? The black codes, and Johnson's unanticipated defense of their creators, frustrated the expectation that Reconstruction would be swift and uneventful, requiring no special government action.

By and large, as the war came to an end, it seemed to have caused less social polarity than might have been expected. Some significant private-sector institutions, including Protestant churches, remained stubbornly split along sectional and racial lines; and this was a time when religion permeated American life. Yet the enduring post-Appomattox church schisms, if distasteful, did not threaten social stability or national survival. Habit and constitutional law kept churches separate from government. No political response to the church divisions was appropriate. But the black codes and the President's Reconstruction policies polarized politics. Democrats in Union states, in association with renascent southern party organizations, maintained that the nation now possessed no special powers in the southern states. Republicans felt that for an unspecified period the nation still possessed war powers in the South. Confused by evidence of southern white intransigence, Republicans looked first to their party's leader, President Johnson, for direction.

Andrew Johnson and Party Politics

Several presidential proclamations, issued between May and December in 1865, assigned regular army units to aid southern whites (whom Johnson quickly pardoned or amnestied in very large numbers) in resurrecting state and local governments. In superficial ways, Johnson's approach resembled the policies Lincoln had offered tentatively in December 1863. But by April 1865, Lincoln evidenced the intent to alter his policies in the direction of greater biracial participation in the government and politics of the Reconstructed states. Johnson had grown not at all during that period.

War Department funds paid Johnson's appointed pardoned provisional governors and their staffs. Employing war powers, Johnson required the ex-Confederate states to repudiate secession and to ratify the Thirteenth Amendment. But in general, Johnson took no action against the exclusion of southern white Unionists from the provisional governors' staffs or the new governments. And southern Negroes were not protected.

By his orders to federal attorneys and Freedmen's Bureau officers in the South, Johnson blocked effective enforcement of the 1862 confiscation and test oath laws and the 1865 Freedmen's Bureau statute. Forthrightly executed, these laws might have allowed relatively large numbers of southern Negroes to become economically self-sufficient, and thereby diminished the economic, social, and political dominance of the old white leadership.

Similarly, Johnson appointed many hundreds of pardoned recent rebels to positions in federal courts and land, postal, and revenue offices. This ignored the "ironclad test oath" statute passed by Congress in 1862 and signed by Lincoln. The statute required all federal officeholders to swear to their past loyalty. In short, Johnson disregarded his presidential responsibility to execute all the laws. Instead he picked and chose among them, thereby creating confrontations on such questions as whether a presidential pardon obviated the loyalty-oath requirement.

His Republican party colleagues had assumed that Johnson would give federal jobs, if not to Negroes, then at least to white southern Unionists, like himself, who could swear to their past loyalty, as the law required. Lincoln had done precisely this in Johnson's own instance, in order to encourage viable two-party organization in Tennessee. Johnson's devious course, nourishing only recent rebels (who were all Democrats) puzzled fellow Republicans.

Recent scholarship makes clear that Johnson aimed covertly to build a new national political coalition as a base from which he could win the Presidency in 1868.[1] He retained his Republican cloak, but he had to have the support of the South's Democrats in order to build a national constituency. Further, Johnson's racial views were reactionary, in any case. For these reasons, he favored quick acceptance by Congress of the southern states' delegations, even though the test oath law barred most ex-rebels from Congress as well as from executive and judicial offices.

Executive Power

Lincoln, at the war's height, had never claimed such extensive rights in determining Reconstruction policy as those Johnson assumed. Unlike Johnson, Lincoln had played politics openly, with full consideration of alternatives, and with respect for congressional views. Instead of holding to rigid executive-power theories, Lincoln, for example, voluntarily appeared before a congressional committee to explain why his wife corresponded with her southern relatives. Most of the Republicans elected to the Thirty-ninth Congress in November 1864, when Lincoln won his second term, shared his view that the Constitution was a source of government power more than a negation of it. Lincoln hoped, therefore, that he, cooperating with Congress, the Republican party, and the voters, could achieve reasonable harmony on national policy.

Andrew Johnson could not see a need for harmony. Despite his congressional service, Johnson as President exhibited little patience for delicate separation-of-power, check-and-balance politics. Convinced by his own exaggerated rhetorical claims for executive powers, Johnson dug a great gulf between himself and Congress. He transported his border state's hurly-burly political style and racial attitudes to the most sensitive national questions. Secretive and devoid of humor or humility, he saw foul conspiracies where honest disagreements existed. Imbued with an overblown sense of the office he occupied, Johnson stretched presidential prerogatives to unprecedented lengths, thereby creating crisis.

Democrats

In light of their need to restore links to the reviving party organizations in the southern states, the northern Democrats' haste in Reconstruction is understandable. Looking to 1866, Democrats hoped to capture Congress, especially the House, and, in 1868, the White House. With the ratification of the Thirteenth Amendment, the Constitution's three-fifths clause was obsolete; with each freed slave counting as a full constituent, the southern states would have more representatives in the House. A political position favoring extreme views of states' rights would help the Democrats recapture the South for their party. Therefore, northern Democrats supported the black codes and insisted on immediate and unqualified national acceptance of the southern states, reconstructed according to President Johnson's terms.

Republicans

Many Republican congressmen and their constituents, by reason of their conservatism, worried at Johnson's swift Reconstruction pace and unprecedented grants of pardon and amnesty. His use of the army for civilian policy objectives not approved by Congress re-raised the specter of runaway military power. Republicans opposed the black codes because they represented an excessive extension of state power. Moreover, the enhanced sense of decency and patriotism that arose during the war could not accept swift, full equality for states that refused fair legal equality to blacks and rewarded recent rebels.

The black codes spelled danger to the Republican party. This youthful, seemingly fragile coalition, held together primarily by patriotism and antipathy to slavery, could, ironically, fall apart now that the war and slavery had ended. The hazard was easy to discern; the remedy, more difficult. Republicans had first to realize, then to teach, that a national concern for black Americans' civil rights and remedies before state laws did not mean a loss of whites' civil liberties or states' rights.

Civil *rights* are individuals' workaday protections, remedies, and responsibilities, involving the security of property and persons. The rights to contract, sue, and testify were bedrock civil rights. They entailed derivative responsibilities, varying somewhat according to state and local laws and customs. Civil *liberties* involved essentially the openness of political avenues. Except for the temporary, bearable diminutions of civil rights and liberties during the Civil War, only the 1798 Sedition Act and the southern states' prewar fetters on antislavery advocacy had limited whites' extraordinary freedom. Americans were confident, despite these deviations, that they understood civil liberties. The assumption was that they were enjoyed as result of bills of rights that restrained federal and state governments.

Democrats insisted that if the federal government intervened to effect equality of civil rights for Negroes within a state, then state rights, and whites' civil liberties, would be diminished. Democrats pointed to the nation's test oath statute as proof of their argument. If enforced, it would have kept the great majority of southern whites out of appointive and elective government offices.

Early in 1866 the Supreme Court of the United States, considering its own rule applying the loyalty oath to lawyers practicing before it, condemned the rule as an unconstitutional bill of attainder and *ex post facto* excess. But contemporary disagreement with the Court's decision was extensive; and its applicability to the situation in the southern states, or even to national executive departments, was dubious. Basically, there was no way other than the oath tests for the nation to give a priority to southern Unionists and blacks, and to keep out the old southern white leadership. But the burden of disproving Democratic contentions lay on Republicans.

It was difficult for Republicans and their constituents to grasp the relationships between economic and political rights and liberties, or to admit a need for national intervention in a state's affairs. Republicans were state-centered constitutional conservatives, else they would have imposed a simple military occupation of the South, mass imprisonments and exiles, and wholesale confiscations of secessionists' property. Instead, whatever selfish purposes moved individual Republicans, they were committed to search for a Reconstruction formula that safeguarded state rights and increased individuals' (including black and white Unionists') rights and liberties.

States' rights were always basic in the Republican approach to Reconstruction. Republican policies evolved not as part of an ideology but in response to events in the South and President Johnson's unanticipated course.

What had Republicans expected the nation's role to be regarding black residents of the ex-rebel states? They had thought that role, based on a final use of war powers, would be brief, inexpensive, and uncoercive. Even the minority Radical Republicans, such as Senator Charles Sumner of Massachusetts, expected that the nation owed the South's blacks no more and no less than it owed to whites—equality of economic opportunity. Temporary, low-budget, heavily voluntaristic national institutions such as the Freedmen's Bureau would quickly accomplish that.

The bureau law, which was signed by Lincoln, should have bound Johnson, and bureau operations should not have been impeded as they were by Johnson and by those he appointed or supported in the South. In the state courts the President had helped to establish, the efforts by bureau agents to defend Negroes, and of blacks to protect themselves, in ordinary civil litigation concerning, for example, employment contracts, were mockeries. As defendants in criminal prosecutions, blacks were in for far worse treatment.

Pardoned ex-rebels initiated harassing lawsuits in state courts against army and bureau officers, claiming damages for a range of alleged offenses. These damage suits seriously interfered with government operations. Worse, they pitted the President either against "his" state institutions and officials or against "his" army, which was obeying presidential orders and Congressional laws—the laws of the land.

Army and bureau officers, including Grant, pleaded with Johnson for backing. His equivocating refusal to come out on the side of law and order is reflected in Grant's desperate decision, in mid-January 1866, on his own authority, to allow officers being sued in state courts to transfer the lawsuits to federal court jurisdictions. Grant did not hide his policy; Johnson did hide his.

Army and bureau leaders then looked to Congress. Increasing numbers of bureau officials reported to Congress (and to the President) that the nation must, somehow, diminish black-code inequities, else slavery in other guises would persist. As expressed by army officer Manning Force, on bureau assignment, the basic point was: "How far are we bound in honor to supervise . . . state laws upon the . . . freedmen?"[2]

In December 1865, congressional Republicans exercised their traditional right to determine the qualifications of members of Congress, and refused to seat elected delegates from the "Reconstructed" southern states. Instead, Congress created a new joint investigating committee to report on conditions there. This famed "Reconstruction Committee" was never, as so long alleged, dominated by vindictive Radicals. Neither did it reflect a conspiracy inspired by northern industrialists to suppress the agrarian South in order to retain high protective tariffs for favored industries, national bank controls, and subsidies for communications. The committee learned quickly that in black-code states freedmen were far less than free-and-equal persons, as defined by those states' own laws.

The 1866 Civil Rights Bill

By early April 1866, a phenomenally short time after assembling, the Congress had drafted a Civil Rights Bill, a pioneering effort to define and protect civil rights. Its author was the conservative Illinois Republican Senator Lyman Trumbull. His bill passed because of the support of moderates in both Houses.

After intensive study of committee reports on the effects of black codes, Trumbull and his colleagues tried, in the Civil Rights Bill, to deny states the power to discriminate racially between their own citizens. In the bill, citizens of states were defined, for the first time, also as national citizens, thus overturning the 1857 Dred Scott decision. If states did not discriminate, they would not be subject to any national presence. But when, overtly, "under color of any state law," a state denied equal civil rights because of race, the bill allowed the federal attorney, or the aggrieved party, to seek a shift of the resulting lawsuit to the federal district courts (whose jurisdiction was expanded by the bill) or the Freedmen's Bureau temporary courts (in areas where federal civil courts were not yet fully functioning). In the federal courts, of course, Negroes could sue and witness; judges and jurors were required to meet the loyalty-oath test. It was hoped that by means of this inexpensive, unbureaucratic device, citizens could themselves secure their own civil rights. The nation need not directly confront state power. Rather, the confrontations would be initiated by individual litigations, to be resolved in a forum where, it was hoped, more decent standards of justice prevailed than in state courts.

The real question the nation faced in early 1866 was not what the relationship should be between nation and states, as most Democrats, Andrew Johnson, and many historians insisted for so long. Instead, it was what should be the status under state law of state citizens, who were now defined also as national citizens.

Trumbull's clear intent was to secure as a national right what, in legal theory, had always obtained, except for slaves;

practical, marketplace freedom and equality, as each state defined these matters. The Civil Rights Bill was Congress' Reconstruction. No more was needed, or would be approved by Congress, if the white South abided by its terms.

The Civil Rights Bill was the mildest "punishment" for treason and civil war in all history. It was a decent effort to enforce the Thirteenth Amendment, now the supreme law of the land. Obfuscations and distortions of its intent and content by Democrats infuriated such Republican conservatives as Ohio's Rutherford Hayes, who replied to erroneous news-media accounts.

> I know it [the 1866 Civil Rights Act] is grossly misrepresented and greatly misunderstood in Ohio . . . as if it gives increased and unheard of rights as privileges to negroes—as if it would compel the schools to receive negro children, the hotels negro guests &c &c &c now please to note what I say. It undertakes to secure to the negro no right which he has not enjoyed in Ohio since the repeal of the [Ohio] Black Laws in 1848–9.[3]

In addition to passing the Civil Rights Bill, Congress extended the life of the Freedmen's Bureau, whose courts were, under certain circumstances, to enforce the provisions of the bill. Republican backers of both measures were shocked when President Johnson, without warning his party leaders, vetoed their proposed legislation.

Johnson's decision to veto opened a rift between him and the majority of the Republican party. The President's use of the veto was itself exceptional; Lincoln had gone no further in defying Congress, especially his party colleagues there, than the Wade-Davis pocket veto. Johnson's veto message excoriated both bills as unconstitutional infringements on state powers, and dangerous, tyrannical measures.

Responding, Republican congressmen overrode the President's vetoes. Meanwhile, the Congress drafted the Fourteenth Amendment, which, in essence, restated the terms of the Civil Rights Act in vetoproof form (a proposed amendment does not need a Presidential signature). Approved by Congress in mid-1866, the amendment went to the states for ratification, which occurred in July 1868.

The Fourteenth Amendment

Under the Fourteenth Amendment, states continued to have the authority to define and secure their citizens' rights, remedies, and responsibilities. But the amendment reversed permanently the tradition, sanctified by the Dred Scott decision, that Negroes could be denied citizen status. A state could no longer overtly diminish the rights of minority citizens. The states were now obliged to respect and uphold each citizen's right to the equal protection under state law with respect to life, liberty, and property, and the right to be subject to or enjoy the same procedures (processes) that were applied to all other citizens of the state. Civil rights were federalized, but state rights were not thereby lessened.

While ratification of the Fourteenth Amendment pended in the states, Johnson increasingly obstructed the laws of the land concerning Reconstruction, with which he disagreed. His like thinking attorney general issued constraining instructions that hampered the enforcement of the Civil Rights Law, such as orders to delay submission of pleadings or to send testimony and evidence to Washington for review. Commander-in-chief of the army, Johnson hamstrung army and Freedmen's Bureau officers on southern duty, transferring those who were too zealous in their obedience to federal laws.

Encouraged by the President's policies, southern whites descended to violence. In New Orleans, rioting whites, including city policemen, murdered helpless Negroes. The mayor and city council (mostly pardoned ex-Confederates, as were the police) failed utterly to restrain the mobs. The governor made no move to assemble state militia, which may have been as well, since its members were also pardoned ex-rebels. Nearby, federal soldiers remained immobile, because the President issued no orders to intervene.

In many places in the South, whites who assaulted federal soldiers, white Unionists, and Negroes, epecially black soldiers, went unpunished in state courts. In some instances, all-white juries, court officers, judges, and police praised the assaulters, including at least one brazen murderer of a United States soldier.

Still, northern opinion, as of the critical November 1866 congressional and state elections, asked only minimal evidence of southern good-will. Ratification of the pending Fourteenth Amendment by southern states would be an adequate sign of their intention to abide by the standards of the Civil Rights Law.

But of all the seceded states, only Johnson's state, Tennessee, against his objections, ratified the amendment. Congress at once admitted its delegates. Thus, it was clear that the other ex-rebel states, now firmly Democratic, were unwilling to accept the law of the land. And President Johnson's spectacular pro-Democratic and antiamendment efforts during the election campaigns, including his unfortunate "swing around the circle" of major cities, where he resorted to a low level of inflammatory demagoguery, rasped Republicans' sensibilities, still smarting from his abuses of executive power.

In the election, Republicans won every Union state except for formerly slave-owning Delaware, Kentucky, and Maryland.

With clear majorities in hand, Republicans in Congress now had to decide how to move.

The 1867 Military Bill

In 1866, Republicans had been willing to accept non-loyalist officials and representatives in southern state governments, as they did in the case of Tennessee, if observation of minimal civil rights was promised, symbolized by ratification of the Fourteenth Amendment. But by early 1867, impatient congressional Republicans, now able systematically to override presidential vetoes (if party lines held firm), began consideration of legislation that became the Military Reconstruction Act.

Sponsored by middle-of-the-road Republicans Senator George Williams and Representative Roscoe Conkling, the bill, despite its flagrant martial features, attracted broad party support and constituent approval. It at last disavowed the recalcitrant Johnson state governments in the South. Now the Congress, on its independent authority, was initiating Reconstruction anew. No state governments or constitutions created since 1865 in the former Confederacy were legitimate (except Tennessee's). The military was to provide law and order in the ex-rebel states, and to announce new elections. But this time all delegates to constitutional conventions would have to be able to swear to the test oath. The new state constitutions would have to provide equal civil rights and political rights for all citizens. A state legislature, elected by terms of a new constitution, would have to approve the still-pending Fourteenth Amendment before Congress would admit the state's delegates. Having the right to vote, southern Negroes would be able to protect their interests just as the Irish did in New York and the Germans did in Missouri.

Republicans felt they could no longer leave southern Negroes and other Unionists to the mercy of southern whites. The latter had exhibited too clearly what black and white Unionists could expect in such circumstances. But Republicans hoped that the bill would quickly effect Reconstruction and avoid long-term national interventions. Thereafter, the Civil Rights Law and the Thirteenth and Fourteenth Amendments would be adequate safeguards of the progress achieved. Congressman James G. Blaine made specific this intention to withdraw the troops as soon as possible:

> . . . all they [the southern states] have to do, in order to get rid of military rule and military government, is to present to the Congress of the United States a constitutional form of State government in accord with the letter and spirit of the Constitution and laws of the United States, together with a ratification of the pending constitutional amendment.[4]

Secretary of War Stanton, properly obedient to a federal law, proceeded to enforce the act in the southern states. The new state constitutions that emerged greatly improved and modernized many aspects of life there, apart from guaranteeing equal rights. The southern states, following the example of other parts of the country, assumed the functions of modernizing asylums, roads, schools, and taxes. In short, Reconstruction had become an opportunity for general reform in the southern states.

But there was widespread resistance to the national program. Congress had to issue supplements to the Military Reconstruction Law, each vetoed by the President and overridden, as southern whites avoided the law's requirements, sometimes violently. President Johnson and his attorney general interpreted the Reconstruction statutes conservatively, but nevertheless, for almost a year, Johnson did execute these laws, however grudgingly.

Then, in February 1868, Johnson suddenly attempted to seize control of the only means the nation possessed to effect Reconstruction, the army. He discharged Stanton, the Secretary of War. This violated the Tenure of Office Act, which had been passed by Congress a year earlier precisely to prevent the President from discharging members of the administration Congress favored.

Desperate, with no hope that Johnson would continue to execute the laws during the nine months remaining of his term, Congress impeached him.

The Impeachment

Historians have too long admired Johnson's courage under adversity. But his other, less admirable, traits have recently received better illumination. Today, it is cogently argued that Congress had legitimate reasons to impeach.

Until Johnson, no President had been impeached. The few major earlier impeachments in America had occurred sixty years before. They involved two federal judges, who had seriously abused their offices while conducting Sedition Act trials. During one of these impeachments, of Judge John Pickering, in 1804, the defense counsel misconstrued English constitutional and legal history, and the intentions of the framers of our Constitution, by insisting that a national official's offense, to be impeachable, must also be criminally indictable.

This dubious argument, resurrected in 1868 (and in 1974), had failed in its immediate purpose of 1804, in that Pickering was convicted. It fails also the best tests of law and history. To restrict impeachable offenses to indictable ones, in a federal system of multiple, diverse criminal laws, plays tricks with reason and the history of impeachment law. It is more supportable to conclude that impeachment was incorporated into the 1787 Constitution as a last-resort political process, utilizing paralegal procedures for the definition and prosecution of impeachable offenses as outlined in the Constitution. The framers of the Constitution were involved in a wholly unique effort—the creation of an effective executive for a tripartite federal system. In this system, a President who refuses, as Johnson did, fully to execute his office obstructs all government operations; a President who ignores the other branches of government risks the political legitimacy of the whole.

Johnson, as noted, had abused executive powers. And by removing Stanton from office, he confronted the nation with wholly unsatisfactory alternatives. Acquiescence in his retrograde policies was the first option, and, of course, Democrats favored it. Second, Republicans could wait until the November 1868 elections offered a new popular verdict on all public policies. But even if voters repudiated Johnson, he would hold office until March 1869. Obviously he would employ the period to appoint to major offices men who were sympathetic to his views. Southern Unionists and Negroes would suffer further. The next President and Congress might never be able to make up lost ground. And if Johnson won, he would be President at least until 1873, if not 1877.

Republican congressmen felt the electorate had expressed clear support of Republican policies. Their mutual goal was economic, social, and racial stability. Impeachment was a way toward that goal.

Johnson's Democratic defenders denounced the impeachment as a partisan plot. They predicted the permanent emasculation of the Presidency if a congressional majority could impeach, and convict, for allegedly transitory policy reasons. Johnson's very able counsel in the Senate impeachment proceedings dredged up the Pickering defense and maintained that the

President, having done nothing criminally indictable, could not be convicted and should not have been impeached at all.

The House Republican impeachment managers, acting as prosecutors, had a tougher job. Less adept than Johnson's counsel, they were already known as partisans, an inescapable feature of our presidential-impeachment arrangements. They committed gross errors of style and argument. Unable to specify precisely the limits of executive power, the impeachment managers presented the Senate with a mélange of poorly conceived articles of impeachment, and conducted a confused and undignified Senate debate.

From February to May 1868, as the impeachment trial proceeded, seemingly extraneous concerns intruded into the senators' considerations. Were Johnson convicted and removed, his successor would be Ohio Senator Benjamin Wade, an exponent of fiscal heresies, which troubled even Republicans who wanted Johnson out. Recent racial violence in the nearby British West Indies—where emancipation was thirty-five, not five, years old—sapped the zeal of some impeachers. Must the United States face three decades of violence and national intervention in the southern states? The President's subdued demeanor during the trial suggested to undecided senators that impeachment was enough, that conviction was unnecessary. When, during the impeachment trial, Grant evidenced his willingness to accept the 1868 Republican presidential nomination, it was obvious that no Democrat, including Johnson, had a hope to win in November. Therefore, in May 1868, enough Republicans voted against conviction to let Johnson escape the deserved consequences of his conduct by one vote, 35–19.

Myths immediately commenced to accumulate about the impeachment. They should be dispelled. The seven Republican senators who voted against conviction were *not* hounded unmercifully by their party majority. Johnson was *not* vindi-

Below, a view of the Senate chamber during the impeachment trial of President Johnson (March–May 1868). Standing in the right foreground is Johnson's defense attorney, Benjamin R. Curtis; the President did not attend. At right, a pass of admission to the trial.

NOSTALGIA PRESS, INC.

NEW YORK PUBLIC LIBRARY

cated by the verdict. He was repudiated by the Democrats, who refused him the presidential nomination for which he lusted. His policies were further rejected by passage (1868) and ratification (1870) of the Fifteenth Amendment, prohibiting denial of the right to vote because of race.

State of the Nation

At the height of the impeachment trial, the keenly observant English reformer John Bright marveled to Senator Sumner that in America's "progressing revolution . . . it is wonderful that your government securities remain unshaken whilst your Congress and Executive are almost at open war!"[5]

United States government finances were indeed in excellent health. Substantial annual Treasury surpluses, derived primarily from excise and import taxes and land sales, were at the President's disposal even during the impeachment. (We know now that Johnson had toyed with extralegal uses for surplus funds. He had considered establishing, at Baltimore, an unauthorized new army department, under his rather than Congress' orders. But Grant had smelled out the scheme in its preliminary stages: he sent General Sherman, Johnson's credulous uniformed supporter, who might have taken the Baltimore command, out west to cope with Indians. Otherwise, Johnson's scheme remained secret.)

The business community exhibited noteworthy confidence throughout the impeachment. Despite prophecies of stock market collapse if impeachment, conviction, or near-conviction occurred, Wall Street and commercial indicators generally were stable rather than chaotic.

Farmers were becoming Grangers, taking advantage of the provisions of the Homestead and Mineral Land acts, and benefiting from expanding markets. Cities flourished as immigration soared. Minor wars in Europe further increased demand for American products. A few labor unions had organized since Appomattox. They were less upsetting than many employers and middlemen had feared. Unemployment was low. Jobs in railroad and home construction, lumbering, milling, and consumer-goods production more than absorbed returning veterans and immigrants. Indeed, in the west, mass importations of Asian laborers seemed to be necessary.

Political stability underlay the benign economic indicia. Impeachment was not a crisis, as predicted; it was a constitutional and political process, brought into operation because, without it, crisis was imminent. Within weeks after the impeachment's close, the Republicans' nominating convention, for the first time blessed with delegations from southern states, named Grant the party's presidential candidate and Indiana's Schuyler Colfax the vice-presidential candidate. The platform attended especially to Reconstruction progress, to gratification in the July 1868 ratification of the Fourteenth Amendment, to pleasure in the southern states' improved constitutions and laws, to affirmations of the validity of the public debt, and to a restatement of Johnson's offenses.

The Democrats, once more a nationally vigorous second party with delegates from all states, convened in July. They reiterated that Reconstruction should have ended in 1865 with the states' repudiations of secession and slavery, that further Reconstruction measures were excessive and unconstitutional, and that civil liberties and state rights were casualties of the war and its aftermath. A midwestern wing, long associated with antiwar militantism, encumbered the platform with a demand, repugnant to creditors, that the government continue to issue paper money. The Democrats' presidential nominee, Horatio Seymour, former New York governor, bore the burden of having been unable to control wartime antidraft riots. The party's vice-presidential choice, Missouri's Montgomery Blair,

Result of the Presidential Election of 1868

States	*Electoral vote*		*Popular vote*	
	Grant	*Seymour*	*Grant*	*Seymour*
New Hampshire	5		38,191	31,224
Massachusetts	12		136,477	59,408
Rhode Island	4		12,993	6,548
Connecticut	6		50,641	47,600
Vermont	5		44,167	12,045
New York		33	419,883	429,883
New Jersey		7	80,121	83,001
Pennsylvania	26		342,280	313,382
Delaware		3	7,623	10,980
Maryland		7	30,438	62,357
Virginia*				
North Carolina	9		96,226	84,090
South Carolina	6		62,301	45,237
Kentucky		11	39,566	115,889
Tennessee	10		56,757	26,311
Ohio	21		280,128	238,700
Louisiana		7	33,263	80,225
Indiana	13		176,552	166,980
Mississippi*				
Illinois	16		250,293	199,143
Alabama	8		76,366	72,086
Maine	7		70,426	42,396
Missouri	11		85,671	59,788
Arkansas	5		22,152	19,078
Michigan	8		128,550	97,060
Florida†	3			
Texas*				
Wisconsin	8		108,857	84,710
Iowa	8		120,399	74,040
California	5		54,592	54,078
Minnesota	4		43,542	28,072
Oregon		3	10,961	11,125
Kansas	3		31,049	14,019
West Virginia	5		29,025	20,306
Nevada	3		6,480	5,218
Nebraska	3		9,729	5,439
Georgia		9	57,134	102,822
Total	214	80	3,012,833	2,703,249

*No vote   † By legislature

From Edward McPherson, ed. *The Political History of the United States of America during the Period of Reconstruction, 1865-1870* (New York, 1865; reprint, ed. H. M. Hyman and H. Trefousse [New York: DaCapo, 1972]), p. 499.

had seemingly encouraged violence among anti-Reconstruction zealots.

Grant's victory was overwhelming in the Electoral College. But the popular-vote pattern (see accompanying chart) repeated the message of 1864 and 1866: The Democrats were strong. Whether Republican Reconstruction policies would continue to attract votes, with Johnson's obstructionism out of the White House, was problematic. The night before Grant took office, novice Republican congressman Robert Ingersoll expressed this concern:

> We can't run the machine [any longer] merely by making faces at Andy Johnson. . . . The people said why in hell . . . don't we have peace in the South—Andy Johnson—Why are not some of the traitors hung?—Andy Johnson— . . . What the devil makes the roads so muddy—measles so bad—whooping cough so prevalent—Why G–d d– –n it, Andy Johnson. We can sing this song only until tomorrow.[6]

Tomorrow came. Republicans no longer had Andy Johnson to kick around. Ingersoll's jocular analysis of the problem facing Republicans was soon tested. The outcome of Grant's first two years in office, 1869–70, determined the final configurations of Reconstruction, and brought the decade to an end with most Americans in confident spirit.

FOOTNOTES

1. The best recent evaluation is M. L. Benedict, *A Compromise of Principle: Republicans and Reconstruction* (New York: Norton, 1974).
2. To Peter Force, Dec. 3, 1865, Force Papers, Boston University Library.
3. Quoted in Bernard Schwartz, *The Law in America: A History* (New York: McGraw-Hill, 1974), p. 94.
4. *Congressional Globe,* 39th Cong., 2d sess., p. 1076 (Feb. 7, 1867).
5. March 7, 1868, in Massachusetts Historical Society *Proceedings* (1912), p. 159.
6. *Letters of Robert G. Ingersoll,* ed. E. I. Wakefield (New York: Philosophical Library, 1951), pp. 156–57.

EPILOGUE / CONFIDENT AMERICANS of 1869-70

Retreats from Reconstruction

"THE REPUBLICANS have exploited the negro too intensely," Walt Whitman mused at the height of the impeachment trial, "and there comes a reaction."[1] Reaction, or, better, many reactions, to Reconstruction occurred. But in the century since Whitman set down his impression, and especially during the last twenty years, scholarship has modified and refined his insight into the nature of white America's lessening concern for black Americans.

This new scholarship does not confirm that Republicans, in a merely opportunistic sense, had overexploited the southern Negro issue. Nor does it support claims that northern racism or Republicans' subservience to business interests caused the shift away from racially liberal Reconstruction policies. Reconstruction as it related to blacks had never been a central issue to most white Americans. Republicans had only reluctantly acknowledged that any national Reconstruction commitment existed, and, as a party, had been inclined to drop it ever since Appomattox. Driven toward grudging, temporary recommitments, reluctant Republicans wished quickly to lay down the Reconstruction burden. Now, in 1870, even relatively steadfast Reconstructionists concluded either that the substance of what they had sought had been won, or that further effort was no longer worthwhile.

Pride in Reconstruction achievements, more than prejudice against blacks, was what motivated Republicans' choices of ends and means. Grant's 1869 inauguration symbolized the passing of a turbulent decade. Johnson was out. Republicans were dominant in Congress. Seemingly, a real two-party structure existed in the southern states at last. The crises that had recurringly threatened the American federal system since 1820 were finished, it appeared. The 1868 election results, and those of the 1870 congressional and state contests, indicated that the political center was attracting voters in large numbers.

Aging abolitionist zealots saw in Grant's inauguration and the ratification of the Fifteenth Amendment, proofs that three decades of antislavery agitation were, at last, fittingly concluded. White Unionists (scalawags), northern immigrants to southern states (carpetbaggers), and Negroes, including black veterans of the Union's armies, now voted and held office. A Negro took Jefferson Davis' United States Senate seat. Another black was admitted to practice before the United States Supreme Court. It appeared in 1870 that the old secessionist, slave-owning leadership was displaced forever. Frederick Douglass and Wendell Phillips agreed that American antislavery societies should close up shop. These organizations had long sparked the movement for racial reform. Now that spark dimmed.

Many other sparks faded by 1870. Some of the great humanitarian leaders were retired or dead, and their loss was significant. No cause could suffer the death of a Thaddeus Stevens without loss of thrust and vigor. Such leaders were not replaced by like-minded younger recruits. History was reshaping social thought and directions. For a fateful span of years, 1862–70, a consensus existed that patriotic goals were pinned to improvement in the condition of blacks. Once those goals were realized, as seemed to be true in 1870, disassociation from Reconstruction politics was in order.

With the ratification of the Fifteenth Amendment, many reformist Republican frontrunners turned to other pursuits, convinced that southern Negroes would now protect their own interests by voting and litigation. Lawyers, for example, plunged again into the work of law codification. By 1873, several states had emulated New York's "Field Code" of the 1850s, and the United States statutes had been revised, if not wholly rationalized.

In 1870, almost no one, certainly no black, suggested that the status of Negroes had not risen. Negroes were now struggling to gain mastery over the white man's tools—education and literacy—denied to slaves. In 1860, of every 100 American children, 60 whites were enrolled in schools, and 2 Negroes. In 1870 the white figure was virtually unchanged, but the number of Negroes had risen to about 20. And in the next decade, though white enrollment still remained about the same, Negro enrollments climbed to 34. Howard University, including a law school, now existed.

In 1860, something close to 100% of Negroes were illiterate. By 1870, this figure was reduced to about 80% (compared to about 11% for whites). Within twenty years, Negro illiteracy was reduced to 57%; white, to 8%. Twenty years more, and the black rate was reduced to 30%; the white, to 5%. In short, by 1910, the difference in illiteracy rates between the races was reduced from approximately 70% to 25%.

In 1870, increasing numbers of Negroes, lacking capital and credit, were engaging in various forms of sharecropping. We know now that sharecropping contracts were to degenerate to mere exploitation, with social costs all Americans still pay. But in 1870 the whites as well as blacks, Kansans as well as Carolinians, were entering into tenant relationships. Sharecroppers were, after all, responsible contractors, a far prouder status than slave. In general, white America saw nothing amiss in such arrangements. A century ago, sharecropping seemed somewhat analogous to Congress' encouragement of transcontinental railroads by land grants.

A heartening number of Negroes escaped or transcended tenancy, despite horrific obstacles. By 1870, Virginia Negroes for example, were beginning painfully to buy land, to such effect that by the century's end they owned over 1 million acres, involving more than 25,000 farms. Land and building assessments on Negroes were almost $13 million. Nowhere did blacks enjoy a fair return on their labor, or truly equal opportunity. Yet, for the first time, they had *some* opportunity, and used it. These were Herculean achievements over vast odds. It was white Americans' judgment in 1870 that an adequate base had been built for further progress. Now it was up to black would-be climbers to climb. Self-help, struggle, and self-improvement was the gospel preached by Frederick Douglass as well as by Andrew Carnegie.

A substantial impulse toward reunion and Reconstruction had come from evangelical Protestant churches. These churches were intimately connected with the Republican party. They volunteered the funds, personnel, and votes that made possible the Christian Commission and the Freedmen's Bureau, among many other voluntaristic enterprises. By 1870, several of the most important church denominations had won, or lost, their southern missionary campaigns. Churches' central boards shifted attention away from the American South to new missionary bonanzas in Africa and Asia. Freedmen were now registered Baptists and Methodists, in the main, and were organizing racially segregated congregations. It was already clear that Negroes were welcome as co-congregationists only in the rarest white church or synagogue. Nevertheless, free now to engage in worship and Bible instruction as they chose (slaves had been forbidden to learn to read even the Bible), Negroes were beginning to build a remarkable spiritual community, with such energy and commitment that within one generation (by 1906), 37,000 Negro churches, claiming 3.7 million communicants and owning church property valued at over $56 million, served black America.

White women were among the prime movers of the Protestant churches' Civil War and Reconstruction auxiliaries. By 1870, untold numbers of female workers in good causes were more sensitive to distant Asia and Africa or, paradoxically, to very local distresses and evils, than to the problems of southern blacks. SPCA and antivice crusades close to home preempted the interest, energy, and zeal of Ladies Bountiful. Some militants, erstwhile Reconstructionists, were organizing to win equal civil and political rights for women. They were indignant that the nation had seen fit, in the Fourteenth and Fifteenth Amendments, to accord black men rights denied almost all white women.

Intellectuals among Republicans had invigorated Reconstruction. Their common conviction had been that equality of all men was a self-evident truth; that race was not a factor in a man's worth. But by 1870, Charles Darwin's writings, especially as distorted by disciples and exploiters in the theories of "social Darwinism," led to the erroneous view that white dominance was somehow the result of "natural selection"—a view not advocated by Darwin himself. Men of good will found it more difficult to argue against science, even perverted science, than against frank racism.

By 1870, it was clear that former slaves were not yet competing on the same terms as whites. But the fact that white resistance to the Constitution and laws prevented black self-defense and economic advance was increasingly obscured or ignored. Endless, wearying violence and threats of violence directed against Negroes in the South became common. Blacks who dared to practice the rights, remedies, and responsibilities of Americans were, increasingly, left without supporters. Northern workmen and farmers were more concerned about associating in unions and Granges for their self-defense than about the plight of blacks. The energy, patience, and will that had been devoted to Reconstruction flagged. In 1870, the South, and Negroes, were on the downward swing of the pendulum of social conscience. They were disappearing below the horizons of most Americans' awareness. The return motion was a long time in coming, and in the 1970s consistent concern appears again to be in ebb.

Whatever else troubled the South, the region's Negroes were remarkably pacific. The degree of blacks' devotion to law-and-order, even while denied rewards for their devotion, is difficult to appreciate today. The explanations offered in 1870 included a judgment that the orderliness of blacks proved their innate inferiority, another view was that blacks' patient good citizenship showed their lack of interest in exercising citizenship's rights and responsibilities. The patience of blacks made it even easier for increasing numbers of whites to turn away from southern matters, even though, during the early 1870s, southern blacks were occasionally to suffer such outrageous publicized injuries (no one knows the unrecorded troubles blacks saw) as briefly to swing national attention back to their hurts and needs.

Time was on the white South's side. It possessed enduring willingness to violate by private acts (allegedly private acts, at least) the Constitution and laws, and to concentrate on maintaining white supremacy. Short of a semipermanent, bureaucratized, coercive national presence to protect Negroes (a political impossibility), northern whites saw no way to assure the survival of Reconstruction's civil rights policies. By 1870, Andrew Johnson and his supporters had substantially won their war against further uncomfortable changes in race relations.

The Republicans' View

By 1870, severe splits were developing among majority Republicans in Congress and in the states concerning many policy questions, including Reconstruction. Most Republicans concluded in 1869–70 that almost all the southern states had adequately reformed themselves. As promised, Republican congressmen admitted "reconstructed" states' delegations.

Some worried Republicans insisted that acceptance was going too fast. Once it readmitted a state, Congress lost the capacity to monitor the state's adherence to commitments. Minority Radicals begged Republican colleagues in Congress to make readmission of a state contingent upon permanent guarantees by the state never to alter its equal-suffrage commitment, in its constitution, laws, or practices. This went too far for most Republicans, however. It implied a long-term national presence in state affairs.

Taking another approach, some Radical congressmen perceived considerable potential in the Constitution's "guarantee" clause. By its terms, the nation must guarantee each state a broadly representative (republican) form of government. But again, actually applying this clause in order to perpetuate Reconstruction involved a greater use of federal power than the majority of Republicans cared to contemplate. The party majority was willing only to "jawbone" at readmitted southern states.

The Fifteenth Amendment, ratified in 1870, salved consciences, and Congress was prepared to ignore subterfuges devised to evade its intent, such as voting requirements involving property, literacy, or length of residence. Indeed, Congress specifically excluded from the amendment's final text race discrimination related to state officeholding as an infringement of the national rights of citizenship. Nevertheless, the Fifteenth Amendment could have created the revolution so many had hoped for, if its clear intent had prevailed.

Wider Vistas

Here and abroad, this was a generation of materialists who exalted principles of compromise and did not think of them as compromises of principle. To Americans, the Union, fiscal-social stability, and abolition were inseparable measures of a good society. Evidence came from abroad as well as at home that these precious goals were won. Two international conferences held at Paris in 1867, on global antislavery and monetary-stability developments, made the American delegations their Cinderellas. Not only had the world's largest slave-owning nation become abolitionist, it was returning swiftly to specie-based hard money policies, and delegates to these conferences applauded.

Commentators asserted that Americans were also learning to

maintain domestic stability by limiting the tendency of states and cities toward democratic excesses. Foremost among the books analyzing limitations on government powers were Thomas McIntyre Cooley's *A Treatise on the Constitutional Limitations Which Rest Upon the Legislative Power of the States of American Union* (1868), the earlier-noted John Dillon's *Law of Municipal Corporations* (1867), John Jameson's *The Constitutional Convention: Its History, Powers, and Modes of Proceeding* (1867), and John U. Taylor's *Treatise on the American Law of Landlord and Tenant* (1866). All quickly became standard law-school texts, and remained basic treatises well into the twentieth century. The message of these astonishingly influential volumes was that state power was not plenary after all. Even the state constitutional convention, that expression of *vox populi*, was not sovereign in nature. State powers, including those delegated to counties and municipalities, were innately limited. These limits could be appropriately defined via lawsuits brought by individuals under the Constitution as amended since 1865, rather than by confrontations between nation and states.

This approach appealed to Republicans. The legal techniques worked out for southern-state Reconstruction might be applied to all states to blunt the increasingly worrisome class attacks on private property and entrepreneurship that merchants and manufacturers discerned in northern states and cities.

Class antagonisms and violence were emerging in Europe in the mid-nineteenth century. France was soon to be bloodied in the Paris Commune uprisings. During the 1860s, ideas deriving from Marx's *Das Capital* and from Ferdinand LaSalle's workingmen's organizations, had, it was feared, filtered into America. Southern whites depicted racial egalitarians as advocates of class war and racial strife. Reconstruction amendments and laws were interpreted as undermining the principles of property ownership.

By 1870, political corruption and social turbulence in northern cities appeared to many persons as more dangerous than less visible events in southern states. Northern leaders focused on problems in their own back yards. The new class radicalism appeared to be centering in cities, and property owners were comforted by evidence that the law and custom were on their side. For example, owners of urban rental property were greatly disturbed during the '60s because tenants had found loopholes in landlords' prior rights. Taylor's book on rental law became the landlords' bulwark. And during the '70s the principles outlined here and in other basic legal treatises were incorporated into newly codified state and federal laws. In 1870, the fight against dangerous ills in northern cities, like that against those in southern states, appeared to be winnable, if not won; success was possible on all fronts, it seemed.

More Pride than Prejudice

As time passed, pride grew in Civil War and Reconstruction accomplishments. "Touched with fire," in Oliver Wendell Holmes' phrase, Lincoln's generation apologized for little. The post-1870 retreat from Reconstruction was a result of confidence as well as prejudice.

In 1870, Robert Dale Owen, the internationally famous utopian reformer, antislavery congressman, diplomat, and entrepreneur, looked back across the enormous "war-gulf," as he termed it, that Americans had traveled since 1860. Owen noted particularly that, the public- and private-sector institutions that in 1860 had floundered in shocking irrelevancy, in 1870 were flourishing. Treasured nation-state constitutional relationships, which allowed great diversity in almost all commercial, legal, and political activities, were not merely preserved but strengthened. The bloodiest war fought since Waterloo had resulted not in mass retributions on the losers, but in improvement in the condition of millions of Americans. Protection of individuals' civil rights and liberties was now a national commitment even if not yet entirely accomplished.

Moreover, applied social science promised to raise the quality of government; and applied science and technology were reshaping the continental environment and extracting new wealth. Silver discoveries in 1870, at the Comstock Lode and elsewhere, implied continued stability for the national currency, despite soaring populations and credit demands. Greenbackers' and other debtors' demands for state stay-laws on debt payments, inflationary policies, or outright debt repudiations appeared to be lessening—permanently, most Republicans hoped. Technological novelties in agriculture, communications, and industry continued to multiply. And Francis A. Walker, superintendent of the 1870 Census, reported to Congress that "so fierce and vast [was] the growth of the nation as a whole," that the decennial census could not fully keep up with the country's "internal changes."[2]

In this climate, new businesses proliferated. The development of petroleum-derived dyes for use in wool manufacturing benefited Philadelphian John Wanamaker, who modernized the production and marketing of men's clothing. In 1861, according to Mercantile Agency credit raters, Wanamaker sold $24,000 worth of goods; in 1870, $2.1 million. Relying on mass inventory turnover and standard sizes and patterns for his product, Wanamaker was respected for reliability of personal notes and product quality. At Durham Station in North Carolina, Washington Duke, a penniless Confederate veteran and a scalawag, began producing tobacco products in 1865. Three

Wanamaker & Brown's clothing store in Philadelphia, about 1869. John Wanamaker started the business in 1861, with his brother-in-law Nathan Brown. Within ten years they owned the largest retail men's store in the United States.

NEW YORK PUBLIC LIBRARY

years later his "Bull Durham" company was one of the three leading manufacturers in the state. The industry snowballed as a result of improved communications and changing consumer tastes in its favor. By 1870 Duke's was only one of 111 Tarheel tobacco manufactories, but his family's vast fortune was in the making.

Radical changes in manufacturing were stimulated by the availability of the vernier caliper and the far better quality and increased quantity of pig iron and steel (increasingly significant by 1870). The caliper was first made in the United States in 1851. In 1860 it was still rare, but in 1870 it was common in machine-tool manufacture. Its use enabled relatively specialized factory hands to produce machines that made, for instance, far more precise steam-engine valves, cash registers, lathes, clocks, sewing machines, and sewer pipes. The dependability and ease of maintenance of new machine tools and consumer items were rapidly altering American styles of industry, labor, and life.

Self-schooled factory and farm workers were able now to maintain lathes, McCormick reapers, and numerous other machines, and neighborhood laborers or tinkerers could keep street railways and water-supply and sewage systems in working order. Gangs of untutored laborers, under skilled direction, were able to build the Brooklyn Bridge and the transcontinental rail lines. Machines were entering daily life in a manner that still endures. There were those who, like Thoreau, responded negatively to this change, but they were increasingly regarded as anachronistic fossils.

In 1870, reports by field agents of the credit-rating Mercantile Agency reflect a healthy economy manned by tireless, effective entrepreneurs. On one end of the scale, John D. Rockefeller's refinery was estimated ". . . to have made over $700 [thousand] clear during the past 3 years." On the other, a minor merchant in Charleston, South Carolina, William Lobby, who had lost all his prewar assets by mid-1865, in 1870 again owned his own store and was worth $3,000.[3] For its part, the Mercantile Agency, after a wartime halt in growth, was on the verge of substantial expansion in its operations. The Agency had 17 urban branches in 1858, 28 by 1870, and now known as R. G. Dun & Company was to establish 41 more in the '70s (15 in 1872 alone).[4] A rival credit agency, founded by John M. Bradstreet in 1849 in Cincinnati, also was on the move as com-

A. J. Russell photographed this steam shovel at Echo Canyon, Utah, in 1869. The manual labor of immigrants was much more significant in railroad construction than machinery such as this.
THE OAKLAND MUSEUM

merce flourished, opening offices in many cities, often identical to those of its competitor.

Looking back, we can see how the economy and society of the re-United States were bending toward modern ways. Samuel P. Hays has shown how labor was becoming increasingly specialized and management was separating itself from labor. Similarly, expert, efficient merchandisers and manufacturers like John Wanamaker began to displace the general store and the wholesalers and jobbers who served it. Among financiers, investment specialists were drifting off from commerical bankers; the wider and more complex price-and-market network of 1870 required more specialized concentrations of skills and information than bankers could provide. This trend was later seen as leading to the manipulation of "the little man by irresponsible financiers." But in 1870 almost no commentator discerned such a danger. Instead, the liquid capital that money managers made available to finance commerce and industry was seen as a blessing, in terms of the profits and improved consumer goods that emerged.

Specialization became the mark of modernization. Chicago commodity merchants were developing a unified grain-marketing system. The mountains of wheat that were once carried bag by bag on laborers' backs to ships or rail termini for transport to the East and to Europe, by 1870 were transported largely in freight-car bulk loads to huge grain elevators. Immense steam-driven buckets dumped the grain from elevators into the rail cars or ships. Labor and distribution costs plummeted; the capital investments required for such innovations soared.

Like manufacturers and merchants, farmers and ranchers were on a road leading to specialization and high capitalization. More than 90% of Americans in 1870 were farmers, but subsistence farming was giving way to commercial, cash-crop agriculture. Combines, harvesters, and reapers lowered the need for labor and increased efficiency, but also increased demand for accessory machines, fertilizers, improved seeds, and credit. The new land-grant colleges and industry (including transportation) provided the research and skills needed to supply the new machines, fertilizer, and seeds; new banking and investment institutions supplied the credit. Only southern agriculture remained labor-intensive. The ebbing of Reconstruction tended to insulate the South from the currents that were changing the rest of agrarian and industrial America.

Government and law remained dedicated to the least possible interference with private enterprise, no matter how huge enterprises became; government action was still largely directed to releasing entrepreneurial energies, not regulating them. The many new law schools and bar associations in existence by 1870 further rationalized corporation law, and adapted agency, contract, and tort law to more modern needs. The first public and private law schools west of the Mississippi (Iowa's and Washington University in St. Louis), were in operation by 1870, as was the first Negro law school (at Howard).

Government stability, especially in states, greatly stimulated corporation development. Corporations, which were better organized to collect investment capital and to manipulate the environment than single ownerships or partnerships, increased their advantage by recruiting experts, influencing legislators, and applying the most modern actuarial and marketing techniques. Their potential stature in the universe of business is indicated in a Dun & Bradstreet report, dated January 29, 1870, on the Standard Oil Company of Ohio.

> This is now an incorporated company under the name of the "Standard Oil Company" with an authorized capital of 1 million dollars all of which is paid in. The stockholders are John D. Rockefeller (who is President of the Co.), Henry M. Flagler (who is the Treasurer & Secretary), William Rockefeller of NY (who is Vice President).

> Samuel Andrews (who is Superintendent), B. Jennings of Fairfield Ct. and we think A. Stone . . . all of whom represent a joint responsibility of some $4,000,000. Their Refinery is the largest in the U.S. having a daily refining capacity of some 1200 packages. The officers and stockholders are all men of high standing and have capacity. Wealthy, reliable and safe for any credit they may need. Aside from the paid up capital they hold some $150,000 borrowed capital invested. A + A1.[5]

Corporations had been merely state-created artificial persons, possessed of no agreed privileges. But by the end of the '60s, corporation managers and their lawyers were beginning to insist that corporations should enjoy special privileges against adverse state action such as the Grangers' rate-setting regulations, no matter how big the popular majorities that demanded the action. A drift among some lawyers whose major clients were corporations was becoming noticeable, to employ the Fourteenth Amendment as a shield for their clients. By the terms of a legal theory that was beginning to develop, the Fourteenth Amendment's restraints on a state depriving its citizens of life, liberty, or property without due process of state law, applied also to artificial citizens such as corporations. The courts were seen not only as the best instruments for protection of freedmen's rights, but also as a means of securing new freedoms for corporations.

This, perhaps ironic, conjunction is apparent in the appointment to the nation's Supreme Court, in December 1869, of Edwin M. Stanton, who had served the Union heroically during the war and Reconstruction and was also an outstanding commercial and patent lawyer. The Court that Stanton joined as Associate Justice was a Court whose condition contrasted sharply with what had obtained in 1860. Since 1789 the Supreme Court had lacked jurisdiction in basic, workaday matters of property, civil, and political rights. Then, in the 1857 Dred Scott decision, the Court had misconstrued the Constitution so outrageously, with respect to the adequacy of national power and functions and the nature of American citizenship, as to lose almost all credibility. As a result, the high Court became virtually irrelevant to public and private needs.

During the Civil War and Reconstruction decade, however, successive Congresses gambled that the Court had reformed itself, and, with presidential approval, impressively increased its jurisdiction to include many more classes of appeals from state courts and from lower federal courts. The court also benefited from Lincoln's wise appointments, such as Salmon Chase, David Davis, Stephen Field, and Samuel Miller. By 1870 the Supreme Court and the federal district courts once again functioned as an effective branch of government. With exceptions, the Supreme Court's decisions on both war issues and commercial-law questions were meaningful and respected. And, by 1870, in coping with litigation rising from the Civil War, Reconstruction, and the rapid changes in industry, communications, agriculture, and urban environments, the Court had at hand a vastly improved Constitution over what had obtained ten years earlier.

These alterations in only one public-sector institution, the Supreme Court, reflect the enormous distance the nation had traveled from 1860 to 1870. In 1870 the President and the Congress, and states, counties, and cities as well as the Supreme Court, all functioned far more meaningfully and effectively than could even have been imagined in 1860. And private institutions, ranging from charitable to professional to entrepreneurial, manifested a similar competence.

This strength and sufficiency of public- and private-sector institutions was an essential element in the restoration of confidence in the rewon Union. That disputes could be resolved by means of ordinary constitutional, legal, and political procedures was again taken for granted. Lobbyists, adversary litigants, and alternative candidates replaced the negative politics of secession, to which American institutions had no effective response other than soldiers.

By 1870, it made sense again to aspire and strive, whether for selfish or humanitarian purposes, because it was possible again to achieve almost any aim. Visions were worth having. As the decade of the '60s ended, this generation, excited by the potential of a reunified nation and the new advances in science, technology, and social science, looked forward more than back.

This alteration in outlook, from pessimism at the decade's start to confidence at its end, reflected accurately the steps American society had taken between 1860 and 1870. In 1860 safe passage was at best a dim possibility. But despite all odds, Americans had found goals worth striving toward and new means that were consistent with their traditional institutions, customs, and concepts. So equipped, they reached a more perfect Union of states and a markedly better condition of life for millions of their countrymen.

FOOTNOTES

1. Walt Whitman, *The Correspondence, 1868–1875,* ed. Edwin Miller (New York: New York University Press, 1961), p. 15.

2. U.S. Secretary of the Interior, Census Office, *Compendium of the Ninth Census, June 1, 1870* (Washington, 1872), p. 5.

3. Dun & Bradstreet Papers, Ohio, vol. 41, p. 154, on Rockefeller. On Lobby, *ibid.,* South Carolina, vol. 6, p. 73.

4. J. H. Madison, "The Evolution of Commercial Credit Reporting Agencies in Nineteenth Century America," *Business History Review,* XLVIII (Summer, 1974), 174.

5. Dun & Bradstreet Papers, Ohio, vol. 41, p. 228.

INDEX

abolitionists (*see also* slavery), 28–29, 40, 43, 45, 50, 55, 93, 101, 113, 119, 120, 121, 132, 187, 272, 278
Across the Continent: A Summer's Journey to the Rocky Mountains . . . and the Pacific States, with (House) Speaker (Schuyler) Colfax (Samuel Bowles), 171
Adams, John Quincy, 185
agriculture (*see also* farms, farming):
  during Civil War, 123, 170
  during Reconstruction, 198, 199, 205–208, 281, 287
  prior to secession, 9–12, 18, 43, 182
Alabama, 47
Alaska purchase, 172
Andersonville Prison, 167
Antietam, Md., 118, 119
Appalachian mountains, 102, 103, 158
Appleton's Annual Cyclopedia, 179, 219
Appomattox, 3, 57, 71, 99, 143, 159, 166, 169, 170, 172–173, 182, 184, 198, 213, 214, 217, 267, 272
Arkansas, 49, 150
army, 247, 251, 253–254, 257, 261, 266
  Confederate, 72–74, 79, 84, 96, 98, 103–109, 115, 116–119, 125–127, 129–137, 146–149, 152, 158–163
  draft, 138, 146, 166

army (*cont.*)
Negro troops in, 88, 123, 126, 127, 144, 146, 151, 163, 272
Union, 72–74, 79, 84, 86, 88, 89, 90, 91, 93, 95–96, 99, 101, 103–109, 110, 111, 112–113, 115, 116–119, 121–127, 129–137, 138, 139, 140, 143, 144, 146–149, 153, 154–155, 158–163, 165, 166, 167, 183, 230, 272
Army Medical Bureau, 195
Army of the Potomac, 86, 105–107, 117–119, 124, 129–134, 146
Articles of Confederation, 70
Articles of War, 114, 141
associations, 13–17, 26, 90, 97, 125, 194–198, 221–222, 234–241
bar, 16–17, 287
exclusions from, 16
and government, 14, 194–198, 237
and slavery, 32, 194–198
Atlanta, Ga., 149, 151, 152, 158, 182
Atlantic cable, 173, 213

Bache Corporation, B. F., 180
Bagehot, Walter, 184
Baltimore, Md., 83–84
Baltimore and Ohio Railroad, 176
banks, banking, 11, 17, 43, 45, 122, 180, 194, 199–200, 203–205, 286, 287
federal reserve system, 203–205
national banks, 203–205, 254
Barlow, S. L. M., 86
battles (*see also* Civil War):
Antietam, 119
Bull Run, 105, 109, 117, 119, 131
Chattanooga, 136–137
Gettysburg, 131–134
Manassas, 117–119, 131
naval, 115–116
Peninsular Campaign, 115–117, 125
battles (*cont.*)
Vicksburg, 134-137
Beard, Charles, 4
Beauregard, Pierre, 105
Bell, John, 43, 45
Belmont, August, 86
Bergh, Henry, 234
Beringer, Richard, 96
Bill of Rights, 230
black codes, 240–241, 243–247, 250, 251, 254, 255
blacks, *see* Negroes
Blaine, James G., 260
Blair, Montgomery, 186–187, 267
Blodgett, William, 214
Booth, John Wilkes, 163
border states, 72, 74, 79, 86, 101
Bradstreet, John M., 283–284
Brady, Mathew, 124, 135
Breckinridge, John, 43, 45
Bright, John, 266
Broglie, Albert de, 214
Brooklyn Bridge, 226–227, 283
Brown, John, 45, 50
Bryce, James, 21, 38
Buchanan, James, 1, 42–43, 52, 61, 185, 206
and secession, 53–54, 60–61, 62, 71, 88
"Bull Durham" Company, 282
Bull Run, battle of, 105, 109, 117, 119, 131
business (*see also* commerce; industry):
postwar expansion, 223–229, 244, 256, 266, 281–282
during secession, 32–33, 142, 181–183
Butler, Benjamin, 124, 125

Calhoun, John C., 47, 72
caliper, 282–283
Cameron, Simon, 186–187
Campbell, John A., 52, 98
Carlyle, Thomas, 5, 12, 20, 93

Carnegie, Andrew, 92, 274
census:
  of 1860, 11, 12
  of 1870, 281
Central Pacific Railroad, 110–211
Charles River Bridge case, 19
Charleston, S.C., 72, 77
Charleston Mercury, 48
Chase, Salmon P., 145, 180, 186–187, 200, 203, 289
Chattanooga, Tenn., 136–137, 142, 148
Chicago, Ill., 176, 239
Christian Commission, 91, 125, 166, 195, 222, 234–236, 275
churches, 32, 274–275
city government, 20, 21, 22, 232–236, 248
civil liberties, 28, 40, 82, 83, 86, 122, 151, 251–253, 267, 281
civil rights, 28, 42, 163, 197, 251–253, 254–257, 258, 259, 260, 275, 277, 281
Civil War, 3, 4, 5, 6, 57, 71–88, 97, 99, 101–119, 120, 122, 124–137, 138–144, 146–149, 151, 153, 158–163, 185, 222–223, 230, 251, 256, 259, 275, 280, 289
  battles, 105, 115–119, 131–137, 146, 159
  eastern theater, 102–107, 115–119, 125–127, 129–134, 136–137, 146–148, 151, 158–163
  race relations during, 110–114
  security policies during, 110
  Union administration of South during, 125–127
  Union blockade during, 109–110, 115–116
  western theater, 107–109, 125, 134–137, 148–149
Clemenceau, Georges, 21, 184
Coast and Geodetic Survey, 199
Colfax, Schuyler, 170, 267
commerce, 17–18, 19, 35, 52, 62, 123, 171–172, 181–184, 198, 230–231, 244, 245, 266
communications, 9, 12–13, 52, 108, 136, 172–173, 199, 212–213, 281
"compromises" of 1820–1854, 39–40, 42, 45
Comstock, Anthony, 195, 235
Comstock Lode, 281
Confederacy, the (*see also* Civil War; Reconstruction; secession; slaves, slavery; South), 52, 60–74, 79, 82–83, 93–99, 101, 121
  Congress of, 67–70, 96, 98, 109
  constitution of, 52, 64–71, 74, 94–95, 99, 197, 222–223
  economic problems of, 97–98
  national government of, 93–99, 160–161
  presidency of, 68, 69
  state government of, 97–98
  and states' rights, 96–99
  structure and resources of, 93–96, 98, 99
  Supreme Court of, 94, 99
confiscation acts, 190
Congress, the, 26, 141, 153, 168, 197, 248, 249, 250, 264–265, 266, 272, 277, 289
  and civil rights, 254–261
  and Civil War, 82, 83, 84–86, 91, 95, 114, 122, 188–190
  and Fifteenth Amendment, 266, 272, 273, 275, 278
  and Fourteenth Amendment, 241, 257–259, 260, 267, 275, 288
  vs. Johnson, Andrew, 243, 247, 249–250, 260–266, 267, 271
  and the military establishment, 137–143, 188–189, 251
  and Military Reconstruction Act, 259–261

Congress (*cont*).
and Reconstruction, 144, 150, 188–190, 197–198, 201, 203–208, 246, 254–261
during secession, 49, 52–53, 54–56
and slavery, 39–40, 42, 43–45, 47, 120, 121, 158, 197
and Thirteenth Amendment, 57, 146, 158, 181, 241, 244, 246, 248, 250, 256, 260
and Thirteenth Amendment proposal, 56–57, 158
Conkling, Roscoe, 259
Constitution, the, 22, 43, 51, 53, 54–55, 56, 65, 66, 93, 94, 95, 99, 142, 146, 158, 249–250, 261–262, 276, 277–278, 279, 288, 289
Constitutional Convention: Its History, Powers, and Modes of Proceeding (John Jameson), 279
Cooke, Jay, 180, 203
Cornell University, 207
corporations, 17–18, 23, 223–229, 287–288
Country School, The (Winslow Homer), 24–25
courts (*see also* law), 244, 246
federal, 139–140, 182–184, 189–191, 248, 254, 255, 256
state, 140, 245, 253, 254, 258
credit reporting, 13, 32, 171, 177, 180, 283
Crittenden, John, 54–56
Cumberland, Virginia, 117
Currier & Ives, 61
Curtis, Benjamin R., 264–265

Darwin, Charles, 275–276
Das Kapital (Karl Marx), 279
Davis, David, 289
Davis, Henry W., 150–151, 152
Davis, Jefferson, 52, 65, 71, 72–74, 96, 136, 159, 162, 166, 272
Degler, Carl, 77
Delaware, 83, 90, 94, 156, 258
democracy, political, 17, 50, 55, 83, 88, 90, 96, 164–166, 188, 217
Democrats, Democratic Party, 40–43, 45, 49, 53, 88, 111, 124, 194, 249, 255, 256, 262, 263, 266
and Civil War, 74, 86–96, 112, 119, 131, 194, 199
in election of 1860, 45–47
in election of 1862, 89–96, 122–123, 194
in election of 1864, 151–157
in election of 1866, 258, 259
in election of 1868, 267–269
and Lincoln Reconstruction Proclamation, 145
and Negroes, 40–47, 86, 112, 120–121, 144, 252
in North, 42, 43, 45, 56, 74, 82, 86–88, 89–96, 101, 119, 120, 122, 131, 144, 145, 151–157, 193, 194, 197, 199, 247, 250–251
De Republica (Cicero), 244
Detroit, Mich., 80–81
Dicey, Edward, 20, 21, 23
Die Presse, 164
Digest of Opinions (Joseph Holt), 141
District of Columbia, 55, 90, 94
Donald, David Herbert, 70
Douglas, Stephen, 42, 45
Douglass, Frederick, 163, 246, 272, 274
Drake, Charles, 170
Dred Scott decision, 40, 43, 54, 84, 255, 257, 288
Duke, Washington, 281–282
Dun and Bradstreet, 13, 287
Dun & Co., R. G., 283
Dynamics of Modernization (Cyril Black), 3

Early, Jubal A., 149

Eaton, John, 113
Echo Canyon, Utah, 284–285
ecology, post-Civil War concern about, 229–231
economy:
during Civil War, 122–123
post–Civil War, 170–180, 213–214, 224–231, 281–288
during secession, 49
prior to secession, 7–8
education, 38, 43, 199, 273–274
Freedmen's Bureau schools, 196, 207
and Negroes, 28, 29, 273–274
parochial schools, 25
public schools, 16, 24–26, 29, 159
truant officers, 25–26, 29
universities, 199, 207, 273, 287
elections, 35–37, 38, 40, 88–89, 223
acceptance of, 35–36, 43–45
in the Confederacy, 96
corruption in, 36–37
of 1860, 29–30, 31–33, 38, 39, 45–47, 55
of 1862, 89, 119, 120, 121, 122–123
of 1864, 89, 144, 145–146, 151–158
of 1866, 258–259, 262, 263, 266
of 1868, 267–269, 272
emancipation, 51, 145, 151, 153, 181, 186–188, 263
Emancipation Proclamation, 119, 120–121, 122, 123–124, 144, 145, 146, 164, 198, 206
Emerson, Ralph Waldo, 5, 12, 93
Erie Railroad, 176, 225, 239
Europe, 21–22, 51, 74, 176, 217–218, 267, 279
exports, 9–11, 173

factories, 173, 179, 180, 283
farms, farming (*see also* agriculture), 122, 173, 179, 180, 266, 286–287
Farragut, David, 148
Farrar, Timothy, 38
federal agents, 42, 50
federal government:
during Civil War, 71–74, 77–88, 185–192, 200–202
control of military establishment, 137–145
and Negroes, 41–42, 43, 45, 253, 254–257
and patronage, 34, 90, 94, 96, 185–186
postal service, 21, 52, 95
during reconstruction, 205–208, 243, 245–247, 252, 255, 259–261, 266
rivalry among branches of, 185–191
during secession, 31–39, 49, 52–53, 54–57, 61–62
prior to secession, 19–21, 26, 97
and states, 193–200, 255, 279, 280–281
subsidies and aid, 202–212
federalism, 17, 21–23, 29–30, 32, 36, 38–40, 42, 43, 89–90, 91, 168, 173, 184, 231–232
Federalist Party, 42, 43, 68, 123, 194
Fessenden, William Pitt, 200
Field, Stephen, 289
"Field Code," 273
Fifteenth Amendment, 4, 266, 272, 273, 275, 278
57th Article of War, 88
First Amendment, 55–56
Florida, 47, 72, 97
Force, Manning, 254
Fort Donelson, 109
Fort Henry, 109
Fort Pickens, 61, 65–66, 71–72, 74
Fort Sumter, 4, 61, 65–66, 71, 72–74, 77, 78, 79, 84, 90, 107, 120, 123, 173, 199, 200
Fourteenth Amendment, 241, 257–259, 260, 267, 275, 288

Fredericksburg, Va., 124, 131, 146
freedmen, 195–199, 243–244, 250, 254, 275
Freedmen's Bureau, 166, 167, 195–199, 222, 245, 248, 253, 255, 256, 257, 275
  schools, 196, 207
free states, *see* North; Union
Frémont, John C., 107, 111–112, 120, 142, 144

Gardner, Alexander, 118, 160–161
Gelpcke v. *Dubuque*, 191, 219, 232–233
"General Orders #100" (Francis Lieber), 141
Georgia, 47
Gettysburg, Pa., 130, 131–134
grain farming, 9, 176, 179, 238–239, 241, 286
Granger Commission (Ill.), 238–239, 241
Grant, Ulysses S., 74, 109, 127, 134–137, 143, 146–149, 151, 159, 179, 254, 263, 266, 267–269, 272

Habeas Corpus Act, 84–86, 139–140
Harper's Weekly, 44, 162
Harrington, George, 200
Harvard University, 207
Haupt, Herman, 93
Hayes, Rutherford, 256
Hays, Samuel P., 286
Holmes, Oliver Wendell, 149, 280
Holt, Joseph, 141
Homestead Act, 199, 205–208, 229, 266
Hooker, "Fighting Joe," 129
Hopkins, John Baker, 12
Houston, Sam, 47
Howard, O. O., 245, 246
Howard University, 207, 273, 287
Howe, Timothy O., 105
Hurst, Willard, 205

Illinois, 223, 228
Illinois Central Railroad, 230, 239
Illustrated London News, 132
immigration, 8, 207–208, 266–267
import tariffs, 199, 203
Indians, 8, 21, 97, 167, 198, 266
industry:
  during Civil War, 123, 142, 170
  post–Civil War expansion of, 173, 205–208, 213–214, 244, 245, 254, 281, 282–283, 286
  prior to secession, 9, 11, 17, 43
inflation, 180–181
Ingersoll, Robert, 269
Inspector General's Office, 141, 142, 143
internal security, 79–83, 87–88, 89, 91, 109, 138–140, 166
Iowa, 191, 233
Irish, the, 16, 259

Jackson, Andrew, 33, 39, 47, 54, 185
Jackson, "Stonewall," 116–117, 131, 222
Jefferson, Thomas, 34, 40, 84, 185, 205–206, 222
Jews, 8, 16
Johnson, Andrew, 145–146, 166, 237, 243, 253, 255, 266, 267, 269, 272, 277
  abuse of executive power by, 243, 249–250, 262, 263
  and the army, 257, 258
  Fourteenth Amendment, opposition to, 257–259
  and the Freedmen's Bureau, 253–254, 256, 257
  impeachment of, 4–5, 243, 261–266, 267
  and party politics, 247–249
  pro-southern Democrats, 240, 243, 248–249, 251, 258–259, 260–261
  reconstruction plan of, 240, 247, 251, 253

Johnson, Andrew (*cont.*)
  struggle with Congress, 243, 247, 250, 256–257, 260–261
  vetoes by, 256, 257, 259, 260
Johnston, Joseph E., 116, 159
Joint Standing Committee on the Conduct of the War, 114, 141
Judge Advocate General Bureau, 141, 142

Kansas-Nebraska Act, 39–40, 54
Kentucky, 107–109, 153, 156, 258

labor, 9, 123, 198, 244, 267, 283–286
La Salle, Ferdinand, 279
law, 17–19, 23, 24–26, 28, 33, 83, 84, 90, 108, 118, 142, 144, 182–184, 197, 240, 245, 262 223–229, 247, 257, 273, 276, 287
  civil and criminal, 18, 144, 150, 182–184, 197, 240, 245, 262
  civil rights, 254–257, 260
  confiscation and test oath, 189–190, 223, 247, 248, 249, 252, 255, 259
  federal, 189–190, 199, 205–206, 223, 228, 247–249, 252, 255, 259, 280
  fugitive slave, 41, 42, 55, 111, 112, 183
  Habeas Corpus, 84–86, 139–140
  municipal, 83, 90, 184, 232–234, 244, 251
  national conscription, 138, 146, 166
  state, 90, 184, 218–241, 244, 245, 251, 280
law journals, 16–17
Law Magazine and Review, 217
Law of Municipal Corporations (John Dillon), 233, 279
lawyers, 15, 16, 23, 184, 273, 288
Lee, Robert E., 4, 117, 119, 131–134, 136, 146, 147, 149, 159
Lieber, Francis, 141
Lincoln, Abraham, 1, 4, 5, 7, 26, 30, 31, 33, 45, 49, 53, 64, 77–79, 89, 92, 95, 96, 98, 120, 131, 140, 148, 163–166, 168, 169, 194, 224, 249, 250, 253, 280
  assassination of, 163, 166, 171
  and Civil War, 78–79, 82, 84–86, 91, 92, 105, 109, 111, 113–114, 115–119, 131–134, 136, 138–143, 149, 153, 159, 168, 187, 191
  in 1860 election, 45–47
  in 1862 election, 122–123
  in 1864 election, 145–146, 152, 153–158
  Emancipation Proclamation, 119, 120–121, 123–124, 127, 144, 146, 153, 164
  executive power, use of, 144, 187–188, 249–250
  Habeas Corpus Act, 84–86, 139–140
  inaugural addresses of, 66, 71, 159
  and the military establishment, 138–143, 153
  Reconstruction Proclamation of, 144–145, 146, 149–151, 184, 197
  relationship with other government branches, 185–191, 201, 206
  and secession, 61, 62, 71, 73–74, 77–79
  and slavery, 50, 56, 113–114, 119, 120–121, 158, 163, 197
  Wade-Davis pocket veto of, 150, 256
literacy, 273–274
Lobby, William, 283
Louisiana, 47, 97, 125, 150, 159, 223, 225–228, 231, 239–241
Louisiana Purchase, 39

Lowell, James Russell, 57

McClellan, George B., 86, 93, 105, 106, 111–114, 115–119, 120, 123–124, 125, 127, 131, 142, 151–152, 156–157, 168
McCormick's reaper and harvester, 11, 282
McCulloch, Hugh, 200
McDowell, Irwin, 105
McKitrick, Eric, 95
Madison, James, 40
Maine, 39, 236
Mallory, S. R., 72
management-labor relations, 244, 286
Maryland, 83–86, 90, 94, 131, 232, 258
Marx, Karl, 164, 184
Massachusetts, 19, 228
Meade, George, 131–134
meat industry, 173, 174–175, 176, 179, 225–228, 231, 239–241
medicine, progress in, 180, 193–194, 237
Mercantile Agency, 13, 32, 171, 177, 180, 283
Mercer, John F., 55
Merryman, John, 84
Merryman case, 83–86, 190–191
Metropolitan Health Board, 237–238
Mexican War, 63, 103, 109
Military Director and Superintendent of Railroads, 136, 142
military establishment, 21, 137–143, 245, 251, 252
  civilian control of, 138–143, 168, 188–189
  1867 Military Bill, 259–261
  and the private sector, 141–143
Military Reconstruction Act, 259–261
militiamen, 78, 79, 80–81, 83, 97, 105, 137–138
Miller, Samuel, 289
Miller Farm, 178–179
Mineral Land Act, 206, 266
Mississippi, 47, 125
Mississippi River, 107, 109, 125, 136, 137
Missouri, 107, 109, 259
Missouri Compromise, 39–40, 54
Mobile, Alabama, 151
monetary-stabilization conference, 172, 278
Monitor, 115–116
Montgomery, Alabama, 52, 65–67, 71
More Perfect Union, A: The Impact of the Civil War and Reconstruction on the Constitution (Harold M. Hyman), 4
Morrill Land Grant College Act, 206–208, 209, 224, 236
Munn Brothers Corporation, 225, 230, 239

National Academy of Science, 199
navy, 72, 109–110, 116, 125
Negroes (*see also* slaves, slavery), 4, 5, 8, 16, 100, 144, 163
  abuse of, under black codes, 244–246, 251, 260, 262
  and civil rights, 163, 251–253, 255–258, 259
  during Civil War, 110–114, 123, 132
  and education, 163, 196, 273–274
  Emancipation Proclamation and, 119, 120–121, 122, 123, 144, 151, 164
  in North, 39, 42, 90, 132, 153
  and Reconstruction, 150, 252–253, 271–274, 275, 276–277
  and Thirteenth Amendment, 57, 146, 158, 181
  in Union army, 88, 123, 126, 127, 131, 144, 146, 151, 188, 272
  unprotected under Andrew John-

Negroes (*cont.*)
son administration, 248–249, 258, 260, 262
Neustadt, Richard E., 143
Nevins, Allan, 137
New Orleans, La., 124, 125, 231, 258
New York, N.Y., 234–238
New York Central Railroad, 176
New York Commercial and Financial Chronicle, 214
New York Tribune, 164
North, the (*see also* Civil War; Reconstruction; secession; slaves, slavery; Union), 3–4, 24–26, 39–40, 49, 51, 279, 280
post–Civil War achievements in, 169–180, 217–229, 266–267, 281–288
North Carolina, 49, 98
Northwest Ordinance, 34

Ohio River, 107, 109
oil industry, 178–179, 225–228
Oliphant, Laurence, 184
Owen, Robert Dale, 280

Pacific Railroad Act, 209
Panama Canal, 172
patents, 173, 198
Pendleton, George, 151
Peninsular Campaign, 115–117, 125
Pennsylvania, 131, 177, 179
Pennsylvania Railroad, 176
Pensacola, Fla., 71, 72
Petersburg, Va., 146–148, 151, 159
Peto, S. Morton, 170, 184
petroleum industry, 177, 281
Philadelphia, Pa., 282
Phillips, Wendell, 272
Pickens, Francis, 61
Pickering, John, 261
politics, political parties, 22–23, 34, 42–47, 91–93, 95–96, 98, 156–158, 194, 221, 231, 247, 250–254, 267, 280, 281
and Confederate government, 68, 70, 95–96
and government, 34, 35–36, 82, 89, 91–92, 95, 99, 158, 168
and two-party system, 34, 95, 101, 102, 156–158, 168, 190, 194, 249, 272, 275
Pope, John, 117–119
population, 8–9, 94, 281
Porter, David D., 148
postal service, 20–21, 52, 95, 248
Potomac River, 102, 103, 107, 116, 119
Potter, David, 95
presidency, the, 53, 185–187, 243–250, 262, 266, 289
private enterprise, 172–173, 221, 287
private sector, the (*see also* business; industry), 3, 5, 142, 208, 221, 247, 280
professional licensing boards, 236
Protestant churches, 222, 247, 274–275
Provost Marshal General's Bureau, 138–140, 142
public health, 15, 219, 222–223, 231–241
Public Health Board (New York), 236–238
public sector, the, 3, 5, 173, 221, 280

Radical Republicans and Reconstruction, The (Harold M. Hyman), 4
railroads, 191, 199, 267, 283, 284–285
in Civil War, 52, 107, 122, 123, 136–137, 142
growth of, 10, 11, 13, 43, 172–176, 198, 208–212, 225, 238–239

Reconstruction, 3–4, 5, 6, 60, 90, 99, 125, 144, 150, 156, 159, 167, 181–185, 193–194, 197–199, 218–241, 247–249, 250, 251–254, 256, 257, 259–261, 267, 269, 279, 280, 289
Congress and, 254–257, 259–261
Johnson and, 240, 247, 251, 253
Lincoln Proclamation of, 144–145, 146, 149–151, 184
retreat from, 271–278, 280, 287
and Wade-Davis Bill, 150–151, 163
Reid, Whitelaw, 92
Republicans, Republican Party, 4, 30, 31, 43–47, 49, 68, 78, 82, 86, 88, 144, 194–198, 222, 247, 249, 250, 262
and Civil War, 74, 86–88, 96, 112, 119, 120
conflict with Andrew Johnson, 256–257
in election of 1860, 45–47
in election of 1862, 122–123
in election of 1864, 145–146, 151–158, 194–198
in election of 1866, 258–259
in election of 1868, 267–269
and Negroes, 251–254, 256–260
and Reconstruction, 149–151, 194–198, 201, 205–206, 251–261, 271–273, 274, 275, 277–278
and secession, 56, 62, 63, 194–198
and slavery, 43–47, 50, 56, 62, 71, 112, 113–114, 120–121, 144, 158
Resources and Prospects of America, Ascertained During a Visit to the States in the Autumn of 1865, The (S. Morton Peto), 170
Richmond, Va., 98, 102, 103, 115, 116, 117, 146, 159, 160–161, 182
riots, 131–134, 258, 267
Rockefeller, John D., 179, 225, 283, 287
Rosecrans, W. S., 136
Russell, A. J., 210–211, 284–285

Sanitary Commission, 91, 125, 166, 195, 198, 222, 234–241
Savannah, Georgia, 159
Schumpeter, Joseph, 143
Scott, Thomas A., 93
secession, 2, 3, 4, 19, 29–30, 31–39, 47–99, 109, 119, 144, 169, 190, 240, 243, 252, 258, 267, 272
attempts at compromise, 54–56
effects of, on business, 32–33, 52
effects of, on government, 38–39, 60–62
reasons for, 50–51, 60–64, 70–71, 99, 121
and southern unionists, 47–49, 107
securities manipulators, 225–228
Seddon, James, 98
Sedition Act, 40, 82, 251, 261
Seward, William, 172, 186–187
Seymour, Horatio, 267
sharecropping, 274
Shenandoah River Valley, 103, 105, 117, 149
Sheridan, Philip, 148
Sherman, William T., 148–149, 151, 152, 158–159, 266
slaves, slavery (*see also* Negroes), 2, 3, 7, 26–29, 30, 34, 39–40, 41–42, 43, 45, 47, 50–51, 54–57, 60, 62, 64, 65, 71, 95, 96, 99, 102, 103, 107, 111–114, 119, 120, 124, 126, 151, 153, 169, 181, 230, 245, 251, 252, 254, 267, 272–273, 276, 279
and Civil Rights Bill, 255
and "compromises" by Congress, 39–40, 42, 54–56
and Confederate constitution, 64–65, 67, 71

slaves, slavery (*cont.*)
and Emancipation Proclamation, 119, 120–121, 122, 123–124, 145, 146, 206, 220
in North, 39, 42, 43, 50, 90, 94
police patrol of, in South, 28–29, 30, 96
and political parties, 40–47, 151, 195–198, 206
property rights in, 26–29, 30, 39–40, 41–42, 43, 50–51, 54–57, 60, 65, 120, 124, 150, 190, 230
runaways, 27, 28, 41, 42, 43, 50, 51, 55, 111–113
and secession, 32, 50–51, 121
and Thirteenth Amendment, 57, 158, 220
slave states, *see* Confederacy; South
social reform, post–Civil War, 231–241
Society for the Prevention of Cruelty to Animals (SPCA), 234–235, 275
South, the (*see also* Civil War; Confederacy; Reconstruction; secession; slaves, slavery), 2, 4, 26–29, 45, 243, 247, 248, 250, 251, 280, 287
Negroes in, after Reconstruction, 276–277
political parties in, 40–43, 272
Unionists in, 47–49, 107, 245, 248–249, 258, 260, 262, 272
South Carolina, 4, 7, 48, 54, 72, 79
Springfield, Mass., *Republican*, 170
Squibb Corporation, E. R., 180
Standard Oil Company, 287–288
Stanford, Leland, 210–211
Stanton, Edwin M., 1, 6, 93, 115, 136, 142–143, 163, 186–187, 260, 261, 262, 288
state government, 14, 20, 21, 22–23, 24–29, 191, 218–241, 252, 255, 257, 259, 277–278
state government (*cont.*)
in South, 26–29, 66–67, 144, 150, 219, 243–246, 248, 251–253, 259–260
state power, 24–29, 184, 218–219, 232–236, 240–241, 243, 246, 251, 255, 270
states' rights, 40, 42, 43, 45, 66–67, 86, 96–99, 122, 151, 199–200, 250–253, 257, 267
Steamboat Inspection Service, 199
steam shovel, 284–285
Stephens, Alexander, 52, 65, 159
Stevens, Thaddeus, 273
Strong, George T., 93
Sumner, Charles, 198, 253, 266
Supreme Court, 19, 40, 43, 49, 53, 54, 57, 86, 121, 189, 240–241, 252, 255, 272, 288–289

Taney, Roger B., 84–86, 98, 121, 186, 190
taxes, 23, 199, 203
telegraph, 11, 13, 52, 108, 136, 172–173, 199, 212–213
Tennessee, 49, 107, 125, 136, 146, 249, 258, 259
Tenure of Office Act, 261
territories, 34–40, 43, 50, 54–57
Terry, A. H., 245, 246
test oath statute, 189–190, 252, 255
Texas, 47, 232
Thirteenth Amendment, 57, 146, 158, 181, 241, 244, 246, 248, 250, 256, 260
Thirteenth Amendment proposal of 1861, 56–57, 158
Thomas, George, 148
Thoreau, Henry David, 36, 283
Titusville, Pa., 178–179
tobacco, 9, 281–282
Tocqueville, Alexis de, 21
transportation, 52, 199, 205–208
Treasury, Department of, 186, 199, 266

Treatise on the American Law of Landlord and Tenant (John U. Taylor), 279, 280
Treatise on the Constitutional Limitations Which Rest Upon the Legislative Power of the States of American Union, A (Thomas McIntyre Cooley), 279
truancy, 25–26, 29
Trumbull, Lyman, 255
Turner, Jonathan Baldwin, 207
Tyler, John, 54

Union, the, (*see also* Civil War; North; Reconstruction; secession; slaves, slavery), 2–3, 6, 96–97, 98, 146, 240–241, 258
  structure and resources of, 93–96
  wartime economic problems in, 122–123, 200–205
  wartime elections in, 88–93, 122–123, 144, 145–146, 151–158
  wartime government in, 185–192
Unionists in South, 145–146, 150, 252, 260, 262, 273
Union Pacific Railroad, 210–211
Union Party, 92, 146, 188, 194
Union Stockyards, 174–175
United States:
  during Civil War, 71–159
  government of, 34–39, 43, 50, 53, 55, 88–96, 217–218, 279, 287
  post–Reconstruction growth of, 266–290
  during Reconstruction, 166–266
  during secession, 47–74
  prior to secession, 7–30

Vallandigham, C. L., 151
Vicksburg, Miss., 125, 134–136
Virginia, 49, 105, 107, 109, 119, 125, 131, 136, 149, 245
Virginia, 115–116
Von Holst, Hermann, 56
voting, 89, 222, 273

Wade, Benjamin, 150–151, 152, 263
Wade-Davis Bill, 149–151, 256
Walker, Francis A., 281
Wanamaker, John, 281, 286
Wanamaker & Brown (Philadelphia), 282
War Department, 91, 98, 114, 138–143, 146, 153, 159, 166, 180, 186, 195, 198
War Powers Under the Constitution of the United States (William Whiting), 141
Washington, D.C., 60, 71, 79, 82, 83, 90, 102, 103, 105, 115, 119, 124, 143, 149, 159, 160, 165, 236
Washington, George, 20, 78, 185
Washington University, 287
Webster, Daniel, 38
Welles, Gideon, 186–187, 194
Western Union, 228
West Virginia, 90, 223, 228–229
wheat, wheat farming, 9, 173, 286
Whig Party, 42, 43, 68, 123, 194
Whiting, William, 140–141
Whitman, Walt, 93, 164–166, 185, 271
Williams, George, 259
Wirz, Henry, 166
women, 16, 90, 153, 275

Yorktown, Va., 116–117